Anti-Inflammatory Diet Cookbook

A Guide With a Sample Meal Plan, Tips and Simple Recipes To Help
Your Immune System Rebuild and Enjoy Healthy Food Every Day

Sebastian Young

Your Free Gift

As a way of saying thanks for your purchase, to our readers we

offer as a gift a printable recipe book, to download for free:

"Cookbook Journal",

a diary in which to keep track of all your culinary inventions,

assigning each one an evaluation, the difficulty of execution

and much more.

Click this link to free download https://dl.bookfunnel.com/i3sq7ljm6z

Table of contents

Chapter No 1: Introduction to   Anti-Inflammatory Diet **19**

1.1 What is Inflammation?...*19*

1.2 What Causes it?...*20*

1.3 What is Anti-Inflammatory Diet? *20*

1.4 Types of Anti-Inflammatory Diet *21*

1.5 Benefits *21*

1.6 Who can it help? *22*

1.7 How Anti-Inflammatory Diet Works?...*22*

1.8 What Research Says About Dietary Inflammation Reduction? *23*

1.9 Most Anti-Inflammatory Foods to Eat...*23*

1.10 Foods That Cause Inflammation...*27*

1.11 Diet Tips to Help You Fight Inflammation *30*

1.12 A Complete Anti-Inflammatory Meal Plan for a Week..*34*

Chapter 2: Breakfast Recipes Recipes **37**

1. Cherry coconut porridge *38*

2. Gingerbread Oatmeal *38*

3. Rhubarb, apple + ginger muffins {gluten + dairy-free}...*38*

4. Mushroom and Spinach Frittata *39*

5. Overnight Oats with Peanut Butter and Banana *39*

6. Eggs Benedict with Easy Hollandaise Sauce...*40*

7. Nutella Pancakes...*40*

8. Monkey-Bread Danish *41*

9. Sheet Tray Pancakes with Peaches and Strawberries *42*

10. 'Everything Bagel' Cauliflower Rolls *42*

11. The Nourishing Healthy Scramble *43*

12. Golden Milk Chia Seed Pudding..*43*

13. Vanilla Turmeric Orange Juice..*43*

14. Berry & Chia Breakfast *44*

15. No-Bake Turmeric Protein Donuts..*44*

16. Paleo Pancakes Nutty Choco-Nana...*44*

17. Sweet Potato Cranberry Breakfast Bars *45*

18. Paleo Turmeric Scones *45*

19. Chocolate Avocado Blueberry Muffins *46*

20. Raspberry-Grapefruit Smoothie *46*

21. No-Stress Shroom Iced Mocha *47*

22. Savory Indian Pancake...47

23. Scrambled Eggs with Smoked Salmon Recipe 47

24. Dark Chocolate Orange Chia Pudding 48

25. Paleo Crêpes Sprinkled with Nutella 48

26. Keto Avocado Smoothie with Ginger, Coconut Milk, and Turmeric.....................................49

27. Maple-baked rice porridge recipe with fruit..49

28. Coffee and Mint Yogurt Parfait 49

29. 5-Minute Herb-Baked Eggs...50

30. Crunchy Cinnamon Granola..50

31. Energizing pineapple anti-inflammatory smoothie 50

32. Pecan Banana Bread Overnight Oats 51

33. Yogurt parfait recipe with raspberries and chia seeds 51

34. Winter Morning (Or Any Time!) Breakfast Bowl 52

35. Greek yogurt recovery smoothie 52

36. Cacao Berry Smoothie 52

37. Tropical turmeric smoothie bowl...53

38. Spinach and Smoked Salmon Breakfast Recipe 53

39. Prosciutto-Wrapped Avocado Egg..54

40. Keto Breakfast Burger with Avocado Buns 54

41. Crispy Bacon and Baked Eggs in a Portobello Mushroom 55

42. Chocolate Paleo Donuts..55

43. Sweet Cherry Almond Chia Pudding 56

44. Smoked salmon eggs benedict 56

45. Anti-inflammatory cherry & beet smoothie...57

46. Chocolate Breakfast Milkshake 57

47. Feel-good pineapple smoothie 58

48. Gluten Free Paleo Cherry Muffins 58

49. Anti-inflammatory smoothie 58

50. Ginger, Tropical Carrot, & Turmeric Smoothie 58

51 Smoothie with cherries and mocha 59

52 Omelet with avocado and kale 59

53 Breakfast Salad with Baby Kale, Quinoa, and Strawberries 60

54 Lemony Labneh with Pistachios..60

55 Toast with Mascarpone and Berries 60

56 Granola Bars with Almond Joy 61

57 Smoothie with Peanut Butter and Jelly..61

58 Baked Oatmeal with Banana, Raisins, and Walnuts 61

59 Pancakes with Avocado 62

60 Burrata and Avocado Toast 62

61 Smoothie with strawberries, blueberries, and bananas 63

62 Overnight Oatmeal with Dates and Pine Nuts 63

63 Pancakes with Orange Whole-Wheat Flour 63

64 Scrambled Eggs with Smoked Trout and Spinach 64

65 Breakfast with Greek Yogurt 64

66 Oranges with Cinnamon 64

67 Blood Oranges with Yogurt and Cardamom Brulle 65

68 Energy Bites from Carrot Cake 65

69 Apple Butter with Chai in the Slow Cooker 65

70 Smoothie with Anti-Inflammatory Cherry and Spinach 66

71 Spinach, Tomato, and Feta Waffle 66

72 Overnight Oats with Cherry and Walnuts 66

73 Smoothie with berries and kefir 67

74 Quinoa Cakes from Southwest 67

75 Sandwich with egg and salmon 67

76 Recipe for maple-baked rice porridge with fruit 68

77 Herb-Baked Eggs in 5 Minutes 68

78 Cinnamon Granola with a Crunchy 68

79 Parfait with Coffee & Mint Yogurt 69

80 Anti-Inflammatory Smoothie with Energizing Pineapple 69

81 Toasted Avocado with Egg 70

82 Porridge of Chia Quinoa 70

83 Overnight Oats Pecan Banana Bread Recipe 70

84 Smoothie with Greek yogurt for recovery 71

85 Smoothie with Cacao and Berries 71

86 Turmeric Scramble with Nutrients 71

87 Breakfast with Chia and Raspberry 71

88 No-Bake Protein Turmeric Donuts 72

89 Paleo Pancakes with Nutty Choco-Nana 72

90 Turmeric Scones for anti Inflammation 73

91 Breakfast Bars with Sweet Potatoes and Cranberries 73

92 Muffins with Chocolate Avocado and Blueberries 74

93 Smoothie with raspberries and grapefruit 74

94 Shroom Iced- Mocha 74

95 Pancakes with a Savory Flavor 75

96 Chia Pudding with Dark Chocolate and Orange 75

97 Smoothie Bowl with Tropical Turmeric 75

98 Breakfast with Smoked Salmon & Spinach 76

99 Avocado Buns for a Keto Breakfast Burger 76

100 Avocado Egg with Prosciutto Wrapping 77

101 Chickpea and Cauliflower Tikka Masala 77

102 Turkey Stuffed Peppers in the Air Fryer 78

Chapter 3: Lunch Recipes Recipes Recipes **79**

1. Mediterranean Tuna Salad 80

2. 5 Ingredient Thai Pumpkin Soup 80

3. Kale Caesar Salad including Grilled Chicken Wrap 80

4. Persimmon salad with pears and grapes 81

5. Roasted Red Pepper and Sweet Potato Soup 81

6. Smoked salmon potato tartine 82

7. Red lentil and squash curry stew 82

8. White Bean & Veggie Salad 83

9. Chopped Veggie Grain Bowls with Turmeric Dressing 83

10. Salmon Salad-Stuffed Avocado 83

11. Green Salad with Edamame & Beets 84

12. Sweet Potato, Kale & Chicken Salad with Peanut Dressing 84

13. Sprouted-Grain Toast with Peanut Butter & Banana 84

14. Brussels Sprouts Salad with Crunchy Chickpeas 85

15. Avocado Egg Salad Sandwiches 85

16. Vegan Superfood Buddha Bowls 85

17. Chicken, Arugula & Butternut Squash Salad with Brussels Sprouts 86

18. Red, White, and Blueberry Fruit Salad 86

19. Pan Seared Salmon 86

20. Easy Roasted Broccoli 87

21. Tomato and Avocado Salad 87

22. Grilled Peppers 87

23. Mushrooms and Spinach Italian Style 88

24. Turmeric Milk 88

25. Cherry Coconut Smoothie 88

26. Homemade Melt-In-Your-Mouth Dark Chocolate (Paleo) 89

27. Faux Fried Coconut Chicken with Honey Mustard 89

28. Walnut Crusted Salmon with Honey & Rosemary 89

29. Citrus Salad and Ginger Yogurt 90

30. Indian Spiced Carrot Soup with Ginger 90

31. Red Bell Pepper, Spinach, and Goat Cheese Salad with Oregano Dressing 91

32. Pan Seared Salmon on Baby Arugula 91

33. Arctic Char with Chinese Broccoli and Sweet Potato Purée 91

34. Roasted Salmon with Orange-Herb Sauce 92

35. Carrots and Brussels Sprouts 93

36. Chilled Red Bell Pepper and Habanero Soup 93

37. Curried Chicken Salad with Spiced Chickpeas and Raita 94

38. Beet Chips with Turmeric-Yogurt Dip 94

39. Mighty Melon Green Tea Smoothie 95

40. Grilled Tuna Steaks with Grape and Caper Salsa 95

41. Turmeric Ginger C Boost Life Juice 95

42. Salmon Avocado Salad 96

43. Healthy Turmeric Chicken Stew 96

44. Tuna and Chickpea Salad 96

45. Heirloom Salad including Tomatoes and Rosemary 97

46. Strawberry Spinach Salad 97

47. Broiled Spanish Mackerel 97

48. Easy Roasted Broccoli and Bok Choy with Balsamic Glaze 98

49. My Big Fat Greek Salad 98

50. Spinach Salad with Chicken, Avocado, and Goat Cheese 99

51 Fruit Salad with Red, White, and Blueberries 99

52 Seared Salmon in a Pan 100

53 Salad with Tomatoes and Avocados 100

54 Broccoli Roasted with Ease 100

55 Peppers grilled 101

56 Italian Style Mushrooms with Spinach 101

57 Turmeric Milk 101

58 Dark Chocolate Melt-In-Your-Mouth Homemade 102

59 Tuna Steaks with Grape & Caper Salsa on the Grill 102

60 Smoothie with cherries and coconut 102

61 Smoothie with Mighty Melon and Green Tea 102

62 Life Juice with Turmeric and Ginger 103

63 Turmeric Chicken Stew 103

64 Salad with Salmon and Avocado 103

65 Chickpea salad & Tuna 104

66 Salad of Heirloom Tomatoes with Rosemary 104

67 Salad with strawberries and spinach 104

68 Spanish Mackerel, broiled 105

69 Big Fat Greek Salad 105

70 Salad with Chicken, Avocado, & Goat Cheese on Spinach 105

71 Sandwich with Smashed Chickpea Avocado Salad & Cranberries + Lemon 106

72 Salmon Patties with Butternut Squash 106

73 Sweet Potato Fries 107

74 No Mayo Mediterranean Tuna Salad 107

75 Greek Salad Chicken Wrap 107

76 Avocado Sauced Grilled Salmon Taco Wraps 108

77 Glowing Spiced Lentil Soup 109

78 Bowls of Turkey Taco Meal Prep 109

79 Pasta with Golden Sun-Dried Tomatoes and Red Lentils 110

80 Glow getter Roasted Carrots Butternut Squash Soup 110

81 Chickpea and Vegetable Coconut Curry 111

82 Egg and Veggie Breakfast Bowl 111

83 Apple Slaw & Kale Broccoli 112

84 Champagne Vinaigrette with Orange Muscat 112

85 Salmon with a Walnut-Rosemary Crusted 112

86 Latte with Matcha Green Tea 113

87 Spicy Cranberry Relish on Roasted Salmon 113

88 Lentil Soup 114

89 Pecans with Spices 114

90 Curry Soup with Roasted Cauliflower and Potatoes 115

91 Smoothie Bowl with Berries and Almonds 116

92 Chamomile Herbal Health Tonic 116

93 Salmon with Miso and Maple 116

94 Green Smoothie Bowl with Almonds and Matcha 117

95 Bagna Cauda with Salmon and Fall Vegetables 117

96 Green Salad with Beets and Edamame 118

97 Salad of Purple Fruits 118

98 Cup of Noodles in Miso Soup with Shrimp and Green Tea Soba 118

99 Avocado Chickpea Salad Sandwich with Lemon and Cranberries 119

100 Wild Rice and Buddha Bowl with Avocado, Kale and Orange 119

101 Chickpea & Vegetable Coconut Curry 120

102 White Turkey with Avocado 120

Chapter 4: Dinner Recipes Recipes Recipes Recipes **122**

11. Slow Cooker Turkey Chili 123

2. Baked Tilapia Recipe with Pecan Rosemary Topping 123

3. Italian Stuffed Red Peppers 124

4. One pan lemon herb salmon and zucchini 124

5. Spicy Sweet Potato Black Bean Burgers with avocado-cilantro crema + sprouts 125

6. Turkey & Quinoa Stuffed Peppers 126

7. Greek Roasted Fish with Vegetables 126

8. Mediterranean Chicken Quinoa Bowl 127

9. Kale & Avocado Salad with Blueberries & Edamame 127

10. Skillet Lemon Chicken & Potatoes with Kale 128

11. Spinach Salad with White Beans, Roasted Sweet Potatoes, and Basil 128

12. Roasted Salmon with Greens & Smoky Chickpeas 129

13. Jason Mraz's Guacamole 129

14. Celeriac & Walnut Tacos 130

15. Vegan Coconut Chickpea Curry 130

16. Basil Pesto Pasta with Grilled Vegetables 131

17. Mediterranean Chicken with Orzo Salad 131

18. Quinoa Power Salad 132

19. Quinoa, Chicken & Broccoli Salad with Roasted Lemon Dressing 133

20. Spicy Shrimp Tacos 133

21. Walnut-Rosemary Crusted Salmon 134

22. Panzanella with Tomatoes & Grilled Corn 134

23. Chicken, Quinoa & Sweet Potato Casserole 135

24. Citrus Vinaigrette 135

25. Chicken Massaman Curry with Turmeric Brown Rice 136

26. Mediterranean Cod with Roasted Tomatoes 136

27. Slow-Cooker Mediterranean Stew 137

28. Greek Stuffed Portobello Mushrooms 137

29. Mediterranean Ravioli with Artichokes & Olives 138

30. Provençal Baked Fish with Roasted Potatoes & Mushrooms 138

31. Sheet-Pan Mediterranean Chicken, Brussels Sprouts & Gnocchi 139

32. Vegan Pesto Spaghetti Squash with Mushrooms & Sun-Dried Tomatoes 139

33. Simple Grilled Salmon & Vegetables 140

34. Goat Cheese Pizza 140

35. Slow-Cooker Mediterranean Chicken & Chickpea Soup 141

36. Romesco Sauce with Whole-Grain Pasta & Parmesan 141

37. Farfalle with Tuna, Lemon, and Fennel 142

38. Slow-Cooker Pasta e Fagioli Soup Freezer Pack 142

39. Guacamole Chopped Salad 143

40. Greek Salad with Edamame 143

41. Honey Walnut Shrimp 144

42. Mushroom Shawarma with Yogurt-Tahini Sauce 144

43. Cucumber & Avocado salad 145

44. Ginger-Tahini Salmon and Vegetables (Oven-Baked)..145

45. Peanut Zucchini Noodle Salad with Chicken..146

46. Everything Bagel Avocado Toast..146

47. Tomato, Cucumber & White-Bean Salad with Basil Vinaigrette..146

48. Pesto Pasta Salad..147

49. Slow-Cooker Mediterranean Stew..147

50. Greek Stuffed Portobello Mushrooms..148

51 Chicken & Snap Pea Stir-Fry..148

52 Greek Turkey Burgers alongside Tzatziki Sauce..149

53 Easy One-Pan Ratatouille..149

54 Hula Ginger vinaigrette with Seared Ahi Tuna Poke Salad & Wonton Crisps..150

55 Chicken marinated in Balsamic Vinegar, Brussels sprouts, Cranberries, and Pumpkin Seeds..151

56 Pineapple Fried Rice..152

57 Baked Sesame-Ginger Salmon in Parchment..152

58 Mediterranean roast chicken with turmeric & fennel..153

59 One-Pan Eggs with Tomatoes & Asparagus..153

60 Citrus Salad with Sweet Potato Bulgur..154

61 Citrus Salad with Sweet Potato Bulgur..154

62 Roasted Salmon in a Single Pan with Potatoes and Romaine..155

63 Peppers stuffed with ground turkey and sweet potatoes..155

64 Smoky Chickpeas & Greens with Roasted Salmon..156

65 Quinoa Bowl with Mediterranean Chicken..157

66 Salad with Tomatoes, Cucumbers, and White Beans with Basil Vinaigrette..157

67 Pasta Salad with Pesto..158

68 Roasted Greek Fish with Vegetables..158

69 Mediterranean Stew in a Slow Cooker..159

70 Portobello Mushrooms with Greek Stuffing..159

71 Ravioli with Artichokes and Olives from the Mediterranean..160

72 Provençal Baked Fish with Mushrooms and Roasted Potatoes..160

73 Mediterranean Chicken, Brussels sprouts, and Gnocchi on a Sheet Pan..160

74 Spaghetti Squash with Vegan Pesto, Mushrooms, and Sun-Dried Tomatoes..161

75 Grilled Salmon with Vegetables..161

76 Pizza with goat cheese..162

77 Soup with Mediterranean Chicken and Chickpeas in a Slow Cooker..162

78 Pasta with Whole-Grain Sauce and Parmesan..163

79 Farfalle with Tuna, Fennel & Lemon..163

80 Chicken on a Sheet Pan with Brussels sprouts..164

81 Pasta e Fagioli Soup in a Slow Cooker Freezer Pack..164

82 Baked Turkey Meatballs 165

83 Bean Bolognese in the Crock-Pot 165

84 Salmon & Cauliflower Rice Bowl for Gut Healing 166

85 White Bean & Chicken Chili with Winter Vegetables 166

86 Chicken Tenders with Harissa and Yogurt Marination 167

87 Buffalo cauliflower baked 167

88 Bolognese with Polenta and Wild Mushrooms 167

89 Recipe for Chinese chicken salad 168

90 Saag Paneer 169

91 Alfredo Spaghetti Squash 169

92 Green Fried Rice 170

93 Recipe for Baked Tilapia with Pecan Rosemary Topping 170

94 Lentil Shrimp Jambalaya 171

95 Lasagna with Tofu and Winter Squash 172

96 Buddha Bowls with Chicken and Quinoa 172

97 Salad of Greek Kale with Quinoa and Chicken 173

98 Chicken Fajita Bowls on a Sheet Pan 173

Chapter 5: Snacks and Quickies Recipes 175

1. Turmeric bars (paleo, AIP) - Anti-inflammatory 176

2. Turmeric Gummies (Anti-Inflammatory, Paleo) 176

3. Spicy Kale Chips 177

4. Paleo ginger-spiced mixed nuts 177

5. 10-minute spicy tuna rolls 178

6. Easy Peasy Ginger Date Bars 178

7. Vanilla Turmeric Orange Juice 178

8. AIP / Paleo Hibiscus Ginger Gelatin Gummies (Sweet n' Sour) 179

9. Baked Veggie Turmeric Nuggets (Freeze-Friendly) 179

10. Pineapple Ginger Slaw (Creamy) 180

11. No-Bake Energy Bites with Golden Turmeric 180

12. Ginger Fried Cabbage and Carrots (AIP, Paleo, Vegan) 180

13. Grain-Free Banana Ginger Bars 181

14. Gut-Healing Kombucha Gummies 181

15. Spicy nuts (paleo + whole30) 182

16. Apple Cider Vinegar Gummies 182

17. Cacao Coffee Protein Bars [copycat RXBAR] 182

18. Garlic Plantain Chips 183

19. Roasted Chickpeas with Tumeric 183

20. Mediterranean roasted chicken with fennel and turmeric 184

21. Baked Turkey Meatballs (Makes 25-30 mini meatballs) 184

22. Crock-Pot Bean Bolognese 185

23. Gut-Healing Salmon & Cauliflower Rice Bowl 185

24. White Bean and Chicken Chili with Winter Vegetables 186

25. Blender Olive Oil Hollandaise Sauce 186

26. Spinach-Salmon Salad 186

27. Easy Roasted Chicken Breasts with Tomatoes and White Beans 187

28. Citrus-Salmon Salad 187

29. Crispy Sheet Pan Salmon with Lemony Asparagus and Carrots 188

30. Easy Kimchi 188

31. Matcha Green Tea 189

32. Roasted Haloumi-Stuffed Broccoli Recipe 189

33. Anti-Inflammatory Coconut Fish Curry 190

34. Winter Sausage Stew (Gluten-Free) 190

35. Dan Buettner's coconut cherry parfait recipe 191

36. Tofu and Winter Squash Lasagna 191

37. Harissa & Yogurt Marinated Chicken Tenders 192

38. Ground Turkey Sweet Potato Stuffed Peppers 192

39. Polenta with Wild Mushroom Bolognese 193

40. Baked Buffalo cauliflower recipe 193

41. Glowing spiced lentil soup 194

42. Chinese chicken salad recipe 194

43. Sweet potato and crispy kale tostadas recipe 195

44. Easy Saag Paneer 195

45. Spaghetti Squash Alfredo 196

46. Homemade Green Fried Rice 197

47. Baked Tilapia Recipe with Pecan Rosemary Topping 197

48. Sweet potato and chickpea stew recipe 197

49. Lentil Shrimp Jambalaya {Grain Free} 198

50. Turmeric Ginger Smoothie with Coconut Oil 199

51 Turmeric Bars 199

52 Turmeric Gummies 200

53 Spicy Tuna Rolls 200

54 Mixed Nuts with Ginger Spice 200

55 Spicy Kale Chips 201

56 Ginger Date Bars 201

57 Orange Juice with Vanilla and Turmeric 202

58 Gelatin Gummies with Hibiscus and Ginger 202

59 Baked Turmeric Veggie Nuggets 202

60 Slaw with Pineapple & Ginger Cream 203

61 Muffins with Turmeric & Coconut Flour 203

62 No-Bake Golden Turmeric Energy Bites..204

63 Coconut Oil with Turmeric Ginger Smoothie 204

64 Banana Ginger Coconut Flour Bars 204

65 Kombucha Gummies for Gut Healing..205

66 Protein Bars with Cacao Coffee 205

67 Spicy Nuts 206

68 Gummies with Apple Cider Vinegar..206

69 Recipe for Lemon-Blueberry Bread...206

70 Shortbread Cookies with Lavender..207

71 Energy Balls 207

72 Peanut Butter Chocolate Chex Bars...208

73 Yogurt with Almonds and Blueberries...208

74 Cottage Cheese with Applesauce 208

75 Salad with Asparagus and Artichokes 208

76 Sauce for Barbecue..209

77 Freezer Pops of Berries 209

78 Berry good snack 209

79 Salad with Blackberries and Shrimp 210

80 Breakfast with Blueberries and Yogurt 210

81 Brussels Sprouts in a Garlic-Black Bean Sauce 210

82 Strawberries and Cacao Greek Yogurt 211

83 Dirty Rice in Cajun Style..211

84 Dressing with Carrots and Ginger 211

85 Popcorn made with cauliflower...212

86 Cauliflower-Mash 212

87 Hummus with celery...212

88 Chard Salad with Parmesan 212

89 Plum & Cheese Snack 213

90 Lemon Zucchini with Cheesy Sauce 213

91 Fruit & Cottage Cheese..213

92 Chicken Gravy with a Country Flair 213

93 Yogurt with cucumber and cashews...214

94 Cucumber Cups..214

95 Hummus-Dipped Devilled Eggs 214

96 Dill Sauce..214

97 Easy Creamy Spinach Dip... *215*

98 Eggplant Caviar *215*

My Recipes And Notes **216**

Chapter No 1: Introduction to Anti-Inflammatory Diet

Before you can clearly understand why an anti-inflammatory diet may be beneficial and is now one of the most talked-about diets, you must first comprehend what inflammation is.

1.1 What is Inflammation?

When you hear the term "inflammation," you may think of the swelling and redness that occurs when you stub your toe. There are two obvious visible indicators of inflammation, but there's more to it than that.

Inflammation is a normal aspect of the immune system's response. Inflammatory cells are sent to the rescue when your body is defending against infection or injury. This causes swelling, redness, and discomfort, as well as other symptoms. That's very normal and understandable.

That is, as long as the body remains under control. When inflammation persists and does not go away completely the scenario changes. Chronic inflammation puts your body on high alert all of the time, and it may lead to serious health problems.

Fortunately, you have some influence over your inflammation levels. Inflammation may be increased by factors such as being overweight or obese, smoking and drinking excessively. Your diet also plays a major role, and some doctors believe that changing your diet and drinking habits rather than taking medicine is a better way to reduce inflammation. Taking chronic pain medicine only when absolutely necessary is also a smart idea since many medicines have unpleasant side effects, including sleepiness, fogginess and memory loss.

1.2 What Causes it?

Inflammation may be exacerbated by certain lifestyle variables, particularly those that are repeated. High-fructose corn syrup and Sugar are particularly dangerous when consumed in large quantities. Diabetes, insulin resistance and obesity are all possible outcomes.

Consuming a lot of refined carbohydrates, such as white bread, has also been linked to inflammation, obesity and insulin resistance, according to scientists.

Furthermore, trans fats found in processed and packaged meals have been proven to cause inflammation and damage to the endothelial cells that protect your arteries.

Another suspected reason is vegetable oils, which are found in many processed meals. Regular consumption may cause an omega-6 to omega-3 fatty acid imbalance, which some experts think promotes inflammation.

Excessive alcohol & processed meat consumption may also cause inflammation in the body. In addition, a lack of physical activity with a lot of sitting is a significant non-dietary component that may cause inflammation.

1.3 What is Anti-Inflammatory Diet?

Some foods include ingredients that might cause or exacerbate inflammation. Sugary or processed foods are more likely to do so, while fresh, whole meals are less likely to do so.

Fruits and vegetables are emphasized in an anti-inflammatory diet. Antioxidants may be found in a variety of plant-based meals. However, certain meals may cause the creation of free radicals. Foods that are fried repeatedly in heated cooking oil are an example.

Antioxidants in food are molecules that assist in the removal of free radicals from the body. Somebody activities, such as metabolism, produce free radicals as a natural consequence. External variables like stress and smoking, on the other hand, might raise the quantity of free radicals in the body.

Cell damage may be caused by free radicals. Inflammation is increased as a result of this injury, which may lead to a variety of disorders. The body produces antioxidants that help in the removal of harmful toxins, but dietary antioxidants may also assist.

Anti-inflammatory diets are preferred over foods that stimulate the formation of free radicals in an anti-inflammatory diet.

Omega-3 fatty acids, found in oily fish, may aid in lowering inflammatory protein levels in the body. According to the Arthritis Foundation, fiber can also have this impact.

1.4 Types of Anti-Inflammatory Diet

Anti-inflammatory diets come in a variety of forms. Anti-inflammatory concepts are already included in many popular diets.

For example, Fruits and vegetables, seafood, whole grains, and heart-healthy fats are all part of the Mediterranean and DASH diets.

Although inflammation seems to have an impact on cardiovascular disease, evidence shows that the Mediterranean diet, which emphasizes plant-based foods and healthy oils, may help to minimize inflammation's impact on the cardiovascular system.

1.5 Benefits

Chronic inflammation occurs when the immune system generates chemicals needed to fight damage and bacterial and viral infections, even when there are no external invaders to fight. It is often caused by lifestyle factors such as stress as well as a lack of exercise.

An anti-inflammatory diet may play a major role in various health issues, according to a growing body of evidence.

For example, a 2017 research published in the British Journal of Nutrition looked at the link between dietary inflammation & atherosclerosis in women over 70.

Researchers discovered that dietary inflammatory index scores were linked to subclinical atherosclerosis and mortality from heart disease.

According to research published in the journal Endocrine in 2016, eating an anti-inflammatory diet may assist persons with type 2 diabetes in lowering their levels of inflammatory markers (such as C-reactive protein).

Participants in the research were newly diagnosed type 2 diabetics who followed the Mediterranean or low-fat diet. C-reactive protein levels declined by 37% in persons who followed a Mediterranean diet after a year but remained constant in those who followed a low-fat diet.

1.6 Who can it help?

Many conditions that are worse by chronic inflammation may benefit from an anti-inflammatory diet as a supplemental treatment.
Inflammation involves the following conditions:

- rheumatoid arthritis
- asthma
- psoriasis
- eosinophilic esophagitis
- Hashimoto's thyroiditis
- colitis
- inflammatory bowel disease
- Crohn's disease
- lupus
- metabolic syndrome

1.7 How Anti-Inflammatory Diet Works?

There isn't a formal diet plan that specifies what to eat, how much to consume, and when to consume it. Instead, the anti-inflammatory diet is eating foods that have been found to reduce inflammation while avoiding items that have been found to increase it.

Consider the anti-inflammatory diet as a way of living rather than a diet, says Brittany Scanniello, a nutritionist in Boulder, Colorado. "Anti-inflammatory diet is a way of eating that works to reduce or reduce low-grade inflammation in our bodies," she explains.In an ideal world, you'd consume 8 to 9 servings of fruits and vegetables each day, restrict red meat and dairy consumption, favor complex carbs over simple carbs, and avoid processed foods. Meals high in omega-3 fatty acids, such as anchovies, salmon, halibut, and mussels, are preferable to omega-6 fatty acids, which may be found in maize oil, mayonnaise, vegetables oil, salad dressings, and many processed foods.According to Scanniello, eating this manner is beneficial for everyone since many of the items that promote inflammation are unhealthy in the first place. "I feel that restricting or eliminating sugar and highly processed meals in favor of unsaturated fats, vegetables, fruits, seeds, nuts and lean meats may help everyone," adds Scanniello.

She believes that an anti-inflammatory diet might be particularly beneficial for those who suffer from chronic inflammation as a consequence of a medical condition. Athletes and others who engage in high-intensity exercise and want to reduce their baseline inflammation may benefit from it, she adds.

1.8 What Research Says About Dietary Inflammation Reduction?

Inflammation has been shown to have harmful consequences in several studies; in fact, chronic inflammatory disorders constitute the leading cause of death worldwide. It's linked to health problems, including diabetes, Alzheimer's, and obesity.

A number of additional researches have looked at the impact of consuming an anti-inflammatory diet on various health issues. For example, a study published in Frontiers in Nutrition in November 2017 found that eating anti-inflammatory foods may relieve persons with rheumatoid arthritis (RA). When used as a complementary therapy, the authors believe that lowering inflammation in the diet, such as through a vegetarian diet or a vegan, may help delay disease development, minimize joint damage, and perhaps minimize reliance on RA medication.

Anti-inflammatory foods have been proven to assist in the following ways in other studies:

- In sports training, recovery is important.
- Pain connected with aging may be managed in a variety of ways.
- Protection for the heart
- People with multiple sclerosis have a better quality of life.

1.9 Most Anti-Inflammatory Foods to Eat

Inflammation may be bad or good. On the one hand, it helps in the body's defense against infection and injury. Chronic inflammation, on the other hand, may contribute to disease and weight gain. This risk may be increased by stress, inflammatory meals, and a lack of physical exercise. However, research shows that some foods may help to reduce inflammation.

Here are 13 foods that are anti-inflammatory.

1. Berries

Berries are little fruits with a high fiber, vitamin, and mineral content. Although there are many variants, these are a few of the more famous:

- strawberry
- raspberries
- blueberries
- blackberries

Anthocyanins are antioxidants found in berries. These substances have anti-inflammatory effects, which may reduce your disease risk. Natural killer cells are cells produced by your body that help in the normal functioning of your immune system.

Men who consume blueberries every day generated considerably more NK cells than others who did not, according to one research.

Adults with extra weight who consume strawberries had reduced levels of some inflammatory markers linked to heart disease in another research.

2. Fatty Fish

Protein and long-chain omega-3 fatty acids EPA and DHA are abundant in fatty fish.

Although all varieties of fish contain some omega-3 fatty acids, these are the best sources:

- salmon
- herring
- sardines
- mackerel
- anchovies

EPA and DHA help to prevent heart disease, metabolic syndrome, diabetes, and kidney disease by reducing inflammation. These fatty acids are metabolized by your body into anti-inflammatory compounds called protectins and resolvins.

People who ate salmon or took EPA and DHA supplements had lower levels of inflammatory marker C-reactive protein, according to studies.

In another research, participants with an unbalanced heartbeat who take EPA and DHA daily had no improvement in inflammatory markers when compared to all those who took a placebo.

3. Broccoli

Broccoli is a nutritious vegetable. And including cauliflower, Brussels sprouts, and kale, it's a cruciferous vegetable. Eating a lot of cruciferous veggies has been linked to a lower risk of heart disease. This might be due to the antioxidants in them having anti-inflammatory effects. Sulforaphane, an antioxidant found in broccoli, inhibits inflammation by lowering levels of cytokines & NF-kB, which cause inflammation.

4. Avocados

Avocados are also one of the few supposedly superfoods that are really deserving of the name. They're high in potassium, magnesium, fiber, and monounsaturated fats, which are good for your heart.

They also include carotenoids & tocopherols, both of which have been associated with a lower risk. Avocados also contain a compound that may prevent inflammation in early skin cells.

In one research, persons who ate an avocado slice with their hamburger had low levels of the inflammatory indicators NF-kB and IL-6 than those who ate the hamburger alone.

5. Green Tea

Green tea is among the healthiest teas you can consume, as you've surely heard. It lowers your chances of developing heart disease, Alzheimer's disease, obesity, and other diseases.

Its antioxidant & anti-inflammatory qualities, particularly a compound called epigallocatechin-3-gallate, are responsible for many of its advantages (EGCG).

EGCG reduces pro-inflammatory cytokine synthesis and fatty acid damage in your cells, which helps to reduce inflammation.

6. Peppers

Bell & chili peppers are high in antioxidants and vitamin C, which have anti-inflammatory effects. The Bell peppers contain antioxidant quercetin, that may help patients with sarcoidosis, an inflammatory disease, lower one indication of oxidative damage. Chili peppers include ferulic acid and sinapic acid, which may help you age better by reducing inflammation.

7. Mushrooms

While there are many species of mushrooms on the planet, just a handful are edible and economically farmed. Truffles, shiitake and portobello mushrooms are among them. Mushrooms are high in selenium, copper, and all of the B vitamins yet are low in calories. They also have anti-inflammatory properties thanks to phenols and other antioxidants.

A type of mushroom known as lion's mane may help to lower low-grade inflammation linked to obesity. Cooking mushrooms, on the other hand, drastically reduced their anti-inflammatory compounds, according to one research. As a result, eating them raw or minimally cooked may be the best option.

8. Grapes

Anthocyanins, which are found in grapes, help to prevent inflammation. They may also reduce the risk of a variety of diseases, like diabetes, heart disease, obesity, Alzheimer's disease, and eye problems. Grapes are also a good source of resveratrol, a compound with a variety of health advantages. In one research, persons with heart disease who took grape extract on a regular basis noticed their inflammatory gene markers, such as NF-kB, decrease.

.

9. Turmeric

Turmeric is an earthy-flavored spice that is commonly used in curries as well as other Dishes. Curcumin, a potent anti-inflammatory substance, has received plenty of attention because of its presence. Turmeric may help with arthritis, diabetes & other inflammatory diseases.

In fact, in persons with metabolic syndrome, taking 1 gram of curcumin daily with piperine from black pepper resulted in a considerable reduction in the inflammatory marker CRP. However, it may be difficult to get enough curcumin from turmeric alone to provide a visible benefit.

In one trial, women who took 2.8 grams of turmeric per day for weight loss showed no change in inflammatory markers. It is much more beneficial to take isolated curcumin supplements. Piperine, which may increase curcumin absorption by two thousand percent, is often coupled with curcumin supplements.

10. Olive Oil Extra Virgin

One of the healthier fats you can consume is extra virgin olive oil. It's high in monounsaturated fats as well as a key component of the Mediterranean diet, which has a long list of health advantages. Extra virgin olive oil has been linked to a lower risk of, heart disease and some other major health problems in studies.

CRP and numerous other inflammatory markers fell dramatically in individuals who ingested 1.7 ounces of olive oil daily in one trial on the Mediterranean diet.

Anti-inflammatory medicines like ibuprofen have been likened to the impact of oleocanthal, an antioxidant present in olive oil. It's important to remember that extra virgin olive oil has stronger anti-inflammatory properties than processed olive oils.

11. Cocoa and Dark Chocolate

Dark chocolate is rich, sweet, and satisfying. It's also high in antioxidants, which help to alleviate inflammation. These may lower the risk of disease and help you age more gracefully.

Chocolate's anti-inflammatory properties are due to flavanols, which help maintain the endothelial cells that make up your arteries healthy. In one research, smokers who ate high-flavonol chocolate had significant changes in endothelial function within two hours. To get these anti-inflammatory effects, be sure to purchase dark chocolate that has at least seventy percent cocoa — a higher proportion is even better.

12. Tomatoes

The tomato is a nutrient-dense food. Potassium, Vitamin C and lycopene, an antioxidant with anti-inflammatory qualities, are all abundant in tomatoes.

According to one research, consuming tomato juice reduced inflammatory markers in people who were overweight but not obese. It's worth noting that cooking tomatoes with olive oil might help you absorb more lycopene. That's because lycopene is carotenoid, a vitamin that absorbs better when consumed with fat.

13. Cherries

Cherries are a delicious fruit. Cherries are sweet and high in anti-inflammatory antioxidants, including anthocyanins and catechins. Although sour cherries have been examined more than other types in terms of their health-promoting characteristics, sweet cherries also give benefits. People who ate 280 grams of cherries per day for a month had lower levels of inflammatory marker CRP, which continued low for another 28 days after they stopped consuming cherries, according to one research.

1.10 Foods That Cause Inflammation

Depending on circumstances, inflammation may be beneficial or harmful. On the one hand, it's your body's natural defense mechanism when you're sick or injured. It can assist your body in fighting sickness and promoting recovery.

Chronic, long-term inflammation, on the other hand, has been associated with an elevated risk of diseases including heart disease, diabetes and obesity. Surprisingly, the things you consume might have a big impact on how much inflammation you have in your body.

Here are six foods that can cause inflammation in the body.

1. High-fructose corn syrup and sugar

The two primary kinds of added sugar in the Western diet are table sugar & high fructose corn syrup (HFCS). High fructose corn syrup is around 45 percent glucose and 55 percent fructose, while sugar is 50 percent glucose and 50 percent fructose. Increased inflammation, which may lead to illness, is one of the reasons why additional sugars are hazardous.

The anti-inflammatory benefits of omega-3 fatty acids were reduced in mice given a high-sugar diet in another research. Furthermore, in a randomized clinical experiment in which participants drank regular diet soda, soda, milk or water, only those who drank normal soda had higher uric acid levels, which causes inflammation and insulin resistance.

Sugar also is harmful since it contains an excessive quantity of fructose. While moderate quantities of fructose in vegetables and fruits are OK, ingesting high quantities of fructose from added sugars is indeed not. Obesity, diabetes, insulin resistance, fatty liver disease and chronic kidney disease have all been related to eating much fructose.

Fructose also induces inflammation in the endothelial cells that make up line your blood arteries, which is a risk factor for heart disease, according to studies. In mice and humans, high fructose consumption has been demonstrated to enhance many inflammatory markers. Chocolate, candy, cakes, soft drinks, cookies, sweet pastries, doughnuts and some cereals are all rich in added sugar.

2. Artificial Trans Fat

Artificial trans fats are among the unhealthiest fats you may consume. They are made by adding hydrogen to liquid unsaturated fats to give them the consistency of solid fat. Trans fats are often indicated as partly hydrogenated oils on ingredient labels. Trans fats are found in most margarine and are often used to improve the shelf life of processed foods.

Artificial trans fats, unlike naturally produced trans fats present in dairy and meat, have been demonstrated to promote inflammation and raise disease risk. Trans fats may affect the function of endothelial cells that line your arteries, which is a major risk factor for the heart, in addition to reducing HDL (good) cholesterol.

Artificial trans-fat consumption has been related to elevated levels of inflammatory indicators, including C-reactive protein (CRP). CRP levels were 78 percent higher in one research among women who reported the greatest trans-fat consumption. Hydrogenated soybean oil elevated inflammation substantially more than palm and sunflower oils in a randomized controlled experiment including older ladies with excess weight. Inflammatory indicators increased in both healthy men and individuals with high cholesterol levels in response to trans fats, according to studies.

French fries and other fried fast food, certain microwave popcorn variations, some vegetable shortenings and margarines, packaged cakes and cookies, certain pastries, and other processed goods with partly hydrogenated vegetable oil on the label are high in trans fats.

3. Seeds and Vegetable Oils

Vegetable oil consumption in United States climbed by 130 percent throughout the twentieth century. Because of their high omega-6 fatty acid concentration, some experts think that some vegetable oils, like soybean oil, increase inflammation. Although certain omega-6 fats are required in the diet, the normal Western diet gives significantly more than is required. To increase your ratio, omega-6 to omega-3 and gain the anti-inflammatory effects of omega-3s, health authorities suggest consuming more omega-3-rich foods, like fatty fish.

In one research, rats given a diet with a 20:1 omega-6 to omega-3 ratio showed significantly greater levels of inflammatory markers than rats on a 1:1 or 5:1 diet.

However, there is presently little evidence that high consumption of omega-6 fatty acids causes inflammation in people. Linoleic acid, the most prevalent dietary omega-6 acid, has been shown in controlled experiments to have no effect on inflammatory markers. Before any judgments can be made, further investigation is required.

Cooking oils made from vegetables and seeds are a common element in processed meals.

4. Refined carbohydrates

Carbohydrates also have a bad reputation. The fact is that not all carbohydrates are bad for you. For millennia, ancient people ate grasses, roots, and fruits, which were rich in fiber and unprocessed carbohydrates. Consumption of refined carbohydrates, on the other hand, may lead to inflammation. The majority of the fiber has been eliminated from refined carbohydrates.

Fiber keeps you fuller for longer, helps blood sugar regulation, and feeds your intestinal microbes. The processed carbohydrate in today's diet, according to researchers, may promote the development of inflammatory gut bacteria, raising your risk of obesity as well as inflammatory bowel disease. The glycemic index (GI) of refined carbohydrates is greater than that of unprocessed carbohydrates. Meals with a high GI spike blood sugar levels faster than foods with a low GI. In one research, older persons who ate the most high-GI meals had a 2.9-fold increased risk of dying from an inflammatory condition like (COPD) chronic obstructive pulmonary disease. Young, healthy males who ate 50 grams of refined carbohydrates in the form of white bread had high blood sugar levels and increased levels of a specific inflammatory marker in controlled research.

Candy, pasta, pastries, bread, certain cereals, cakes, cookies, sugary soft drinks, and any processed meals with added sugar or wheat include refined carbs.

5. Drinking too much Alcohol

Alcohol use in moderation has been found to have certain health advantages. Higher doses, on the other hand, might cause serious difficulties.

In one research, participants who drank Alcohol had higher levels of inflammatory marker CRP. Their CRP levels rose in direct proportion to the amount of Alcohol they ingested. People who consume large amounts of Alcohol may have issues with bacterial toxins migrating out of the colon and into the body. This disorder, often known as "leaky gut," may cause extensive inflammation and organ damage.

To prevent alcohol-related health concerns, males should have no more than two standard drinks each day and women should have no more than one.

6. Processed Meat

Processed meat consumption has been linked to a higher risk of diabetes, heart colon & stomach disease. Bacon, sausage, ham, smoked meat and beef jerky are all examples of processed meat.

More new glycation end products (AGEs) are found in processed meat than in most other meats. AGEs are generated when meats and other foods are cooked at high temperatures. They have a history of causing inflammation.

Inflammation may be triggered by a variety of factors, some of which are difficult to avoid, such as injury, pollution or sickness.

You do, however, have a lot more influence over things like your food.

Reduce inflammation by limiting your intake of items that cause it and consuming anti-inflammatory nutrients to remain as healthy as possible.

1.11 Diet Tips to Help You Fight Inflammation

Choosing entire meals like fruits, vegetables & whole grains over processed meals has several health advantages. One of the most important advantages of these nutrient-dense meals is their ability to decrease inflammation in the body.

"Exercise can create short-term inflammation or acute, that is normal," explains Kate Patton, RD, MEd, CSSD, LD, a sports health dietitian. "A healthy diet may help keep inflammation under control."

The risk of chronic inflammation as a consequence of poor diet, stress, and/or incorrect or overtraining in people who exercise regularly is particularly alarming. The above combination puts you at a greater risk of being injured or sick. Reduced inflammation in the body may help you exercise more regularly, heal quicker from injuries, operate at your best, and, in the end, avoid chronic illness.

Because they are your supplies of energy (carbs), the basic building block of cells (protein), and the way to absorb vitamins (fat), foods that treat inflammation have a mixture of carbohydrates, protein, and fat (fat). Muscle contraction, tissue repair, blood flow and healing are all helped by vitamins and minerals.

Dietary Recommendations for Food

Patton offers nine dietary guidelines for reducing inflammation:

- Whole-grain carbohydrates, pure whole fruits and veggies are the best options. These are higher in nutritional density and include a wide range of minerals and vitamins that are essential for maintaining and improving health.
- To get the most nutritious bang for your money, rotate among a range of colorful fruits, veggies, and grains from week to week.

- Refined starches (white variants) and added sugars should be avoided (brown or white sugar, energy drinks, soda). Inflammatory symptoms, including weight gain and increased blood glucose and cholesterol levels, are promoted by these less nutrient-dense diets.

- Skinless chicken, fish, eggs, lentils, and fat-free Greek yogurt are also good choices. These are high-quality protein sources with added calcium, vitamin D, probiotics, and unsaturated fat.

- Processed meats like salami, bologna and hot dogs, as well as high-fat red meats like prime rib, bacon, and sausage, should be avoided. These are high in saturated fat, which may cause inflammation if ingested in excess.

- Omega-3 and Monounsaturated fats are recommended because they are thought to reduce inflammation. Olive oil, avocados, and almonds all contain monounsaturated fats. Consumption of these fats has been linked to a lower risk of heart disease, both of which are linked to inflammation.

- Tuna and wild salmon, walnuts, and ground flaxseed all contain omega-3 fatty acids. Omega-3 is an important fatty acid that our systems cannot produce and must be obtained via food or supplementation.

- Saturated fat should be avoided. Whole milk, cheese, butter, high-fat red meat, and chicken skin all fall under this category. Because our bodies only need a tiny quantity, every day over consumption will increase the inflammatory response.

- Trans fat should be avoided if possible. While trans fats have been prohibited in most foods by the FDA, they may still be found in products like flavored coffee creamers and microwave popcorn. As a result, make sure to read labels carefully. There is no such thing as a safe level of trans fat. It not only lowers good cholesterol while raising bad cholesterol (a pro-inflammatory factor), but it also reuses and recycles it.

Find Vitamins in foods you consume

Here are some suggestions that are most effective for people who exercise frequently:

- **Vitamin A:** is found in sweet potatoes, spinach, carrots, and tomatoes, among other foods.

- **Vitamin C:** is present in fruits and vegetables such as citrus, cantaloupe, and green & red peppers.

- **Vitamin D:** Oily fish, fortified meals, and dairy products are all good sources of vitamin D.

- **Calcium:** Cheese, low-fat milk, kale, broccoli, fortified orange juice, low-fat Greek yogurt, and fortified non-dairy milk are all good sources of calcium.

- **Copper:** To obtain your copper, eat pumpkin, sesame, shitake mushrooms, sunflower seeds and pumpkin, and cashews. Copper is also beneficial during the first several weeks after an injury (a sufficient quantity can be found in a normal multivitamin).

- **Zinc:** Eat crabmeat, chicken, lean beef, cashews, and fortified cereals to increase your zinc intake.
- **Turmeric:** Turmeric is a spice that may be found in curry powder. Curcumin is an anti-inflammatory, antioxidant chemical found in turmeric, which provides mustard and curries their yellow color. Probably add turmeric to your spice cabinet, or take 400 milligrams of turmeric daily in pill form for a more aggressive approach.
- **Garlic:** It may help maintain arteries flexible and clean, enabling oxygen-rich blood to reach working muscles by reducing the production of 2 inflammatory enzymes. Cooking with 2 to 4 garlic cloves each day will enhance taste and help to reduce inflammation.
- **Bromelain:** Bromelain is a pineapple-derived enzyme. After your exercise, drink one glass of pineapple juice or include it in your recovery smoothie for lots of immune-boosting vitamin C & inflammation-fighting effects.

"It's important to think about how you nourish your body," she advises. "A healthy diet and vitamins may help keep inflammation under control."

To make the most of an anti-inflammatory diet, I recommend following these 11 principles:

1. Every day, eat at least 25 grams of fiber.

By offering naturally occurring anti-inflammatory phytonutrients found in fruits, vegetables, and other whole foods, a fiber-rich diet may help decrease inflammation.

Consume whole grains, fruits, and veggies to get your fiber fix. Whole grains, such as oats and barley; vegetables, eggplant, onions, and okra; and a range of fruits, such as blueberries and bananas, are the finest sources.

2. Every day, consume at least 9 servings of fruits & vegetables.

Half a cup of cooked fruit or veg, or one cup of raw leafy vegetables, is one "serving."

Anti-inflammatory spices and herbs, such as ginger and turmeric, may be added to cooked vegetables and fruits to boost their effects.

3. Each week, consume 4 servings of alliums & crucifers.

Garlic, leek, and onions are alliums, whereas crucifers include cabbage, broccoli, mustard greens, cauliflower, and Brussels sprouts.

Consuming an average of 4 servings each week will help lessen risk due to their significant antioxidant effects.

4. Saturated fat should account for no more than 10% of the daily calories.

You may minimize your risk of cardiovascular disease by eating less saturated fat (approximately 20 grams per 2,000 calories).

To decrease the harmful chemicals created while cooking, restrict red meat to once a week and marinate it with spices, herbs, and unsweetened fruit juices, tart.

5. Eat meals that are high in omega-3 fatty acids.

Omega-3 fatty acids have been shown to decrease inflammation and may help lessen the risk of chronic illnesses, including heart disease and arthritis, which all have a high inflammatory process at their root.

6. At least 3 times a week, eat fish.

Fish is another excellent source of omega-3 fatty acids. Cold-water fish like salmon, herring, anchovies, mackerel, sardines, trout, and oysters are good options.

7. Utilize oils that are high in good fats.

The body needs fat, but pick fats that are beneficial to you.

8. Snack on healthful foods twice a day.

Snack on fruit, unsweetened or plain yogurt, carrots, celery sticks, or nuts such as pistachios, almonds, or walnuts.

9. Limit your intake of processed meals and sweets that have been refined.

It includes foods heavy in salt or rich in high-fructose corn syrup, both of which lead to inflammation across the body.

10. Eliminate Trans fats from your diet.

Food makers were obliged to mention Trans fats on nutrition labels by the FDA in 2006, and for a good reason: studies show that persons who consume foods rich in Tran's fats have greater levels of the C-reactive protein, an indicator for inflammation in the body.

11. Use phytonutrient-rich fruits to sweeten meals and spices to flavor dishes.

Phytonutrients are abundant in most fruits and vegetables. Apples, berries, apricots, and carrots may be used to sweeten your meals organically.

1.12 A Complete Anti-Inflammatory Meal Plan for a Week

Meal for an anti-inflammatory diet

For breakfast, lunch, snack time, and dinner, here's a list of anti-inflammatory meals (basically a diet plan)!

Day 1 - Monday

- Coconut (or any other dairy-free) yogurt with fruit and berries for breakfast. Green tea in a cup.

- Lunch - Whole wheat wrap with hummus-slathered chicken breast (roasted previously), spinach, avocado, tomatoes, bell peppers (the list goes on - use whatever vegetables you have in the fridge!)

- (Also, try adding some lemon pepper flavor to it; it's delicious!)

- Snack - a mixture of seeds, nuts, and fresh or dried fruit of your choice (without added sugar)

- Dinner - Shrimp skewers, baked or grilled, with your favorite veggies; finish with a glass of dry red wine, if desired (Hint: place shrimp & vegetables in a bag with herbs, olive oil, a squirt of lemon, and garlic, a few hours before cooking to enhance the flavor).

Day 2 - Tuesday

- Breakfast - Make a zesty omelet with fresh or leftover marinated veggies from the night before (Bell peppers, okra, onions, and mushrooms are good options.)

- A sandwich (whole grain) with veggies and leftover chicken breast for lunch (grapes, cubed chicken, and celery mixed with honey mustard with spinach or romaine lettuce)

- Avocado toast (whole grain) as a snack

- Dinner - Spaghetti squash spaghetti with a substantial dollop of pesto sauce and just a handful of raw walnuts, pine nuts, or raw cashews sprinkled with olive oil

- If you're short on time, spaghetti squash pasta may also be cooked in a crockpot.

Day 3 - Wednesday

- Breakfast - smoothie of your choice (strawberry banana with a lot of spinach and ginger, kale, and a teaspoon of turmeric! Other fantastic ingredients are blueberries, leafy greens, and cayenne pepper; beets and berries.)

- Prepare the smoothie the night prior and let it thaw for an hour the following day.

- Chickpea salad including leafy greens, purple or white onions, chicken, black olives, bell peppers, olive oil, and salt & pepper to taste for lunch

- Set some chickpeas away for tomorrow's snack & bell peppers aside for today's!

- Hummus or bell pepper sticks with guacamole as a snack

- Dinner - Honey garlic salmon with steamed broccoli.

Day 4 - Thursday

- Whole wheat bagel with almond or peanut butter & honey for breakfast

- Lunch - a salad with leftover salmon & spinach, red onions, parsley, celery, and your favorite dressing (preferably olive oil-based)

- Roasted chickpeas as a snack

- Dinner - Mediterranean chicken in a single pan (ignore the Feta cheese!). Dairy is not a friend when it comes to fighting inflammation via diet.)

Day 5 - Friday

- Breakfast - warm oatmeal with honey drizzle, chia seeds, plant-based milk or water, and your favorite fruit (either on top or on the side)

- Lunch - Golden tofu scramble with turmeric, tomatoes, spinach, and anything else you have on hand

- Matcha green tea milkshake as a snack or a handful of raw almonds as well as a cup of ginger tea if you're short on time

- Meal - Make this pesto spaghetti squash with shrimp dish using leftover spaghetti squash & pesto from Tuesday's dinner. Plus, it just takes 20 minutes to cook and prepare!

Day 6 - Saturday

- Whole grain bread with your preferred bananas, nut butter, & chia seeds for breakfast

- Lunch - Rice with cooked spinach and a sunny-side-up egg, served with a fruit side.

- Snack - Protein bar of your choosing

- Prepare a batch of oatmeal protein bars with chia seeds or flaxseed, peanut butter, almonds, & honey on a free day and store them later.

- Dinner: Sweet potato, broccoli, cauliflower, and carrots in a vegetable curry. Add your favorite plant-based protein on top (tofu cubes, golden roasted chickpeas, or crispy tempeh).

Day 7 - Sunday

- Whole wheat pancakes with your favorite fruit for breakfast

- (Combine 1 big egg, 1/2 cup nondairy yogurt, 1 cup whole-wheat, 1/4 cup flaxseed or buckwheat pancake mix, and 3/4 cup nondairy milk in a mixing bowl.)

- Lunch - whole wheat crusted Mediterranean pizza

- Snack - Chia pudding with coconut milk and fresh berries and fruit

- Dinner - Grilled chicken with a side of veggies of your choice.

Chapter 2: Breakfast Recipes

1. Cherry coconut porridge

Prep Time: 10 min, Serving: 2, Difficulty: Easy

Ingredients

- maple syrup
- 3-4cups of coconut drinking milk
- cherries (fresh or frozen)
- 3 tbsp raw cacao
- dark chocolate shavings
- 1.5cups oats
- coconut shavings
- 4 tbsp chia seed
- pinch of stevia

Instructions

1. In a saucepan, combine the chia, oats, cacao, coconut milk, and stevia. Bring to a boil over medium heat, reduce to low heat and continue to cook until the oats are soft.
2. Toss with coconut shavings, dark chocolate shavings, maple syrup, and cherries to taste in a bowl.

2. Gingerbread Oatmeal

Prep Time: 5 min, Serving: 8, Difficulty: Medium

Ingredients

- maple syrup to taste
- 1 ½ tbsp ground cinnamon
- ⅛ tsp ground nutmeg
- ¼ tsp ground coriander
- ¼ tsp ground allspice
- ¼ tsp ground cloves
- ¼ tsp ground cardamom
- 4 cups water
- 2 cup old fashion oats
- ¼ tsp. ground ginger

Instructions

1. Fill a pot with water and take to a boil.
2. In a big pot, bring water to a boil.
3. Toss in the oats.
4. In a large mixing bowl, combine the oats and hot water.
5. Toss in the spices.
6. In a large mixing bowl, mix the spices with the oats.
7. Stir the oats now and then until they're done. To taste, add your sweetener and serve.

3. Rhubarb, apple + ginger muffins {gluten + dairy-free}

Prep Time: 25 min, Serving: 2, Difficulty: Easy

Ingredients

- 1 tbsp ground linseed meal
- 1 small apple, peeled, finely diced and cored
- 1/4 cup raw sugar (unrefined)
- 1 tsp vanilla extract
- 2 tbsp organic corn flour
- 95ml almond milk or rice
- 1/2 tsp ground ginger
- 1/4 cup olive oil
- sea salt
- 1/2 cup almond meal
- 1/2 tsp ground cinnamon
- 1 large free-range egg

- 2 tsp sugar-free baking powder
- 2 tbsp ginger (crystallized), finely chopped
- 1/2 cup buckwheat flour
- 1 cup finely sliced rhubarb
- 1/4 cup rice flour (fine brown)

Instructions

1. Preheat the oven to 360 degrees Fahrenheit. Using paper cases, grease or line 8 1/3 cup size muffin pans.
2. In a medium mixing bowl, combine the sugar, almond meal, linseed meal, and ginger. Whisk together the baking powder, flours, and spices after sieving them in. Toss the apple and rhubarb in the flour mixture to coat. In a separate smaller bowl, whisk together the egg, oil, milk, and vanilla extract before putting into the dry ingredients and whisking just until mixed. Evenly divide the batter between muffin tins/paper cases (spread with a few rhubarb slices if wanted) and cook for 25 minutes, or until risen, brown around the edges, and a skewer inserted in the middle comes out clean. Remove the pan from the oven and cool for 5 minutes before moving to allow to cool completely. They're best eaten the day they're baked, but they'll keep in an airtight jar for 2-3 days or maybe frozen in a zip-lock bag for longer.

4. Mushroom and Spinach Frittata

Prep Time: 10 min, Serving: 2, Difficulty: Easy

Ingredients

- 1 onion, thinly sliced
- 6 eggs
- Salt and pepper
- 1 cup (250 ml) grated cheddar cheese
- 2 cups (500 ml) baby spinach
- 1/4 cup (60 ml) milk
- 4 oz (115 g) white button mushrooms, sliced
- 3 tbsp (45 ml) butter

Instructions

1. Preheat the oven to 350°F with the middle rack in place. A 20-cm square baking dish should be butter-coated. Put aside.
2. Whisk together the eggs and milk in a large mixing dish. Toss in some cheese. Pour Salt & pepper to taste. Set the dish aside.
3. Put brown onion & mushrooms in butter in a large nonstick pan over medium heat. Salt & pepper to taste. Cook, frequently stirring, for approximately 1 minute after adding the spinach.
4. In a mixing bowl, combine the mushroom mixture and the egg mixture. Stir everything up well before pouring it into a baking dish. Bake for approximately 25 minutes or until the frittata is gently golden and puffed. With a spatula, cut the frittata into 4 squares & remove them from the plate. Place on a platter, and you're good to go, warm or cold.

5. Overnight Oats with Peanut Butter and Banana

Prep Time: 5 min, Serving: 1, Difficulty: Easy

Ingredients

- ½ banana
- Oats and toppings
- ½ to ¾ cup milk (such as skim, whole, soy, almond, or coconut)
- ¾ cup old-fashioned oats
- 2 tbsp peanut butter
- 1 tbsp honey
- 2 tbsp peanut butter
- ½ banana, sliced

Instructions

1. Fill a 1-pint mason jar with oats.
2. Using a fork, mash half of a banana in a small bowl. Combine the peanut butter and honey in a mixing bowl.
3. Pour the milk over the oats in the container. (If you want your oatmeal to be thicker, add less milk.)
4. Refrigerate overnight (approximately 8 hours) after putting on the lid.
5. Sprinkle the banana slices and oatmeal with the peanut butter mixture in the morning. Eat right away, or put the top on & take it with you.

6. Eggs Benedict with Easy Hollandaise Sauce

Prep time: 15 min, Serving: 4, Difficulty: Easy

Ingredients

Hollandaise sauce

- 6 tbsp butter, melted and still warm
- 2 egg yolks
- Pinch of cayenne pepper (optional)
- 2 tsp lemon juice
- ¾ tsp salt
- ¼ tsp freshly ground black pepper

Eggs benedict

- 8 poached eggs
- 4 English muffins, halved and toasted until golden
- 8 slices thickly cut cooked ham
- 8 tsp butter, softened

Instructions

1. Toss the egg yolks with the lemon juice in a blender to mix.

2. Pour the melted butter into the blender in a slow, steady stream while it's running. Blend for 30 seconds to 1 minute, or until you have a thick sauce.
3. Pulse in the salt, pepper, and cayenne to mix. Remove from the equation.
4. 1 tsp soft butter, spread over every English muffin half. Top each dish with two muffin halves, two ham slices, and one poached egg. Top each muffin with 2 tbsp of the hollandaise sauce that has been made. Serve right away.

7. Nutella Pancakes

Prep Time: 1 hr 15 min, Serving: 3, Difficulty: Medium

Ingredients

- 1½ tsp baking powder
- ¾ tsp baking soda
- 6 pancakes
- Maple syrup, for serving (optional)
- 2 cups all-purpose flour
- 1 cup buttermilk
- 2 tbsp sugar
- 4 tbsp butter, melted
- 6 tbsp Nutella
- Nonstick cooking spray, as needed
- A pinch of salt

Instructions

1. Using parchment paper, line a baking sheet. Place 6 dollops (1 tbsp each) of Nutella on the baking sheet, allowing space between them. Spread every dollop into a thin circle (approximately 18-inch thick and 2-2 1/2-inches in diameter) using a knife.
2. Place the baking sheet in the freezer & freeze the Nutella for at least an hour until it is firm.
3. Make the pancakes after the Nutella pieces are frozen. Whisk together the flour, sugar,

baking powder, baking soda, and salt in a large mixing basin. Make a well in the middle of the dry ingredients. Add the butter & buttermilk to the ingredients. To blend, stir everything together.

4. Over medium heat, heat a big skillet or griddle. Using a nonstick spray, coat the heated pan.

5. 13 cup pancake batter, ladled or scooped onto the heated skillet. Put a Nutella round in the middle and top with a little amount of pancake batter.

6. Cook for 3 to 4 minutes until golden, then turn and cook for 2 to 3 minutes longer until golden on the other side. Remove the rounds from the pan and put them aside while you finish the rest of the batter & Nutella rounds.

7. Stack 3 pancakes on each dish to serve. Serve immediately with a side of maple syrup (if using).

8. Monkey-Bread Danish

Prep time: 30 min, Serving: 12, Difficulty: Easy

Ingredients

Streusel topping

- 1/3 cup all-purpose flour
- 2 tsps ground cinnamon
- 1/3 cup brown sugar
- ¼ cup (4 tbsp) unsalted butter, at room temperature
- 1/3 cup sugar

Cream-cheese filling

- 2 tbsp all-purpose flour
- One 8-ounce package of cream cheese, at room temperature
- ½ cup confectioners' sugar
- 1 egg
- ¾ cup sugar

- One 16-ounce package puff pastry, diced and thawed
- ¼ cup (4 tbsp) unsalted butter, melted
- 1 tbsp ground cinnamon

Instructions

1. Preheat oven to 350°F. Line two baking pans with parchment paper.

2. Combine the sugar, brown sugar, flour, and cinnamon in a medium mixing basin. Mix in the butter until the sugar mixture is crumbly and moist.

3. Preheat the oven to 350°F. Combine the cream cheese, confectioners' sugar, flour, and egg in a medium mixing bowl.

4. Toss the chopped puff pastry in the melted butter in a large mixing dish to moisten and coat. Combine the sugar & cinnamon in a small bowl. Toss the greased puff pastry with the cinnamon sugar and toss lightly to coat.

5. Fill the baking sheets with 14 cups puff pastry, allowing at least 1 1/2 inches between every mound. Slightly flatten the pieces, but make sure they're all touching. Create a small depression in the middle of each mound with your fingertips or the back of a spoon to make a place for the filling.

6. Fill each mound with 2 tbsp cream cheese filling. Add 2 tbsp streusel topping to the top.

7. Bake, the Danish for 15 to 20 minutes, or until the puff pastry is light brown and the filling is bubbly. Allow cooling before serving.

9. Sheet Tray Pancakes with Peaches and Strawberries

Prep Time: 25 min, Serving: 6, Difficulty: Easy

Ingredients

- Nonstick cooking spray
- 1½ cups sliced strawberries
- 2 ½ cups all-purpose flour
- 2 peaches, pitted and sliced
- 3 tbsp granulated sugar
- ½ tsp pure vanilla extract
- 1 tbsp baking powder
- 2 large eggs
- ¼ tsp salt
- ¼ tsp ground cinnamon
- 2 cups buttermilk
- maple syrup and Confectioners' sugar, for serving

Instructions

1. Preheat the oven to 425 degrees Fahrenheit. Using parchment paper, line a baking sheet and coat the paper & the sides of the pan with nonstick spray.
2. Whisk together the sugar, flour, salt, baking powder, and cinnamon in a big mixing bowl. Take a separate bowl, mix the buttermilk, eggs, and vanilla extract.
3. Pour the batter onto the prepared baking sheet & spread evenly. Arrange the strawberries and peaches over the top.
4. Bake for 12 to 15 minutes.
5. To serve, top the pancake with confectioners' sugar, cut it into squares, and drizzle with maple syrup.

10. 'Everything Bagel' Cauliflower Rolls

Prep time: 10 min, Serving: 4, Difficulty: Easy

Ingredients

- 1 medium head cauliflower, riced (4 cups)
- 3 tbsp "everything bagel" spice
- ⅓ cup almond flour
- 1 tsp garlic powder
- ½ tsp kosher salt
- 3 large eggs, lightly whisked

Instructions

1. Preheat the oven to 400 degrees Fahrenheit. Spray a baking sheet with nonstick spray before lining it with parchment paper.
2. Combine the cauliflower rice, almond flour, garlic powder, and salt in a large mixing basin.
3. Toss in the whisked eggs and mix well.
4. Make 8 equal portions of the mixture and roll them into balls. Place the balls on the baking sheet and sprinkle 1 heaping tsp of "everything bagel" spice on top of each one.
5. Bake for 35 to 40 minutes, or until the rolls are lightly browned around the edges & dry to the touch.
6. Allow the rolls to rest on the baking sheet for 10 minutes before gently transferring to a cooling rack to cool entirely.

11. The Nourishing Healthy Scramble

Prep Time: 10 min, Serving: 2, Difficulty: Easy

Ingredients

- 1 tbsp turmeric
- 2 tbsp coconut oil
- 2 shredded kale leaves
- Radish and clover sprouts to top
- 1 small clove garlic, minced
- 2 radishes grated
- 2 pastured eggs
- 1 pinch cayenne pepper

Instructions

1. Heat the coconut oil in a pan and softly sauté the garlic.
2. Scramble the eggs in a pan.
3. Add the turmeric, shredded kale, and cayenne when the eggs are nearly done.
4. Enjoy the radish and sprouts on top!

12. Golden Milk Chia Seed Pudding

Prep Time: 10 min, Serving: 4, Difficulty: Easy

Ingredients

- 4 cups full-fat coconut milk
- ¼ cup toasted coconut chips for garnishing
- 3 tsp honey
- 1 cup fresh mixed berries for garnishing
- 1 tsp vanilla extract
- ¾ cup coconut yogurt for topping
- 1 tsp ground turmeric
- ½ cup chia seeds
- ½ tsp ground cinnamon
- ½ tsp ground ginger

Instructions

1. In a large mixing bowl, combine the honey, coconut milk, turmeric, vanilla extract, ground ginger, and cinnamon. To blend, whisk everything together well, resulting in a bright yellow liquid.
2. Mix in the chia seeds, then put them aside for 5 minutes to allow them to absorb the liquid. When you're ready, give it another stir.
3. Cover the bowl with plastic wrap and refrigerate for 6 hours or overnight. It will plump the chia seeds and give the mixture the consistency of thick pudding.
4. Top each serving glass with a dollop of coconut yogurt and a spoonful of chia seed pudding. Garnish with toasted coconut chips and mixed berries.

13. Vanilla Turmeric Orange Juice

Prep Time: 5 min, Serving: 2, Difficulty: Easy

Ingredients

- 3 oranges, peeled + quartered
- Pinch of pepper
- 1 cup unsweetened almond milk
- 1 tsp vanilla extract
- ½ tsp cinnamon
- ¼ tsp turmeric

Instructions

1. In a blender, combine all of the ingredients.
2. Blend until completely smooth, then serve in a glass.

14. Berry & Chia Breakfast

Prep Time: 10 min, Serving: 1, Difficulty: Easy

Ingredients

- 1 cup / 125 g fresh or thawed frozen raspberries
- 1 cup / 240 ml plant milk
- 1 pinch ground vanilla
- 3 tbsp desiccated coconut, unsweetened
- 3 tbsp chia seeds

Topping

- kiwi
- nut butter
- hemp seeds
- fresh mint

Instructions

1. In a bowl, use a fork to mash the berries. In a separate bowl, add the vanilla, coconut, and chia seeds.
2. Add the milk and stir to combine. Allow to soak in the fridge for at least 30 minutes or overnight. Top with fruit, hemp seeds, nut butter, and mint, and serve in a bowl or jar.

15. No-Bake Turmeric Protein Donuts

Prep Time: 5 min, Serving: 4, Difficulty: Easy

Ingredients

- 1½ cups raw cashews
- ¼ cup dark chocolate (for topping)
- ½ cup (7 pieces) Medjool dates, pitted
- 1 tsp turmeric powder
- 1 tsp vanilla protein powder

- ¼ cup shredded coconut
- 2 tsp maple syrup
- ¼ t vanilla essence

Instructions

1. Mix all ingredients (except the chocolate) and process on high until a thick and sticky cookie dough forms.
2. Form the batter into 8 balls and press them firmly into the silicone donut form.
3. Wrap the molds in plastic wrap and freeze for 30 minutes to set.
4. Fill a pot with water and bring to a boil for the chocolate topping.
5. Then, on top of the pan, set a smaller saucepan and pour the chocolate into it. Gently stir until the chocolate has melted completely.
6. Remove the donuts from the molds after they have set, sprinkle with dark chocolate, and store in a container in the fridge.

16. Paleo Pancakes Nutty Choco-Nana

Prep Time: 5 min, Serving: 5, Difficulty: Easy

Ingredients

For the Chocolate Sauce:

- 4 tsp raw cacao powder
- ¼ coconut oil, melted

For the Pancakes:

- 2 tbsp creamy almond butter
- 1 tbsp pure vanilla extract
- 2 large eggs
- 2 ripe bananas
- Coconut oil, for greasing
- 2 tbsp raw cacao powder
- 1/8 t salt

Instructions

1. First, melt the coconut oil and then add the cacao powder. Set aside after mixing until thoroughly incorporated.
2. Preheat a big pan over medium heat & grease it with a tbsp of coconut oil.
3. In a food processor, combine all pancake ingredients & pulse until smooth.
4. Scoop the batter into a 1/4 measuring cup & add onto the skillet to make one pancake. Cook for 5 minutes before gently flipping over and cooking for two more minutes. Repeat until you've made 10 pancakes and all of the batters is disappeared.
5. Before serving, place the pancakes on a baking rack to cool for 5 minutes.
6. Pancakes may be stored in the refrigerator for up to 5 days or frozen for up to 30 days.

17. Sweet Potato Cranberry Breakfast Bars

Prep Time: 10 min, Serving: 4, Difficulty: Easy

Ingredients

- 1 ½ cups sweet potato purée
- 1 cup fresh cranberries
- ¼ cup water
- 1 ½ tbsp baking soda
- 2 tbsp coconut oil, melted
- ⅓ cup coconut flour
- 2 tbsp maple syrup
- 2 eggs
- 1 cup almond meal

Instructions

1. Preheat the oven to 350 degrees Fahrenheit.
2. Mix the sweet potato purée, water, melted coconut oil, maple syrup, and eggs in a large mixing bowl. Stir until everything is well combined.
3. Sift together the almond meal, coconut flour, and baking soda in a separate bowl.
4. Mix in the dry ingredients. Combine all of the ingredients in a large mixing bowl and stir thoroughly.
5. Line the bottom of a 9" square baking sheet with parchment paper and grease it with coconut oil.
6. Use a moist spatula to level down the top and fill in the corners of the batter in the prepared baking pan. Place the cranberries on top and press them down.
7. 30–40 minutes in the oven, or until a probe inserted in the center comes out clean. Remove it from the pan and cut it into squares once it has cooled fully.

18. Paleo Turmeric Scones

Prep Time: 15 min, Serving: 6, Difficulty: Easy

Ingredients

- 1 1/3 cup almond flour
- 1 tsp vanilla extract
- 1 cup almonds
- 3 tbsp maple syrup
- 1/4 cup arrowroot flour
- 1/4 cup red palm oil
- 1 tbsp coconut flour
- 1 egg
- 1 tsp turmeric
- 1/2 tsp black pepper
- Pinch salt

Instructions

1. Preheat the oven to 350 degrees Fahrenheit.
2. In a food processor, finely chop almonds. Combine the chopped almonds with the other dry ingredients.

Combine the ingredients and fluff with a spoon.

3. In a separate bowl, whisk together the egg, oil, syrup, and vanilla extract; add to the dry ingredients. Mix until everything is well incorporated, then move the dough to a chopping board or a plastic-wrapped countertop. Cut into sixths after patting into a spherical form about one inch thick.

4. Bake for 15-20 minutes in a preheated oven or until a toothpick inserted in the middle comes out clean.

19. Chocolate Avocado Blueberry Muffins

Prep Time: 10 min, Serving: 9, Difficulty: Easy

Ingredients

- 2 tsp dark chocolate chips
- 1 small avocado, ripe
- ¼ cup fresh blueberries
- 1/3 cup coconut sugar
- ½ cup unsweetened almond milk
- ¼ tsp salt
- 1 cup almond flour
- 1/4 cup raw cacao powder
- 2 tsp baking powder
- 2 large eggs, room temperature
- 2 tsp coconut flour

Instructions

1. Preheat the oven to 375 degrees Fahrenheit. Grease a muffin tray with coconut oil or use muffin liners.

2. Combine the eggs, avocado, sugar, and salt with 1 tablespoon cocoa powder in a blender. Blend on high until the avocado is completely broken down & the mixture has the consistency of a silky custard.

3. Sift together 1/4 cup cocoa powder, baking powder, coconut flour, and almond flour in a small bowl.

4. Pour the almond milk into the liquid mixture, then fold in the dry ingredients gently. Don't overmix! Mix until everything is combined.

5. Combine the blueberries & chocolate chips in a mixing bowl.

6. Divide the batter equally among the 9 cavities of the prepared muffin tray.

7. Bake for 18 minutes.

8. Take the muffins out from the pan and let them cool on a wire rack.

9. Keep refrigerated for up to one week or frozen for up to 1 month.

20. Raspberry-Grapefruit Smoothie

Prep Time: 10 min, Serving: 1, Difficulty: Easy

Ingredients

- 1 banana peeled and sliced (frozen or fresh)
- Juice of 1 pink grapefruit
- 1 cup raspberries (frozen or fresh)

Instructions

1. Put all ingredients in a blender, then blend until smooth.

2. Serve and Enjoy.

21. No-Stress Shroom Iced Mocha

Prep Time: 5 min, Serving: 1, Difficulty: Easy

Ingredients

- ½ tbsp raw cacao powder
- 1 packet of Mushroom Coffee
- Handful ice cubes
- 8 oz hot water
- 1 tsp coconut oil
- ½ cup unsweetened almond milk

Instructions

1. In a pot of boiling water, dissolve the packet. Allow 2 minutes to cool after stirring to dissolve the powder.
2. Mix in the coconut oil & cacao powder until they are completely dissolved.
3. Pour almond milk (unsweetened) over the coffee, top with ice, and enjoy!

22. Savory Indian Pancake

Prep Time: 10 min, Serving: 2, Difficulty: Easy

Ingredients

- 1/2 inch ginger grated
- ½ cup Almond Flour
- 1 serrano pepper minced (or adjust to taste)
- ½ cup Tapioca Flour
- 1 handful cilantro leaves chopped
- 1 cup Coconut Milk canned and full fat
- ½ red onion chopped
- 1 tsp salt adjust to taste
- ¼ tsp freshly ground black pepper
- ½ tsp Kashmiri Chili Powder

- oil/fat of choice use enough to shallow fry
- ¼ tsp Turmeric Powder

Instructions

1. In a mixing bowl, combine almond flour, coconut milk, tapioca flour, and spices.
2. Add the onion, serrano pepper, cilantro, and ginger after that.
3. Fry the Pancakes!
4. Heat a saute pan over low-medium heat, then add enough oil to coat the pan. Pour 1/4 cup of batter into the pan. Pour the ingredients into your pan and spread it out evenly.
5. Cook for 3-4 minutes on each side, pouring a little extra oil on top of the pancake before flipping.
6. Repeat until the batter is finished, adding oil as required.
7. Serve with paleo ketchup or green chutney.

23. Scrambled Eggs with Smoked Salmon Recipe

Prep Time: 10 min, Serving: 2, Difficulty: Easy

Ingredients

- Cooking fat
- 4 eggs
- Scrambled Eggs
- 4 slices smoked salmon, chopped
- 2 tbsp. coconut milk
- Fresh chives, finely chopped
- Sea salt and freshly ground black pepper

Instructions

1. Whisk together the coconut milk, eggs, and fresh chives in a mixing basin. Season with salt and pepper to taste.

2. In a pan, melt some cooking butter and crack the eggs.
3. While the eggs are cooked, scramble them.
4. Add the smoked salmon & cook for 2 minutes after the eggs have settled.
5. Serve with a sprinkle of chives on top.

24. Dark Chocolate Orange Chia Pudding

Prep Time: 5 min, Serving: 2, Difficulty: Easy

Ingredients

- 1 tsp orange zest
- 1/3 cup chia seeds
- Orange peel, for garnishing (optional)
- 3 tsp raw cacao powder
- 1 cup water
- 1/4 cup orange juice
- 1 tsp honey (or maple syrup)

Instructions

1. Combine the raw cacao powder, chia seeds, orange zest, orange juice, and honey in a large mixing dish. Mix thoroughly.
2. Mix in the water until the cacao powder is completely dissolved.
3. Cover the bowl with plastic wrap and refrigerate for at least 3 hours, or until the chia seeds completely absorbed all of the liquid. The chia pudding should have a thick consistency.
4. Serve by dividing the chia pudding equally between two glasses and garnishing an orange peel (if desired).

25. Paleo Crêpes Sprinkled with Nutella

Prep Time: 10 min, Serving: 5, Difficulty: Easy

Ingredients

For the Hazelnut Filling:

- 2 tsp maple syrup
- 2/3 cup dark chocolate chips
- 1 cup hazelnuts
- ½ tsp vanilla extract
- 1 tsp melted coconut oil

For the Crêpes:

- 1 tsp melted coconut oil
- 2 tbsp coconut flour
- 4 large pasture-raised eggs
- ½ cup water

Instructions

1. Preheat the oven to 350 degrees Fahrenheit.
2. Bake for 10 minutes with the hazelnuts on a baking sheet. Remove them from the oven when they're done and set them aside to cool for approximately 5 minutes. To remove the skins, place the hazelnuts on a clean dish towel and massage them together. (It's ok if some skins are left.)
3. Pulse the hazelnuts in a food processor until they are completely broken down. It should have a crumbs-like texture.
4. In a double boiler, melt the chocolate chips & coconut oil. Heat for 4 minutes, stirring regularly, until melted.
5. Toss the melted chocolate with maple syrup, vanilla extract, and crumbled hazelnuts. Place the mixture in a glass jar and put it aside.
6. To make the crêpes, begin by combining all of the ingredients in a large mixing bowl. Whisk together the crêpe ingredients in a mixing bowl until smooth.
7. Grease a pan with coconut oil and cook over medium heat. Cook for 4 minutes, turning halfway through, with 1/3 cup of the crêpe mixture in the pan.

Repeat with the remaining batter after removing the first crêpe from the pan.

8. Fill each crepe with 2 tbsp of the hazelnut filling and fold it in half. Roll up the crêpe with the cut strawberries on top. Drizzle another spoonful of hazelnut filling over the top and serve right away!

26. Keto Avocado Smoothie with Ginger, Coconut Milk, and Turmeric

Prep Time: 10 min, Serving: 2, Difficulty: Easy

Ingredients

- 1/2 avocado
- 1/2 tsp turmeric
- 1/4 cup almond milk
- 1 tsp lemon or lime juice
- 3/4 cup coconut milk
- 1 tsp grated ginger, fresh
- sugar-free sweetener to taste
- 1 cup crushed ice

Instructions

1. In a blender, combine the first 6 ingredients and mix on low until smooth.
2. Mix in the crushed ice and the sweetener. Blend on high speed until completely smooth.
3. Taste and adjust the sweetness and tartness according to your preferences.

27. Maple-baked rice porridge recipe with fruit

Prep Time: 10 min, Serving: 2, Difficulty: Easy

Ingredients

- ½ cup brown rice
- Pinch of salt (optional)
- ½ tsp pure vanilla extract
- Sliced fruit, such as berries, pears, plums, or cherries
- Pinch of cinnamon
- 2 tbsp pure maple syrup

Instructions

1. Preheat oven to 400 degrees Fahrenheit.
2. In a medium-high-heat saucepan, combine the rice & 1 cup of water. Bring to a boil, then mix in the vanilla extract & cinnamon. Reduce heat to medium-low and cover. Simmer for 10-15 minutes. If you're using a rice type that takes longer to cook, follow the instructions until it's soft.
3. Stir the rice and divide it into two heat-safe dishes. Add a spoonful of maple syrup & your favorite sliced fruit to each bowl. If desired, season with salt.
4. Bake for 10-15 minutes, or until the maple syrup begins to bubble and the fruit begins to caramelize. Serve right away.

28. Coffee and Mint Yogurt Parfait

Prep Time: 10 min, Serving: 1, Difficulty: Easy

Ingredients

- ½ cup plain yogurt
- 2 tsp brewed coffee
- 3-4 drops peppermint Stevia (optional)
- ¼ cup chopped pecans
- For garnish: coffee granules and fresh mint

Ingredients

Instructions

1. In a small dish, combine the coffee, yogurt, and stevia.
2. Alternate layers of yogurt and pecans in a tiny glass until you reach the top.
3. Serve with coffee granules & fresh mint as garnish.

29. 5-Minute Herb-Baked Eggs

Prep Time: 5 min, Serving: 1, Difficulty: easy

Ingredients

- 2 eggs
- 1 tsp melted butter
- 1 tablespoon milk
- Sprinkle of dried parsley, dried dill, dried thyme, dried oregano, and garlic powder

Instructions

1. Preheat the oven to "Broil" on low.
2. Using the butter and milk, coat the base of a small baking dish.
3. On top of the butter and milk mixture, break the eggs.
4. On top of the butter and milk mixture, break the eggs. Garlic and dry herbs are sprinkled over the top.
5. Bake for approximately 5-6 minutes, or until the eggs are fully cooked.

30. Crunchy Cinnamon Granola

Prep Time: 10 min, Serving: 3, Difficulty: Easy

Ingredients

- ¼ tsp ground nutmeg
- 2 cups old-fashioned rolled oats
- ¼ cup dried cranberries
- ¼ cup unsweetened shredded coconut
- ¼ cup chopped dried apricots
- ¼ cup chopped walnuts
- ¼ cup raisins
- 2 tbsp pumpkin seeds
- 4 tbsp unsalted butter, melted
- ½ tsp ground cinnamon
- ¼ tsp ground cloves
- ¼ cup honey

Instructions

1. Preheat the oven to 300 degrees Fahrenheit.
2. Using parchment paper, line a baking sheet.
3. Combine the coconuts, oats, pumpkin seeds, walnuts, and spices in a large mixing bowl and set aside.
4. In a separate dish, combine the honey and melted butter and pour over the oat mixture. Stir everything together well.
5. On the baking sheet, spread out the oat mixture. Bake for about 25 minutes, or until golden brown. Remove from the oven and set aside to cool.
6. Once the granola has cooled, break it up and add the dried fruit. Keep the container sealed.

31. Energizing pineapple anti-inflammatory smoothie

Prep Time: 10 min, Serving: 1, Difficulty: Easy

Ingredients

- 4–5 ice cubes
- 2 cups spinach or kale
- 1 Tbsp chia seeds
- 1 cup frozen pineapple chunks
- 1 scoop protein powder
- 2/3 cup cucumber, peeled and cut into large chunks)
- 3 mint leaves – rough chopped
- ½ cup frozen mango chunks
- ¼ tsp ground turmeric
- ½ of a medium banana, peeled
- 1 cup brewed and cooled green tea
- 1/2" fresh ginger – peeled and cut from the stalk (about ½ tsp)

Instructions

1. In a high-powered blender, combine all of the ingredients, excluding the chia seeds.
2. Chia seeds should be added towards the end of the mixing process to avoid sticking to the blender.
3. If you like a thicker smoothie, add ice cubes and mix until the desired consistency is achieved.

32. Pecan Banana Bread Overnight Oats

Prep Time: 15 min, Serving: 2, Difficulty: Easy

Ingredients

- 2 tbsp honey
- 1 cup oats, old-fashioned rolled
- Banana slices, fig halves, roasted pecans, pomegranate seeds and honey, for serving
- 1/4 tsp flaked sea salt
- 2 ripe bananas, mashed
- 2 tsp vanilla extract
- 1/4 cup Greek yogurt, plain

- 1 1/2 cups milk
- 2 tbsp coconut flakes (unsweetened), toasted
- 1 tbsp chia seeds

Instructions

1. Combine the milk, oats, Greek yogurt, unsweetened coconut flakes, bananas, chia seeds, vanilla extract, honey, and sea salt in a medium mixing bowl.
2. Pour the mixture into two dishes or glass jars. Refrigerate for at least six hours or overnight after covering. Stir in the banana slices, toasted pecans, and fig halves, and serve warm if preferred. Drizzle with honey & pomegranate seeds.

33. Yogurt parfait recipe with raspberries and chia seeds

Prep Time: 10 min, Serving: 2, Difficulty: Easy

Ingredients

- ½ cup fresh raspberries
- Fresh fruit, such as sliced blackberries, strawberries, nectarines, etc.
- 2 tbsp chia seeds
- 1 tsp maple syrup
- Pinch of cinnamon
- 16-ounces plain yogurt

Instructions

1. In a small mixing dish, place the raspberries. Mash the berries with the back of a fork until they have a jam-like consistency. In a mixing dish, combine the chia seeds, honey, and cinnamon. Continue mashing until all of the ingredients are completely combined. Remove from the equation.
2. In the base of a medium glass or jar, spread a layer of yogurt.

3. Add a layer of the raspberry chia mixture on top. Finish with a layer of yogurt on top. If preferred, top with fresh sliced fruit and a sprinkle of maple syrup. Replace the second glass/jar and repeat the process.

34. Winter Morning (Or Any Time!) Breakfast Bowl

Prep Time: 10 min, Serving: 2, Difficulty: Easy

Ingredients

- 2 whole cloves
- 1 star anise pod (optional)
- 1 cup of grains such as buckwheat, amaranth, or quinoa
- 1 cinnamon stick
- 2½ cups coconut water or nut milk
- Maple syrup (optional)
- Fresh fruit: apples, blackberries, pears, persimmons, cranberries, etc.

Instructions

1. To create the grain bowls, in a saucepan, bring the grains, nut milk /coconut water, and spices to a boil. Cover and decrease the heat to medium-low after the water has boiled.
2. Cook for 20-25 minutes until the grains are soft. Take the pan off the heat and toss out the entire spices. If preferred, top with chosen fruit and a sprinkle of maple syrup.

35. Greek yogurt recovery smoothie

Prep Time: 10 min, Serving: 1, Difficulty: Easy

Ingredients

- ¼ cup blueberries (frozen or fresh)

- 1 cup nut milk of choice, such as cashew milk, almond milk, etc.
- 3-4 ice cubes
- ½ cup plain Greek yogurt
- (Optional toppings) pinch of cardamom or ground cinnamon, pistachios, or bee pollen
- ¼ cup packed baby spinach
- 1 tablespoon nut butter of choice, such as peanut butter, almond butter, etc.

Instructions

1. Add all ingredients to a blender, and blend until smooth.
2. Serve and enjoy.

36. Cacao Berry Smoothie

Prep Time: 10 min, Serving: 1, Difficulty: Easy

Ingredients

- (Optional) Cacao nibs
- 1/2 cup filtered water
- Ice (use as desired to cool down drink)
- 1 cup fresh baby spinach
- 1 tablespoon honey or maple syrup
- 1 cup raspberries (fresh or frozen)
- 3 tbsp cacao powder
- 1 cup almond, or coconut, milk
- 1 banana

Instructions

1. In a blender, combine all ingredients and mix until smooth. As desired, sprinkle with cocoa nibs.
2. Take a sip and relax!

37. Tropical turmeric smoothie bowl

Prep Time: 10 min, Serving: 2, Difficulty: Easy

Ingredients

- ½ banana
- 1 cup orange juice
- Dash of turmeric - to your taste
- 1 cup frozen pineapple
- 1 cup frozen mango
- 1 spoonful of chia

For the toppings

- Coconut flakes
- Sliced strawberries
- Sliced kiwis
- Chopped almonds

Instructions

1. In a blender, combine all of the ingredients. Blend until the mixture is smooth and creamy. If the mixture becomes too thick, you may need to add a little bit of orange juice. Fruit slices, nuts, and coconut flakes may be sprinkled over the top.

38. Spinach and Smoked Salmon Breakfast Recipe

Prep Time: 20 min, Serving: 4, Difficulty: Easy

Ingredients

- 4 eggs
- Sea salt and freshly ground black pepper
- 8 oz. smoked salmon, sliced
- 2 tbsp olive oil

- 2 russet or sweet potatoes, peeled and diced
- 2 tbsp ghee
- 1/2 onion, sliced
- 1/4 tsp paprika
- 1/2 cup mushrooms, sliced
- 1/2 tsp garlic powder
- 2 cups fresh baby spinach
- 1 garlic clove, minced
- 1/2 tsp onion powder

Instructions

1. Preheat the oven to 425 degrees Fahrenheit.
2. Toss the potatoes with onion powder, olive oil, paprika, garlic powder, and salt & pepper to taste.
3. Preheat the oven to 350°F and bake the potatoes for 30 minutes, flipping halfway through.
4. Over high heat, bring a saucepan of water to a boil.
5. Cook the eggs in the boiling water for 6 to 7 minutes after turning off the heat.
6. Drain the water and rinse the eggs under cold water; peel the eggs and put them aside.
7. Over medium-high heat, melt the ghee and add the onion and garlic.
8. Cook for another 1 to 2 minutes before adding the sliced mushrooms.
9. Season to taste, then cook for another 4 to 5 minutes, or until everything is soft.
10. Cook for 1 to 2 minutes, or until the spinach has wilted.
11. Serve the potatoes with the spinach-mushroom combination, sliced smoked salmon, and an egg.

39. Prosciutto-Wrapped Avocado Egg

Prep Time: 5 min, Serving: 2, Difficulty: Easy

Ingredients

- 2 ripe, ready to eat avocados
- Tomato slices, for garnish
- 2 eggs
- Chopped parsley for garnish
- 6 prosciutto slices
- 2 Tsp olive oil
- Salt and pepper, to taste

Instructions

1. Bring a medium saucepan of water to a moderate simmer over low heat.
2. Line a small bowl with food-safe plastic wrap and drizzle it with olive oil.
3. Pull the edges of the plastic wrap together and make a knot in the egg in the prepared bowl. 3 minutes in the boiling water with the wrapped egg Rep with the second egg.
4. Take the eggs out of the water and place them on a platter. Gently detach the eggs from the plastic wrap by cutting them apart. Remove them from the equation.
5. Flatten the prosciutto slices with the back of a knife before serving.
6. Remove the avocado's outer peel and cut it in half. Scoop out the avocado's center to make it the same size as the poached egg. Carefully place the egg inside and wrap the avocado over it on both sides.
7. Wrap two pieces of prosciutto horizontally and one-piece vertically around the sealed avocado. Carry on with the second egg in the same manner.
8. Fry the wrapped avocado in olive oil for approximately 10 minutes over medium heat, beginning with the loose bacon ends. Turn the bacon regularly until it is crispy all over.
9. Before serving, drain the excess oil on a paper towel. Sprinkle salt, pepper, and chopped parsley over the filled avocado. Serve with tomato slices on the side.

40. Keto Breakfast Burger with Avocado Buns

Prep Time: 5 min, Serving: 1, Difficulty: Easy

Ingredients

- 1 tomato slice
- 1 ripe avocado
- Sesame seeds, for garnish
- 1 egg
- Sea salt, to taste
- 2 bacon rashers
- 1 Tbsp Paleo mayonnaise
- 1 red onion slice
- 1 lettuce leaf

Instructions

1. On a cold frying pan, place the bacon rashers. Start cooking the bacon after the stove is turned on. Flip the bacon with a fork when it begins to curl. Cook the bacon until it has become crispy.
2. Take the bacon out from the pan, break the egg into it, and cook it in the same pan with the bacon grease. Cook until the yolk is still liquid, but the white is set.
3. Cut the avocados in half lengthwise. Remove the pit by scooping it out of the skin using a spoon.

4. Paleo mayonnaise should be used to fill the hole.
5. Lettuce, bacon, onion, tomato, and a fried egg are layered on top.
6. Season with a pinch of salt.
7. Add the 2nd half of the avocado on top.
8. Sesame seeds may be sprinkled on top.

41. Crispy Bacon and Baked Eggs in a Portobello Mushroom

Prep Time: 10 min, Serving: 4, Difficulty: Easy

Ingredients

- 4 portobello mushroom caps
- Salt and pepper, to taste
- 1 cup arugula
- 4 large, pasture-raised eggs
- 1 medium tomato, chopped
- 2 strips thick-cut, pasture-raised bacon, cooked and chopped

Instructions

1. Preheat the oven to 350 degrees Fahrenheit and prepare a baking sheet with parchment paper.
2. Using a spoon, remove the gills from the mushrooms and discard them.
3. Fill each mushroom cap with arugula & tomato and place on a baking sheet. In the middle, carefully place one egg.
4. Bake for almost 20 minutes, or until the egg whites become white, on the center rack of the oven.
5. Add chopped bacon, sea salt, and black pepper to taste.

42. Chocolate Paleo Donuts

Prep Time: 10 min, Serving: 8, Difficulty: Easy

Ingredients

The Donut:

- 4 eggs
- 1 cup coconut flour
- ¼ cup honey
- ¼ cup raw cacao powder
- 1 tsp vanilla
- ½ tsp baking soda
- ¼ cup unsweetened applesauce
- ¼ tsp salt
- ¼ cup coconut oil, melted

The Icing:

- 1 tbsp coconut oil
- ½ cup dairy-free white chocolate

Instructions

1. Preheat the oven to 350 degrees Fahrenheit.
2. Dry ingredients should be mixed. In a large mixing bowl, combine the doughnut ingredients (coconut flour, baking soda, cacao, and salt).
3. Whisk together coconut oil and eggs in a medium mixing basin. Stir in the remaining wet ingredients (honey, applesauce, and vanilla) in the same bowl.
4. Fold wet ingredients into dry ingredients until well combined.
5. Additional coconut oil should be used to grease the donut pan; transfer the dough to the donut pan and push it down to be firmly packed and smooth.
6. Preheat the oven to 350°F and bake the pan for 15 minutes, or until the dough is no longer soft.

7. Remove from oven; invert your donut pan, and the donuts should fall out easily.

8. Allow them to cool for almost 5 minutes before frosting them.

9. In a small saucepan, heat the coconut oil dairy-free and white chocolate together, constantly stirring until completely melted. Ice the doughnuts using a knife.

10. Refrigerate or eat warm to enable the frosting to solidify.

11. Have fun!

43. Sweet Cherry Almond Chia Pudding

Prep time: 20 min, Serving: 4, difficulty: Easy

Ingredients

- 1 can coconut milk
- 1/4 cup maple syrup
- 1/2 cup hemp seeds
- 1/8 tsp sea salt
- 2 cups cherries (whole sweet)
- 1 tsp vanilla extract
- 1 tsp almond extract
- 3/4 cup chia seeds

For Topping:

- 4 cups pitted & halved frozen or fresh cherries

Instructions

1. In a blender, combine coconut milk, 2 cups of cherries, maple syrup, almond and vanilla extracts, and salt. Blend until completely smooth.

2. Blend on low only to incorporate the chia & hemp seeds.

3. Fill containers with the mixture and store them in the refrigerator.

4. Allow 1 hour in the fridge for the chia pudding to solidify before topping with frozen or fresh cherries. If you attempt to put fruit on top of the pudding straight quickly, it will dissolve into the pudding.

5. The puddings may keep in the refrigerator for 4-5 days.

44. Smoked salmon eggs benedict

Prep Time: 35 min, Serving: 2, Difficulty: Easy

Ingredients

- 4 large eggs
- A pinch of black pepper
- 2 English muffins, cut in half
- 3 ounces smoked salmon
- Red onion, thinly sliced
- 4 tbsp cream cheese (omit for Whole30 + paleo)
- 2 tsp capers

For Lemony hollandaise sauce:

- 2 big egg yolks
- Salt
- 2 tbsp butter
- 2 tbsp water
- 2 tsp lemon juice (fresh)

Instructions

1. In a frying pan, combine the water & egg yolks. Beat the eggs till they become frothy & warm, holding the pan over a medium-high element. Put the butter in the pan and mix until the hollandaise becomes thick (do not set the pan on the heat!). Set the pan aside after whisking in the lemon juice and a touch of salt.

2. On high heat, put a pot of water on the stove.

3. Toast your English muffins lightly in a toaster or by cooking them on their cut sides in a little butter. Put them on the dishes you'll be serving them on, then put cream cheese on top. Distribute the smoked salmon among them.

4. Reduce the heat to a low simmer after the water has reached a boil. One at a time, crack the eggs into the pan and cook approximately 4 minutes. Using a slotted spoon, remove them from the saucepan and set one egg on top of every English muffin.

5. Top the eggs with hollandaise sauce and a few pieces of red onion, capers, and black pepper.

6. If serving with arugula, combine a handful of baby arugula with a splash of olive oil and serve with the eggs benedict.

45. Anti-inflammatory cherry & beet smoothie

Prep Time: 10 min, Serving: 1, Difficulty: Easy

Ingredients

- 1 tbsp of almonds/almond butter
- 2 small beets, sliced
- 1/2 cup of pitted cherries (frozen)
- 1/2 banana (frozen)
- 10 oz of vanilla (unsweetened) almond milk

Instructions

1. Add all ingredients to a blender and mix until smooth.
2. Serve and enjoy.

46. Chocolate Breakfast Milkshake

Prep Time: 5 min, Serving: 1, Difficulty: Easy

Ingredients

- 2 large frozen organic bananas
- 4 ice cubes
- 1 cup coconut milk
- 2 tbsp cashew butter
- 1 tbsp raw cacao powder
- 1/2 t vanilla extract

Instructions

1. To begin, place the bananas and coconut milk in a high-powered blender & pulse a few times.
2. Pulse in the cacao powder, cashew butter, and vanilla a few more times.
3. Blend in the ice until it is completely smooth. To get a milkshake consistency, add additional ice cubes or coconut milk as required.

47. Feel-good pineapple smoothie

Prep Time: 5 min, Serving: 1, Difficulty: Easy

Ingredients

- 1 tbsp fresh ginger (finely chopped)
- 1/4 tsp ground black pepper
- 1 orange, peeled
- 1 tsp Ground Turmeric
- 1 cup coconut water
- 1 tsp chia seeds
- 1 ½ cups frozen pineapple chunks

Instructions

1. In a blender, combine all of the ingredients. Pulse until the mixture is completely smooth.
2. Serve right away, with more chia seeds on top if preferred.

48. Gluten Free Paleo Cherry Muffins

Prep Time: 10 min, Serving: 6, Difficulty: Easy

Ingredients

- 1 1/2 cup almond flour
- 1 cup pitted cherries
- 1/4 cup arrowroot flour
- 1/4 tsp sea salt
- 1/4 cup coconut oil
- 1 tsp baking powder
- 1/4 cup maple syrup or 1/2 tsp stevia liquid
- 1 1/2 tsp almond extract
- 3 whole eggs
- 2 tsp vanilla extract

Instructions

1. Preheat the oven to 350 degrees Fahrenheit and prepare a muffin tray with paper liners.
2. Combine all of the muffin ingredients (except the cherries) and mix well. Once the batter is smooth, mix in the cherries.
3. Fill muffin liners halfway with batter and bake at 350°F for 30 minutes, or until golden on top.

49. Anti-inflammatory smoothie

Prep Time: 10 min, Serving: 1, Difficulty: Easy

Ingredients

- 1 cup baby kale
- 1 serving Protein Smoothie Boost (optional)
- 1/2 small beet (peeled and chopped)
- 1 tsp coconut oil
- 1/2 cup water
- 1 tsp fresh ginger (grated or chopped)
- 1/2 orange (peeled)
- 1 cup mixed berries (frozen)
- 1/2 cup pineapple (frozen)

Instructions

1. In a blender, combine the beet, water, baby kale, and orange.
2. Puree until completely smooth.
3. Add the rest of the ingredients.
4. Blend until smooth once again.

50. Ginger, Tropical Carrot, & Turmeric Smoothie

Prep Time: 10 min, Serving: 2, Difficulty: Easy

Ingredients

- 1 tbsp raw hemp seeds (shelled)
- 1 blood or navel orange, peel and white pith removed
- Pinch of kosher salt
- ½ cup mango chunks (frozen)
- Pinch of cayenne pepper
- 1 large carrot, scrubbed, coarsely chopped
- 1½ tsp peeled, finely grated turmeric
- ¾ tsp peeled, finely grated ginger
- ⅔ cup coconut water

Instructions

1. Purée orange, mango, carrot, hemp seeds, coconut water, turmeric, ginger, salt, cayenne, and 1/2 cup ice in a blender until smooth, using the smoothie or ice crush setting.
2. Serve and enjoy

51 Smoothie with cherries and mocha

Ready in 10 min **Servings:** 2 **Difficulty:** Easy

Ingredients

- 2 tbsp of cocoa powder
- 2 tbsp almond butter
- 2 cups of ice cubes
- 1 teaspoon coffee powder
- 1 teaspoon of vanilla
- 1 cup frozen dark sweet cherries
- 1 cup chocolate almond milk
- o to 6-ounce carton vanilla fat-free yogurt
- ½ banana
- 1 tbsp of Dark chocolate

Instructions

1. Mix almond milk, yogurt, cherries, banana, cocoa powder, almond milk, proper coffee powder, and vanilla in a blender and mix until smooth. Blend until smooth, covered. Cover and mix until smooth, adding ice cubes as needed. Pour into glasses and garnish with chocolate-covered espresso beans, chocolate shavings, and more banana slices, if desired.

52 Omelet with avocado and kale

Ready in 10 min **Servings:** 1 **Difficulty:** Easy

Ingredients

- 1 teaspoon sunflower seeds
- 2 teaspoons of extra-virgin olive oil
- 1 tbsp lemon juice
- Pinch of salt
- ¼ avocado, sliced
- 2 eggs
- 1 teaspoon low-fat milk
- Pinch of crushed red pepper
- salt
- 1 tbsp chopped cilantro
- 1 cup chopped kale

Instructions

1. In a small bowl, whisk together the eggs, milk, and salt. In a small fry pan, heat 1 teaspoon oil over medium heat.

2. Cook for 2 minutes, just until the base is set, but the middle is still a little runny. Cook for another 30 seconds on the other side or until the omelet is set. Place on a platter to cool.
3. Toss the kale with leftover 1 teaspoon oil, lemon juice, cilantro, sunflower seeds, smashed red pepper, and a sprinkle of salt in a large mixing bowl. Avocado and kale salad goes on top of the omelet.

53 Breakfast Salad with Baby Kale, Quinoa, and Strawberries

Ready in 15 min **Servings: 1 Difficulty:** Easy

Ingredients

- 1 tbsp olive oil
- 2 teaspoons vinegar
- 3 cups packed baby kale
- ½ cup cooked quinoa
- Pinch of pepper
- ½ cup sliced strawberries
- 1 tbsp pepitas
- 1 teaspoon garlic
- Pinch of salt

Instructions

1. To make a paste, mash the garlic & salt, including the side of even a chef's knife or a fork. In a medium mixing bowl, combine the oil, garlic paste, vinegar, and pepper. Stir in the kale and toss to coat. Serve with quinoa, strawberries, and pepitas on the side.
2.

54 Lemony Labneh with Pistachios

Ready in 12 hrs. **Servings:** 8 **Difficulty:** Easy

Ingredients

- 4 cups of low-fat plain yogurt
- 1 tbsp olive oil or agrumato lemon oil
- 1 tbsp fresh parsley, chopped
- 1 teaspoon of lemon zest
- ¼ teaspoon of salt
- ¼ cup pistachios
- ¼ teaspoon of ground sumac

Instructions

1. Multiple levels of cheesecloth should be used to line a 7-inch and larger fine-mesh sieve. Place over a dish deep enough to allow at least four inches between the sieve's bottom and the bowl's bottom. In a larger bowl, whisk together the yogurt and salt; pour into the cheesecloth.
2. Refrigerate for 12 to 24 hours, or until the yogurt is quite thick, as well as at least a single cup of water has dripped into the bowl. (Remove the liquid.)
3. Sprinkle with lemon zest, oil, pistachios, parsley and sumac to serve.

55 Toast with Mascarpone and Berries

Ready in 5 min **Servings: 1 Difficulty:** Easy

Ingredients

- 1 slice toasted whole-grain bread
- 1 teaspoon of mint leaves
- ¼ cup of berries, such as blueberries, raspberries
- 2 tbsp of cheese

Instructions

1. Mascarpone, berries, and mint go on top of the bread

56 Granola Bars with Almond Joy

Ready in 1 hr. 30 min **Servings:** 24 **Difficulty:** Easy

Ingredients

- ¼ teaspoon of salt
- ⅔ cup of brown rice syrup
- ½ cup almond butter
- 1 teaspoon of coconut extract
- 3 cups oats
- 1 cup brown rice cereal, crispy
- 1 cup of chocolate chips
- 1 cup shredded coconut, toasted

Instructions

1. Heat the oven to 325 ° F. Using parchment paper, line a 9-by-13-inch baking sheet, with excess parchment falling over two edges. Spray the parchment lightly with cooking spray.
2. In a large mixing bowl, combine the chocolate chips, cereal, shredded coconut, oats and salt.
3. In a microwave-safe bowl, mix rice syrup, coconut essence and almond butter, 30 seconds in the microwave. Stir in the wet ingredients until everything is well mixed. Move to the prepared baking dish and use the edge of a spatula to firmly press the dough into the pan.
4. For creamier texture bars, bake for 20 to 25 minutes, or until just beginning to brown around the edges and still moist in the center. Bake for 35 minutes, or until lightly browned around the edges and somewhat hard in the center, for crunchier bars.
5. Allow cooling throughout the pan for 10 minutes before lifting out onto a cutting board with the aid of the parchment paper. Cut into 24 pieces, then set aside for another 30 minutes to cool fully without splitting the bars. Separate the mixture into bars after it has cooled.

57 Smoothie with Peanut Butter and Jelly

Ready in 5 min **Servings:** 1 **Difficulty:** Easy

Ingredients

- 1 cup f banana slices
- ½ cup frozen strawberries
- 1 tbsp peanut butter
- 1 cup of spinach
- 2 teaspoons maple syrup
- ½ cup of low-fat milk
- ⅓ cup plain yogurt

Instructions

1. In a blender, combine the yogurt & milk, then add the banana, spinach, strawberries, peanut butter, and sweetener; mix until smooth.

58 Baked Oatmeal with Banana, Raisins, and Walnuts

Ready in 1 hr. 5 min **Servings:** 6 **Difficulty:** Easy

Ingredients

- 1 teaspoon of vanilla extract
- 1 banana, sliced
- ⅓ cup of raisins
- 1 teaspoon of baking powder
- ½ teaspoon of salt
- ¼ teaspoon of ground allspice
- 2 cups milk
- ¾ cup yogurt
- 2 tbsp canola oil
- ¼ cup brown sugar

- 2 cups oats
- ⅓ cup chopped walnuts
- 1 ½ teaspoons cinnamon

Instructions

1. Preheat the oven to 375 Fahrenheit. Using cooking spray, prepare an 8-inch-square baking dish.
2. In a large mixing basin, combine the walnuts, oats, cinnamon, salt, baking powder, and allspice. In a medium mixing bowl, combine the milk, yogurt, oil, brown sugar, and vanilla. Stir the milk mixture into the dry ingredients until everything is well combined. Combine the bananas and raisins in a mixing bowl. Slowly pour into the baking dish that has been prepared.
3. Bake for 45 to 50 minutes, or until brown on top & firm to the touch.

59 Pancakes with Avocado

Ready in 35 min **Servings:** 4 **Difficulty:** Easy

Ingredients

- 1 cup almond milk
- ⅓ cup ripe avocado
- 2 tbsp sugar
- 1 teaspoon of lemon zest
- 2 tbsp flaxseed meal
- 5 tbsp water
- 1 teaspoon of vanilla extract
- ¼ teaspoon of salt
- 1 teaspoon of baking powder
- 1 teaspoon of canola oil
- ¼ cup of Blueberries
- ¼ teaspoon spirulina powder
- 1 ⅓ cups gluten-free flour

Instructions

1. In a small dish, combine a flaxseed meal and water. Stir in the water well. Allow for a 5-minute rest period.
2. In a blender, purée the almond milk, lemon zest, sugar, avocado, vanilla, salt, and spirulina until smooth, approximately 1 minute. Place in a large mixing basin. Combine the flaxseed and water in a mixing bowl.
3. In a medium mixing bowl, whisk together the flour and baking powder; incorporate into avocado mixture.
4. Preheat a medium-sized nonstick pan or griddle. Spread a thin coating of oil in the pan using a paper towel. For each pancake, use 1/4 cup batter and carefully spread in 3 1/2-inch rounds. Cook the pancakes for 4 to 5 minutes on each side until it's browned and cooked through. Rep with the rest of the batter. If desired, top with blueberries.

60 Burrata and Avocado Toast

Ready in 5 min **Servings:** 1 **Difficulty:** Easy

Ingredients

- ⅛ teaspoon of ground pepper
- 1 ounce of Burrata
- 1 teaspoon of lemon juice
- 1 teaspoon basil, finely sliced
- 1 teaspoon chives, minced
- Aleppo pepper
- 1 slice of whole-grain toast
- ½ large thinly sliced ripe avocado
- ⅛ teaspoon of salt

Instructions

1. Avocado should be spread on the bread.
2. Season with salt and pepper, then sprinkle with lemon juice. Burrata chives, basil, and Aleppo pepper are served on top.

61 Smoothie with strawberries, blueberries, and bananas

Ready in 5 min**Servings:** 1 **Difficulty:** Easy

Ingredients

- ½ cup of strawberries
- ¾ cup of cashew milk
- 1 tbsp of butter
- ½ cup of blueberries
- 1 small ripe banana(optional)
- 1 tbsp of hulled hemp seeds

Instructions

1. In a blender, combine the blueberries, strawberries, banana, cashew butter, cashew milk, and hemp seeds. Blend until smooth, adding additional cashew milk if necessary to get the appropriate consistency. Serve right away.

62 Overnight Oatmeal with Dates and Pine Nuts

Ready in 8 hrs. **Servings:** 1 **Difficulty:** Easy
Ingredients

- Pinch of salt
- 2 tbsp dates, chopped
- 1 tbsp pine nuts, toasted
- ½ cup rolled oats
- ½ cup of water
- ¼ teaspoon of cinnamon
- 1 teaspoon of honey

Instructions

1. Stir together the oats, water, & salt inside a jar or basin. Refrigerate overnight, covered.
2. Heat the oats in the morning are preferred, or eat them cold. Dates, pine nuts, honey, and cinnamon are sprinkled over the top.

63 Pancakes with Orange Whole-Wheat Flour

Ready in 30 min s**ervings:** 6 **Difficulty:** Easy

Ingredients

- 3 oranges
- 1 cup buttermilk
- ½ teaspoon of baking soda
- 1 teaspoon of vanilla extract
- 2 tbsp brown sugar
- 2 tbsp of canola oil
- 1 ½ cups whole-wheat flour
- 3 tbsp of flax meal
- 2 eggs
- 1 teaspoon baking powder
- ¼ teaspoon of ground ginger
- ⅛ teaspoon salt

Instructions

1. In a large mixing bowl, combine baking powder, flour, flax meal, baking soda, ginger, and salt.
2. To acquire 1 tbsp of zest, zest 1 orange. 1/4 cup juice may be obtained by juicing it. The two remaining oranges should be cut into halves. Set aside the parts after cutting them into thirds.
3. In a medium mixing basin, whisk together vanilla, orange juice, brown sugar, eggs, buttermilk, oil, and zest
4. Combine the wet and dry ingredients in a mixing bowl and whisk until just blended. Do not over mix the ingredients. At the same time, you warm the pan, set aside the batter for 5 minutes.
5. Spray a large nonstick skillet or griddle lightly with cooking spray & heat over medium-high heat. 1/3 cup batter each pancake is dropped into the heated pan.

Cook the pancakes for 4 minutes till they start to bubble, then flip & cook for another 3 minutes until gently browned on the other side.

6. Rep with the rest of the batter. Warm the pancakes in a 200°F oven until you're ready to eat them. Serve with the orange segments that were set aside.

64 Scrambled Eggs with Smoked Trout and Spinach

Ready in 15 min **Servings:** 2 **Difficulty:** Easy

Ingredients

- 4 eggs
- ¼ teaspoon ground pepper
- Salt
- 2 tbsp shallot, finely chopped
- 2 teaspoons seed oil
- ½ cup boned & flaked smoked trout
- 2 tbsp milk
- 1 cup spinach, chopped

Instructions

1. In a medium mixing bowl, whisk together the eggs, milk, pepper, and salt until light yellow all over.
2. In a big nonstick skillet, heat the oil over medium heat. Cook, occasionally stirring, until the shallot begins to brown, about 1 to 2 minutes. Reduce the heat to medium-low and add the egg mixture.

Cook, occasionally stirring, until the edges begin to set, approximately 30 seconds. Trout should be strewn over the eggs. Gently press and fold the eggs with a rubber spatula until frothy & barely set, 2 to 4 minutes. Add the spinach and mix well. Remove from the heat, cover, set aside for 2 minutes, or until spinach is barely wilted.

65 Breakfast with Greek Yogurt

Ready in 10 min **Servings:** 1 **Difficulty:** Easy

Ingredients

- ¾ cup yogurt
- ¾ cup of vegetable juice
- 1 cup carrots
- ¾ cup of blueberries
- 2 slices toasted whole-grain bread

Instructions

1. On a platter or in separate containers, arrange carrots, Greek yogurt, and bread. Serve with vegetable juice that is low in salt.
2. To round up this well-balanced dinner, serve with blueberries.

66 Oranges with Cinnamon

Ready in 10 min **Servings:** 4 **Difficulty:** Easy

Ingredients

- 2 tbsp lemon juice
- 1 tbsp sugar
- 4 navel oranges
- 2 tbsp orange juice
- ¼ teaspoon cinnamon

Instructions

1. Remove the rind & white pith from the oranges using a sharp knife. Cut each into five or six slices and place them on four plates. Combine the orange and lemon juices, sugar, and cinnamon in a mixing bowl. Spread the orange slices on top.

67 Blood Oranges with Yogurt and Cardamom Brulle

Ready in 15 min **Servings:** 4 **Difficulty:** Easy

Ingredients

- 1 teaspoon g cardamom
- 1 cup yogurt
- 4 oranges
- 8 teaspoons brown sugar

Instructions

1. Preheat the broiler and place the rack in the top third of the oven (if you have a culinary blowtorch, you can use it instead). Using foil, line a baking pan.
2. Halve the oranges crosswise. Cut the base of each half with a sharp blade or paring knife, so it rests without rolling. Remove any seeds by cutting over each segment. Make a cross in the middle of the fruit and run the knife from around the edge without cutting into the white pith. Place them cut-side up orange halves on the preheated pan.
3. In a small bowl, mix brown sugar and cardamom. 1 teaspoon over top of each half of an orange 3 to 5 minutes under the broiler, until the top is caramelized. Serve with a side of yogurt.

68 Energy Bites from Carrot Cake

Ready in 15 min **Servings:** 22 **Difficulty:** Easy

Ingredients

- ¾ teaspoon cinnamon
- ¼ teaspoon g turmeric
- ¼ teaspoon of salt
- Pinch of pepper
- ½ teaspoon ginger
- 1 teaspoon vanilla extract
- 1 cup dates
- ½ cup of rolled oats
- ¼ cup of chia seeds
- 2 finely chopped carrots
- ¼ cup chopped pecans

Instructions

1. In a food processor, mix dates, oats, pecans, & chia seeds; pulse until thoroughly blended and diced.
2. Process carrots, vanilla, cardamom, ginger, turmeric, salt, & pepper in a food processor until thoroughly diced and a paste form.
3. Using only a little 1 tbsp. of the ingredients, roll into balls.

69 Apple Butter with Chai in the Slow Cooker

Ready in 7 hrs. 45 min **Servings:** 28 **Difficulty:** Easy

Ingredients

- 2 teaspoons cardamom
- 2 teaspoons cinnamon
- 2 teaspoons turmeric
- ½ teaspoon of salt
- 2 teaspoons coriander

- 5 pounds apples
- ⅔ cup brown sugar
- 1 tbsp of vanilla extract

Instructions

1. In a 6-quart or larger slow cooker, mix apple, turmeric, brown sugar, cardamom, vanilla, cinnamon, coriander, and salt. Cover and cook on high for 5 hours, stirring once or twice. Set the cover ajar and simmer, stirring regularly, for another 2 hours, until the apples become practically broken down. Puree in a mixing bowl until smooth, if desired.

70 Smoothie with Anti-Inflammatory Cherry and Spinach

Ready in 5 min **Servings:** 1 **Difficulty:** Easy

Ingredients
- 1 cup plain kefir
- 1 cup cherries
- ½ cup spinach leaves
- ¼ cup ripe avocado
- 1 tbsp salted almond butter
- 1 piece ginger
- 1 teaspoon chia seeds, plus more for garnish

Instructions

1. In a blender, combine the kefir and the water. Puree the spinach, cherries, avocado, ginger, almond butter and chia seeds in a high-powered blender until smooth. Put into a glass and, if preferred, top with extra chia seeds.

71 Spinach, Tomato, and Feta Waffle

Ready in 10 min **Servings:** 1 **Difficulty:** Easy

Ingredients
- 1 whole-grain waffle
- 3 quartered cherry tomatoes
- 1 tbsp feta cheese
- 1/4 cup spinach

Instructions

1. Waffles should be toasted according to the package guidelines. Top with spinach, tomatoes, and feta cheese on a platter. Serve right away.

72 Overnight Oats with Cherry and Walnuts

Ready in 8 hrs. **Servings:** 1 **Difficulty:** Easy

Ingredients
- 1 tbsp dried cherries, chopped
- 1 tbsp chopped walnuts, toasted
- 2 teaspoons of raw sugar
- ½ teaspoon of lemon zest
- ½ cup of rolled oats
- ½ cup of water
- Pinch of salt
- 2 tbsp cream cheese

Instructions

1. Stir together the oats, water, & salt inside a jar or basin. Refrigerate overnight, covered.
2. Heat the oats in the morning if preferred, or eat them cold. Whipped cream, cherries, walnuts, sugar, and lemon zest go on top.

73 Smoothie with berries and kefir

Ready in 5 min **Servings:** 1 **Difficulty:** Easy

Ingredients

- ½ banana
- 2 teaspoons of almond butter
- 1 ½ cups of mixed berries
- 1 cup of plain kefir
- ½ teaspoon of vanilla extract

Instructions

1. In a blender, combine the berries, banana, kefir, almond butter, and vanilla. Blend until completely smooth.

74 Quinoa Cakes from Southwest

Ready in 1 hr. **Servings:** 6 **Difficulty:** Easy

Ingredients

- 14-ounce can of fire-roasted diced tomatoes
- 1 clove of garlic
- 1 chipotle pepper in adobo sauce
- ¼ cup cilantro, chopped
- 1 chopped avocado
- ¾ cup cottage cheese
- ¼ cup scallions, sliced
- 2 tbsp flour
- 1 teaspoon of baking powder
- 1/4 teaspoon salt
- 1 cup shredded pepper
- 2 cups of water
- 1 cup red quinoa
- 4 lightly beaten eggs
- 1 cup rinsed canned black beans

Instructions

1. Preheat the oven to 375 Fahrenheit. Using cooking spray, spray a 12-cup nonstick baking tray.
2. In a medium saucepan, bring to a boil. Add the quinoa and mix well. Reduce to low heat, cover, and cook for 15 minutes, just until the grains become soft and expose their spiraling germ. Allow it cool for 10 minutes in a large mixing basin.
3. Toss the quinoa with the eggs, flour, beans, scallions, cottage cheese, baking powder, and 1/4 teaspoon salt until completely blended. 1/4 cup each) of the mixture should be divided among the muffin cups. 1 tablespoon cheese on top of each quinoa cake.
4. Step 4 Bake the cakes for approximately 20 minutes, or until puffed and golden brown on top. Allow cooling for 5 minutes in the pan. With a paring knife, gently loosen and remove.
5. In a blender, purée the tomatoes, garlic, chipotle pepper, and a touch of salt until smooth. Stir in the cilantro in a small mixing bowl.
6. Toss the cakes with both the salsa & avocado before serving.

75 Sandwich with egg and salmon

Ready in 15 min **Servings:** 1 **Difficulty:** Easy

Ingredients

- 1/2 teaspoon chopped capers
- 1 ounce of smoked salmon
- 1 whole-wheat toasted muffin
- ½ teaspoon of virgin olive oil
- 1 slice of tomato
- 1 tbsp red onion, chopped
- 2 beaten egg whites
- Pinch salt

Instructions

1. In a medium nonstick skillet, heat the oil over medium heat. Cook, occasionally stirring, until the onion starts to soften, approximately 1 minute. Add the egg whites, salt, & capers to cook, frequently stirring, for approximately 30 seconds or until the whites are set.
2. Place the smoked salmon, egg whites, and tomato on an English muffin to construct the sandwich.

76 Recipe for maple-baked rice porridge with fruit

Ready in 35 min **Servings:** 2 **Difficulty:** Easy

Ingredients

- ½ cup of brown rice
- Pinch of salt
- ½ teaspoon of vanilla extract
- 2 tbsp maple syrup
- Sliced fruit, such as plums, pears, berries, or cherries
- Pinch of cinnamon

Instructions

1. Preheat oven to 400 °F.
2. In a medium-high-heat saucepan, combine the rice & 1 cup of water. Bring to a boil, and then mix in the vanilla extract & cinnamon. Turn down the heat to moderate and cover. Simmer for 10-15 minutes (or according to package instructions if using a rice type that takes longer to prepare) or until soft.
3. Stir the rice and divide it into two heat-safe dishes. Add a spoonful of maple syrup & your favorite sliced fruit to each bowl. If desired, season with salt.

4. Bake for 15 minutes or until maple syrup begins to bubble and the fruit begins to caramelize. Serve right away.

77 Herb-Baked Eggs in 5 Minutes

Ready in 5 min **Servings:** 1 **Difficulty:** Easy

Ingredients

- 1 teaspoon butter, melted
- The sprinkling of dried oregano, garlic powder, dried thyme, dried parsley, & dried dill
- 2 eggs
- 1 tbsp milk

Instructions

1. Preheat the oven to "Broil" on low.
2. Using the butter and milk, cover the base of a medium baking dish.
3. Crack the eggs over the butter and milk mixture. Garlic and dry herbs are sprinkled over the top.
4. Cook for 5minutes, just until the eggs become fully cooked.

78 Cinnamon Granola with a Crunchy

Ready in 30 min **Servings:** 1 **Difficulty:** Easy

Ingredients

- 2 cups rolled oats
- ¼ cup shredded coconut
- ¼ cup walnuts, chopped
- ¼ teaspoon of cloves
- 2 tbsp pumpkin seeds
- ½ teaspoon of cinnamon
- ¼ teaspoon nutmeg
- ¼ cup of honey

- 4 tbsp butter, melted
- ¼ cup raisins
- ¼ cup apricots, chopped
- ¼ cup cranberries

Instructions

1. Heat oven to 350°F. Prepare a baking sheet.
2. Mix the oats, pumpkin seeds, coconuts, walnuts, and spices in a big mixing basin and set aside.
3. In a separate dish, mix the honey & melted butter and pour over the oat mixture. Stir everything together well.
4. Pour the oat mixture onto the baking sheet and spread it out evenly. Bake for about 25 minutes, or until golden brown. Remove from the oven and set aside to cool.
5. Once the granola has cooled, break it up and toss it inside the dried fruit. Keep the container sealed.

79 Parfait with Coffee & Mint Yogurt

Ready in 20 min **Servings:** 1 **Difficulty:** Easy

Ingredients

- 3-4 peppermint Stevia drops
- ¼ cup pecans, chopped
- 2 teaspoons coffee
- ½ cup yogurt
- coffee granules & fresh mint

Instructions

1. In a small mixing dish, combine the yogurt, coffee, & stevia (if using).
2. In a tiny glass, alternate layers of yogurt and pecans until you reach the top.
3. Add coffee granules & fresh mint on the top.

80 Anti-Inflammatory Smoothie with Energizing Pineapple

Ready in 10 min **Servings:** 1 **Difficulty:** Easy

Ingredients

- 2/3 cup of cucumber
- ½ cup mango chunks
- ½ of the banana
- 1/2" fresh ginger
- ¼ teaspoon turmeric
- 3 mint leaves, chopped
- 1 cup cooled green tea
- 2 cups spinach
- 1 cup pineapple chunks
- 1 scoop of protein powder
- 1 tbsp of chia seeds
- 5 ice cubes

Instructions

1. In a high-powered blender, combine all of the items, except the chia seeds.
2. To avoid chia seeds sticking to the blender container, add them towards the conclusion of the blending process.
3. If you like a thicker smoothie, add ice cubes and mix until the desired consistency is achieved.

81 Toasted Avocado with Egg

Ready in 13 min **Servings:** 1 **Difficulty:** Easy

Ingredients

- 1 slice of toasted gluten-free bread
- 1 teaspoon of ghee
- 1/2 of an avocado
- 1 scrambled egg
- Red pepper flakes
- Handful of spinach

Instructions

1. Spread ghee on the gluten-free bread & toast it.
2. Place the avocado on the bread and spread it out evenly. Put additional spinach on top of the avocado, and then add a cooked or poached egg and a sprinkling of red pepper flakes to finish.
3. Serve open-faced with a knife and fork, or form a sandwich by adding an extra piece of bread.

82 Porridge of Chia Quinoa

Ready in 7 min **Servings:** 2 **Difficulty:** Easy

Ingredients

- 1 cup cashew milk
- ¼ cup walnuts, toasted
- ½ teaspoon ground cinnamon
- 2 teaspoon raw honey
- 2 cups of quinoa, cooked
- 1 cup frozen blueberries
- 1 tbsp chia seeds

Instructions

1. In a saucepan, mix the quinoa & cashew milk and gently reheat over moderately low heat.
2. Toss in the blueberries, cinnamon, and walnuts and stir to combine. Remove the pan from the heat and add the raw honey. Chia seeds are sprinkled on top.
3. Toss in raw cacao nibs and serve in bowls for a boost of antioxidants.

83 Overnight Oats Pecan Banana Bread Recipe

Ready in 6 hrs. 15 min **Servings:** 2 **Difficulty:** Easy

Ingredients

- 1/4 cup of fresh yogurt
- Banana slices, fig halves, honey, roasted pecans, and pomegranate seeds for serving
- 2 tbsp toasted coconut flakes
- 2 tbsp fresh honey
- 1 cup rolled oats
- 1 cup of milk
- 2 mashed bananas,
- 2 teaspoon vanilla extract
- 1 tbsp chia seeds
- 1/4 teaspoon of sea salt

Instructions

1. Combine the oats, milk, bananas, unsweetened coconut flakes, yogurt, honey, vanilla extract, chia seeds and sea salt in a medium mixing bowl. Pour the mixture into two dishes or glass jars. Refrigerate for at least six hours, preferably overnight after covering. Stir in the banana slices, toasted pecans, and fig halves, and serve warm if preferred. Pour with honey & pomegranate seeds to finish.

84 Smoothie with Greek yogurt for recovery

Ready in 15 min **Servings:** 2 **Difficulty:** Easy

Ingredients
- 1 cup of nut milk
- pinch of ground cinnamon, pistachios, or cardamom, or bee pollen
- ½ cup of yogurt
- ¼ cup spinach
- 4 ice cubes
- ¼ cup frozen blueberries
- 1 tbsp nut butter

Instructions

1. In a blender, combine all ingredients and pulse until smooth.

85 Smoothie with Cacao and Berries

Ready in 10 min **Servings:** 2 **Difficulty:** Easy

Ingredients
- 1 cup almond or coconut milk
- 1/2 cup water
- 3 tbsp cacao powder
- 1 tbsp honey
- Ice
- Cacao nibs
- 1 cup spinach
- 1 cup frozen raspberries
- 1 banana

Instructions

1. In a blender, combine all ingredients and mix until smooth. As desired, garnish with cocoa nibs. Take a drink and relax!

86 Turmeric Scramble with Nutrients

Ready in 10 min **Servings:** 1 **Difficulty:** Easy

Ingredients
- 1 cayenne pepper
- 2 radishes grated
- 2 eggs
- 2 kale leaves
- 1 clove garlic
- 1 tbsp turmeric
- 2 tbsp coconut oil

Instructions

1. Lightly sauté garlic in a skillet with coconut oil.
2. Crack eggs & scramble them in a pan.
3. Adding the shredded kale, saffron, & cayenne when the eggs are nearly done.
4. Garnish with radish and sprouts and serve!

87 Breakfast with Chia and Raspberry

Ready in 30 min **Servings:** 1 **Difficulty:** Easy

Ingredients
- 1 cup of frozen raspberries
- 3 tbsp of chia seeds
- 1 cup plant milk
- 1 pinch of vanilla
- 3 tbsp coconut

Instructions

1. In a bowl, mash all berries with a fork. Mix in the coconut, vanilla and chia seeds. Pour in the milk and stir to combine. Allow to soak for at least 30 mins or overnight inside the refrigerator. Top extra chia seeds, nut butter, fruit, and mint in a dish.

88 No-Bake Protein Turmeric Donuts

Ready in 45 min **Servings:** 8 **Difficulty:** Easy

Ingredients
- 7 pieces dates
- 2 tbsp syrup of maple
- 1 tbsp of turmeric powder
- ¼ teaspoon of vanilla essence
- 1 teaspoon vanilla powder
- ¼ cup of shredded coconut
- ¼ cup dark chocolate
- 1½ cups of raw cashews

Instructions

1. In a food processor, combine all the ingredients (besides the chocolate) & mix on high till a sticky and smooth cookie forms.
2. Form mixture into 8 balls & press into donut mold made of silicone.
3. To set the mold, cover it in plastic wrap and lay it in the freezer for 30 minutes.
4. To make the chocolate coating, fill a pot halfway with water, then bring to a boil.
5. Set a smaller pan over the larger one and pour the chocolate into it. Gently stir even the chocolate has melted completely.
6. Once the donuts have been set, take them from the mold and coat them with the dark chocolate before storing them in a tight jar in the fridge.

89 Paleo Pancakes with Nutty Choco-Nana

Ready in 20 min **Servings:** 10 **Difficulty:** Easy

Ingredients
- 2 teaspoon raw cacao powder
- 2 teaspoon creamy almond butter
- 1 tbsp pure vanilla extract
- Pinch of salt
- 2 eggs
- 2 bananas
- Coconut oil
- 4 tbsp raw cacao powder

Instructions

1. To make the chocolate sauce, first melted the coconut oil and then added the cacao powder. Set aside after mixing until thoroughly incorporated.
2. To make the pancakes, melt a tbsp of coconut oil in a large skillet over medium-low heat.
3. In a mixing bowl (or blender), combine all pancake ingredients & pulse on high till smooth.
4. Scoop the batter into a 14-cup measuring cup & pour onto the griddle to produce one pancake. Cook for 5 minutes before gently flipping over and cooking for two more minutes. Repeat until you've made 10 pancakes and all of the batters have gone.
5. Allow the pancakes to cool for 5 minutes before serving on a wire baking rack.
6. Pancakes may be stored in the refrigerator for up to 5 days or frozen for up to 30 days.

90 Turmeric Scones for anti Inflammation

Ready in 35 min **Servings:** 6 **Difficulty:** Easy

Ingredients
- 1/4 cup of arrowroot flour
- 1 tbsp of coconut flour
- 1 egg
- 1/4 cup of red palm oil
- 3 tbsp maple syrup
- 1 teaspoon turmeric
- 1/2 teaspoon black pepper
- Pinch of salt
- 1 teaspoon vanilla extract
- 1 cup of almond flour
- 1 cup of almonds

Instructions

1. Preheat the oven to 350 degrees Fahrenheit.
2. In a food processor, coarsely chop almonds. Combine the chopped almonds and the remaining dry ingredients in a mixing bowl and fluff with a fork.
3. In a separate bowl, whisk together the syrup, egg, oil, and vanilla extract; add to the dry ingredients. Mix until everything is well incorporated, then move the dough on a cutting board or even a plastic-wrapped countertop. Cut into sixths after patting into a spherical form about one inch thick.
4. Bake for 20 minutes in a preheated oven and until a tester placed in the middle comes out clean.

91 Breakfast Bars with Sweet Potatoes and Cranberries

Ready in 1 hr. 30 min **Servings:** 16 **Difficulty:** Easy

Ingredients
- 1 ½ cups sweet potato
- ¼ cup of water
- 2 tbsp coconut oil
- 1 ½ teaspoon baking soda
- 1 cup cranberries
- 2 tbsp maple syrup
- 2 eggs
- 1 cup of almond meal
- ⅓ cup of coconut flour

Instructions

1. Preheat oven to 350 ° degrees Fahrenheit.
2. Mix the maple syrup, potatoes purée, melted coconut oil, water, & eggs in a large mixing bowl. Stir until everything is well blended.
3. Sift together the coconut flour, almond meal, & baking soda in another dish.
4. Combine the dry ingredients with the potato mixture & thoroughly combine.
5. Line the bottom of a 9-inch square baking sheet with parchment paper and grease it with coconut oil.
6. Pour the mixture into the prepared baking pan & level the top, and fill in the corners with a moist spatula. Place cranberries on the top and press them down.
7. Bake for 40 minutes, till a toothpick inserted near the center, comes out clean. Please remove it from the pan & cut it into squares once it has cooled fully.

92 Muffins with Chocolate Avocado and Blueberries

Ready in 18 min **Servings:** 9 **Difficulty:** Easy

Ingredients

- 1/3 cup of coconut sugar
- ¼ teaspoon salt
- 2 eggs
- ¼ cup blueberries
- 2 tbsp dark chocolate chips
- 1 ripe avocado
- 1/4 cup of raw cacao powder
- 1 cup of almond flour
- ½ cup almond milk
- 2 teaspoon baking powder
- 2 tbsp coconut flour

Instructions

1. Preheat the oven to 375 degrees Fahrenheit. Grease a muffin tray with coconut oil or use muffin liners.
2. In a blender, combine the eggs, avocado, sugar, and salt, along with 1 tablespoon cacao powder. Mix on high until the avocado is completely broken down as well as the sauce has the consistency of silky custard.
3. Sift together 14 cups icing sugar, baking soda, coconut flour, and almond flour in a small basin.
4. Slowly fold in the dry ingredients after adding some almond milk to a liquid mixture. Mix only until everything is incorporated.
5. Combine the blueberries & chocolate chips in a mixing bowl.
6. Pour batter into prepared muffin tins, evenly dividing batter among 9 holes.
7. Bake for 18 minutes, till a toothpick injected in the middle comes out clean.
8. Take the muffins from the pan and let them cool on a wire rack.
9. Keep refrigerated for up to one week or frozen for up to 1 month.

93 Smoothie with raspberries and grapefruit

Ready in 15 min **Servings:** 1 **Difficulty:** Easy

Ingredients

1) 1 pink grapefruit, Juice
2) 1 cup frozen raspberries
3) 1 frozen banana

Instructions

1. In a blender, combine all of the ingredients and mix until smooth.

94 Shroom Iced- Mocha

Ready in 5 min **Servings:** 1 **Difficulty:** Easy

Ingredients

- 1 packet of Mushroom Coffee
- 1 teaspoon coconut oil
- ½ tbsp of cacao powder
- 8 oz hot water
- ½ cup almond milk
- ice cubes

Instructions

1. Dissolve the Four Sigmatic package in boiling water. Allow 2 minutes to cool after stirring to dissolve the powder.
2. Dissolve the coconut oil & cacao powder in a separate bowl.
3. Pour almond milk over coffee, top with ice, and enjoy!

95 Pancakes with a Savory Flavor

Ready in 25 min **Servings:** 2
Difficulty: Easy

Ingredients
- ½ teaspoon of Chili Powder
- ¼ teaspoon Turmeric Powder
- ¼ teaspoon ground black pepper
- ½chopped red onion
- 1 cilantro leaves chopped
- 1 serrano pepper minced
- 1/2-inch ginger
- fat of choice uses enough to shallow fry
- ½ cup of Almond Flour
- ½ cup of Tapioca Flour
- 1 cup Coconut Milk canned
- 1 teaspoon salt

Instructions
Making Batter

1. In a mixing dish, combine tapioca flour, coconut milk, almond flour, and spices.
2. Add onion, cilantro, serrano pepper, and ginger after that.

Fry Pancakes

1. Preheat a sauté pan over low-medium heat, add enough oil/fat to coat the pan and pour 14 cups of batter into the pan. Pour the ingredients into your pan and spread it out evenly.
2. Cook for 3-4 minutes on each side, drizzling a little additional oil on top of the pancake after flipping. (Stoves vary, so fry until golden brown on both sides.)
3. Keep adding oil as required until the batter is finished.
4. Serve with Paleo ketchup or green chutney.

96 Chia Pudding with Dark Chocolate and Orange

Ready in 3 hrs. **Servings:** 2 **Difficulty:** Easy

Ingredients
- 1/3 cup chia seeds
- 3 tbsp cacao powder
- 1 cup of water
- Orange peel
- 1/4 cup of orange juice
- 1 tbsp orange zest
- 1 tbsp honey

Instructions

1. Mix the chia seeds, orange juice, orange zest, raw cacao powder, & honey in a large mixing dish. Mix thoroughly.
2. Stir in the water until all of the cacao powder has dissolved.
3. Cover the bowl with plastic wrap and refrigerate for at least 3 hours until chia seeds completely soaked all of the liquid. The chia pudding must have a thick consistency.
4. Pour the chia pudding into two glasses, top with orange peel and serve.

97 Smoothie Bowl with Tropical Turmeric

Ready in 15 min **Servings:** 2 **Difficulty:** Easy

Ingredients
- 1 cup of orange juice
- 1 cup frozen pineapple
- Turmeric
- 1 cup frozen mango
- ½ banana
- 1 tbsp of chia

For Topping
- Strawberries sliced
- Coconut flakes
- Kiwis' slices
- Almonds chopped

Instructions

1. In a blender, combine all of the ingredients in the order stated. Blend until the mixture is smooth and creamy. If the mixture becomes too thick, you may need to add a dash of orange juice. Fruit slices, nuts, and coconut flakes may be sprinkled over the top.

98 Breakfast with Smoked Salmon & Spinach

Ready in 30 min **Servings:** 4 **Difficulty:** Easy

Ingredients
- 1 garlic clove
- 1/2 teaspoon onion powder
- 1/2 teaspoon garlic powder
- ½ sliced onion
- 1/2 cup of mushrooms
- 2 cups of spinach
- 1/4 teaspoon paprika
- 2 tbsp ghee
- 2 tbsp olive oil
- Sea salt & ground black pepper
- 4 eggs
- 8 oz. sliced smoked salmon
- 2 peeled sweet potatoes

Instructions

1. Preheat the oven to 425 degrees Fahrenheit.
2. Dice the potatoes and season to taste with olive oil, onion powder, garlic powder, and paprika.
3. Arrange the potato on a baking tray and bake for 25 minutes, rotating halfway through.
4. Over high heat, bring a saucepan of water to the boil.
5. Place the eggs in the boiling water, cover, and simmer for 7 minutes.
6. Take the water and rinse the eggs under cold water; peel your eggs and keep them aside.
7. Add the onion and garlic to the melted ghee over medium-high heat.
8. Cook for another 1 to 2 minutes before adding the sliced mushrooms.
9. Season to taste, then simmer for another 5 minutes, or until everything is soft.
10. Mix the spinach and simmer for 2 minutes, or until wilted.
11. Toss the potatoes with the spinach-mushroom mix, an egg, and smoked salmon slices before serving.

99 Avocado Buns for a Keto Breakfast Burger

Ready in 20 min **Servings:** 1 **Difficulty:** Easy

Ingredients
- 1 ripe avocado
- 1 tomato
- 1 lettuce leaf
- 1 tbsp Paleo mayonnaise
- 1 egg
- 2 bacon rashers
- 1 red onion slice
- Sea salt
- Sesame seeds

Instructions

1. In a chilly frying pan, place the bacon rashers. Start cooking the bacon after the stove is turned on.

2. Flip the bacon with a fork when it begins to curl. Cook the bacon till it has become crispy.
3. Take the bacon from the pan and break the egg into it, cooking it in the same pan with the bacon grease. Cook until the yolk remains liquid, but the white is set.
4. Cut the avocados in halves horizontally. Remove the pit by scooping out of its covering using a spoon.
5. Use Paleo mayonnaise to fill the hole in which the pit used to be.
6. Add lettuce, tomato, onion, bacon, and a fried egg to the top layer. Season with a pinch of salt.
7. Add the second part of the avocado on top. Sesame seeds may be sprinkled on top.

100 Avocado Egg with Prosciutto Wrapping

Ready in 15 min **Servings: 2 Difficulty:** Easy

Ingredients
- 2 avocados
- Salt & pepper
- 6 slices of prosciutto
- 2 tbsp olive oil
- Tomato slices
- Chopped parsley
- 2 eggs

Instructions

1. Prepare a medium saucepan of water to a moderate simmer over low heat.
2. Line a small bowl with food-safe plastic wrap and drizzle it with olive oil.
3. Crack one egg into the prepared dish, fold the plastic wrap in half, and make a knot. 3 minutes in the boiling water with the wrapped egg Rep with the second egg.
4. Take the eggs out of the water and place them on a tray. Gently detach the eggs from the plastic wrap by cutting them apart. After that, please remove it from the equation.
5. Flatten the prosciutto slices with the back of a knife before serving.
6. Cut the avocado in half and peel away the outer membrane. Scoop out the avocado's center to make almost the same proportion as the fried egg. Carefully place the egg in and wrap the avocado over it on both sides.
7. Wrap two pieces of prosciutto horizontally and one-piece vertically around the sealed avocado. Carry on with the second egg in the same manner.
8. Fry a prosciutto-wrapped avocado with olive oil for approximately 10 minutes over medium heat, beginning with the loose bacon ends. Turn the bacon regularly until it is crispy all across.
9. Drain any extra oil on such a paper towel before serving. Sprinkle salt, pepper, and chopped parsley over the filled avocado. Serves with tomato slices on the side.

101 Chickpea and Cauliflower Tikka Masala

Ready in 20 min **Servings: 4 Difficulty:** Easy

Ingredients
- 4 cups of cauliflower florets
- ¼ teaspoon of salt
- Fresh cilantro for garnish
- ¼ cup water
- 1 can rinsed chickpeas
- 1 1/2 cups tikka masala sauce
- 2 tbsp butter
- 1 tbsp coconut oil

Instructions

1. In a large skillet, heat the oil over medium-high heat.

2. Cook, occasionally tossing, until cauliflower is lightly browned, approximately 2 minutes. Add the water, cover, and simmer for 5 minutes or when the cauliflower is soft. Cook for 2 minutes until chickpeas and sauce are heated. Remove the pan from the heat and add the butter. If desired, garnish with cilantro.

102 Turkey Stuffed Peppers in the Air Fryer

Ready in 30 min **Servings:** 3 **Difficulty:** Easy

Ingredients
- 3 red bell peppers
- 1 tbsp olive oil
- ¼ teaspoon pepper
- ¼ cup grated Parmesan
- ¼ cup shredded mozzarella cheese
- 12 ounces of ground turkey
- ½ cup brown rice, cooked
- 3 tbsp flat-leaf parsley, finely chopped
- ¼ cup of breadcrumbs
- ¾ cup marinara sauce

Instructions

1. Spray the air fryer basket with cooking spray. Remove the tops of the peppers and set them aside. Remove the seeds from the peppers and keep them aside.
2. In a large skillet, heat the oil over medium-high heat. Cook, occasionally tossing, until turkey is browned, approximately 4 minutes. Cook, tossing periodically until rice and panko are warmed through, approximately 1 minute. Remove the pan from the heat and add the marinara, parsley, pepper, and Parmesan cheese. Distribute the mixture

equally among the peppers that have been prepped.

3. Put the peppers in an air-fryer basket that has been prepared. Place the pepper top in the basket's bottom. Cook for approximately 8 minutes at 350 degrees F, just until the peppers become soft. Cook for a further 2 minutes, or until the mozzarella is melted.

Chapter 3: Lunch Recipes

1. Mediterranean Tuna Salad

Prep Time: 10 min, Serving: 2, Difficulty: Easy

Ingredients

- 2 large vine-ripened tomatoes
- 2 cans (50z) drained Tuna packed in water
- 1/4 cup of mayonnaise
- salt and pepper
- 1/4 cup kalamata, chopped or mixed olives
- 1 tbsp fresh lemon juice
- 2 tbsp red onion, minced
- 2 tbsp fire-roasted red peppers, chopped
- 2 tbsp fresh basil, chopped
- 1 tbsp capers

Instructions

1. In a large mixing basin, add all the ingredients except the tomatoes and mix to combine. To open tomatoes, slice them into sixths without slicing all the way through.
2. Serve by scooping the Mediterranean Salad mixture of Tuna into the middle.

2. 5 Ingredient Thai Pumpkin Soup

Prep Time: 10 min, Serving: 2, Difficulty: Easy

Ingredients

- cilantro for garnish if desired
- 4 cups chicken or vegetable broth about 32 ounces
- 1 large red chili pepper sliced
- 2 cans pumpkin puree
- 2 tbsp red curry paste
- 1 (3/4 cup) coconut milk

Instructions

1. Cook the curry paste in a big saucepan over medium heat for approximately one minute or until fragrant. Stir in the broth & the pumpkin.
2. Cook, occasionally stirring, for approximately 3 minutes, or until the soup begins to boil. Cook for 3 minutes or until the coconut milk is heated.
3. Pour into bowls and top with sliced red chilies and a sprinkle of the reserved coconut milk. If desired, garnish with cilantro leaves.

3. Kale Caesar Salad including Grilled Chicken Wrap

Prep Time: 10 min, Serving: 2, Difficulty: Easy

Ingredients

- 8 ounces chicken (grilled), sliced thinly
- 2 Lavash flatbread or two large tortillas
- 6 cups curly kale, sliced into bite-sized pieces
- Kosher salt and freshly ground black pepper
- 1 cup quartered cherry tomatoes
- 1/8 cup olive oil
- 3/4 cup Parmesan cheese, finely shredded
- 1/8 cup fresh lemon juice
- 1 clove garlic, minced
- 1/2 tsp Dijon mustard
- 1 tsp honey or agave
- ½ coddled egg, cooked for a minute

Instructions

1. Combine half of a coddled egg, mustard, honey, minced garlic, olive oil, and lemon juice in a mixing bowl. Whisk together until you have a dressing. Season with salt & pepper to taste.
2. Toss the kale, chicken, cherry tomatoes with the dressing and 1/4 cup of grated parmesan cheese.
3. The 2 lavash flatbreads should be spread out. Distribute the salad evenly between the two wraps and top with a quarter cup of parmesan cheese on each.
4. Roll the wraps up and cut them in half. Eat right away.

4. Persimmon salad with pears and grapes

Prep Time: 25 min, Serving: 6, Difficulty: Easy

Ingredients

- 1 cup grapes, cut into halves
- 4 Fuyu persimmons, cut in 1-inch cubes
- 3 Bosch pears, cut in 1-inch cubes
- 3/4 cup pecans, cut into half lengthwise to make slivers

Dressing ingredients:

- 1 tsp pomegranate-flavored vinegar
- 1 tsp extra virgin olive oil
- 1 tsp peanut oil
- 2 tsp Monkfruit Sweetener
- pinch of salt, to taste

Instructions

1. Toss the dressing ingredients together in a mixing bowl. While cutting the fruit, combine the ingredients so that the tastes may mingle.
2. Place persimmons, grapes, and pears in a plastic dish and cut them into the same size pieces (approximately 1 inch).
3. Toss the fruit with the dressing and serve. Toss with pecan slices just before serving.

5. Roasted Red Pepper and Sweet Potato Soup

Prep Time: 25 min, Serving: 6, Difficulty: Easy

Ingredients

- 2 medium onions, chopped
- 1 tbsp lemon juice
- 1 jar roasted red peppers, liquid reserved, chopped
- 2 tbsp minced fresh cilantro
- 1 can green chilies, diced
- 4 cups vegetable broth
- 2 tsp ground cumin
- 4 cups peeled, cubed sweet potatoes
- 1 tsp salt
- 2 tbsp olive oil
- 4 oz cream cheese, cubed
- 1 tsp coriander (ground)

Instructions

1. Heat the olive oil in a large soup pot or Dutch oven over medium-high heat. Cook until the onion is soft. Combine the red peppers, green chilies, cumin, salt, and coriander in a large mixing bowl. Cook for approximately 1-2 minutes on each side.
2. In a large mixing bowl, combine the roasted red pepper juice, sweet potatoes, and vegetable broth. Bring to a boil, then reduce to low heat and cover to keep warm. Cook for 10-15 minutes, or until the potatoes are cooked. Combine the cilantro & lemon juice in a mixing bowl.

3. Allow the soup to cool slightly before serving.
4. Blend half of the soup with the cream cheese in a blender. After processing until smooth, return to the soup pot & heat through. If necessary, season with more salt.

6. Smoked salmon potato tartine

Prep Time: 25 min, Serving: 2, Difficulty: Easy

Ingredients

Potato tartine:

- kosher salt
- 1 large russet potato, peeled and grated lengthwise
- 2 tbsp clarified butter (or other neutral-flavored oil)
- freshly ground black pepper

Toppings:

- 4 ounces soft goat cheese, at room temperature
- finely minced chives (for garnish)
- 1 1/2 tbsp finely minced chives
- 1/2 hard-boiled egg, finely chopped
- 1/2 garlic clove, finely minced
- 2 tbsp finely chopped red onion
- half a lemon
- smoked salmon, thinly sliced
- 2 tbsp drained capers

Instructions

1. In a small bowl, combine lemon zest, goat cheese, and garlic. To taste, season with pepper and salt. In a small mixing bowl, gently fold in the fresh chives. Remove from the equation.
2. Season the hard-boiled egg and red onion with salt and pepper.

3. Using the big holes of a grater, shred the potato lengthwise into a huge chunk. Remove any extra liquid by squeezing the potatoes over the sink. Toss with a good amount of salt and pepper.
4. In an 8-10 inch nonstick skillet, melt clarified butter over medium-high heat. When the pan is heated, add the chopped potato and form it into a big circle using a spatula.
5. Cover and cook for 8-10 minutes, or until the bottom is golden brown, pressing down on the mixture with a spoon to compact it.
6. Cook for the next 8-10 minutes, or until light brown and crispy on the opposite side.
7. Allow cooling on a cooling rack until just warm.
8. Spread the cheese mixture on top of the potato cake after it has cooled. Sprinkle the hard-boiled egg, red onion, and capers immediately on top of the smoked salmon. Garnish with chives that have been finely cut. Serve immediately after cutting into wedges.

7. Red lentil and squash curry stew

Prep Time: 13 min, Serving: 4, Difficulty: Easy

Ingredients

- Kosher salt & black pepper, to taste
- 1 sweet onion, chopped
- Freshly grated ginger, to taste (optional)
- 3 garlic cloves, minced
- 1 cup greens of choice
- 1 tbsp good quality curry powder (or more to taste)
- 3 cups cooked butternut squash
- 1 carton broth (4 cups)
- 1 tsp Extra virgin olive oil
- 1 cup red lentils

Instructions

1. Combine the EVOO, chopped onion, and minced garlic in a large saucepan. Over low-medium heat, saute for approximately 5 minutes.
2. Cook for a few more minutes after adding the curry powder. Bring the broth and lentils to a boil. Cook for approximately 10 minutes on low heat.
3. Stir in the cooked butternut squash & your preferred greens. Cook for 5-8 minutes over medium heat. Season to taste with pepper, salt, and freshly grated ginger.

8. White Bean & Veggie Salad

Prep Time: 10 min, Serving: 1, Difficulty: Easy

Ingredients

- Freshly ground pepper to taste
- ¾ cup veggies of your choice, such as cherry tomatoes and chopped cucumbers
- ¼ tsp kosher salt
- ⅓ cup canned white beans, rinsed and drained
- ½ avocado, diced
- 1 tbsp red wine vinegar
- 2 cups mixed salad greens
- 2 tsp extra-virgin olive oil

Instructions

1. In a medium mixing dish, combine the greens, vegetables, beans, and avocado. Season with salt & pepper and sprinkle with vinegar and oil.
2. Toss everything together and move to a big plate.

9. Chopped Veggie Grain Bowls with Turmeric Dressing

Prep Time: 10 min, Serving: 4, Difficulty: Easy

Ingredients

- 2 packages quinoa, cooked
- 1 container veggie mix, chopped
- 1/2 cup turmeric salad dressing (creamy)
- 1 can chickpeas, rinsed

Instructions

1. Prepare the quinoa as directed on the box. Allow it to cool fully in a shallow basin before assembling bowls.
2. Divide the vegetable mixture into four single-serving covered containers. Place one-fourth of the quinoa & one-fourth of the chickpeas on top of each. Refrigerate for 4 days after sealing the containers.
3. Refrigerate 2 tbsp salad dressing in each of 4 small closed containers for up to 4 days.
4. Just before serving, toss every bowl with the dressing.

10. Salmon Salad-Stuffed Avocado

Prep Time: 10 min, Serving: 1, Difficulty: Easy

Ingredients

- 2 tsp minced shallot
- ½ avocado
- ⅓ cup canned salmon
- 5 thin wheat crackers
- 1 tbsp pesto
- 1 tbsp nonfat plain Greek yogurt
- 1 cup baby spinach

Instructions

1. Combine salmon with yogurt, pesto, and shallot.
2. Serve over baby spinach and avocado with the crackers.

11. Green Salad with Edamame & Beets

Prep Time: 15 min, Serving: 1, Difficulty: Easy

Ingredients

- 2 cups mixed salad greens
- Freshly ground pepper to taste
- 1 cup shelled edamame, thawed
- 2 tsp extra-virgin olive oil
- ½ raw beet(about 1/2 cup), peeled & shredded
- 1 tbsp red wine vinegar
- 1 tbsp chopped fresh cilantro

Instructions

1. Arrange edamame, greens, and beet on a big plate. Whisk oil, cilantro, vinegar, pepper and salt in a small bowl.
2. Sprinkle over the salad and eat.

12. Sweet Potato, Kale & Chicken Salad with Peanut Dressing

Prep Time: 15 min, Serving: 4, Difficulty: Easy

Ingredients

- ¼ cup chopped unsalted peanuts
- ⅛ tsp ground pepper
- 6 cups chopped curly kale
- 1 ½ tsp extra-virgin olive oil
- 1 pound sweet potatoes
- 1/2 cup Peanut Dressing
- ¼ tsp kosher salt
- 2 cups shredded cooked chicken breast

Instructions

1. Preheat the oven to 425 degrees Fahrenheit. Using foil, line a rimmed baking sheet and gently spray with cooking spray. Set aside. In a large mixing basin, mix sweet potatoes with salt, oil, and pepper.
2. Put the sweet potatoes in a layer on the baking sheet that has been prepared. Roast for 20 minutes, turning once, until soft and lightly browned & crispy on the outside. Allow it to cool completely before constructing the bowls.
3. Refrigerate 2 tbsp peanut dressing in each of 4 small covered containers for up to 4 days.
4. Divide the kale into four single-serving containers (each approximately 1 1/2 cup). 1/4 cup roasted sweet potatoes & 1/2 cup chicken on top of each. Refrigerate for 4 days after sealing the containers.
5. Drizzle 1 part of peanut dressing over each salad just before serving & toss well to coat. 1 tbsp crushed peanuts on top.

13. Sprouted-Grain Toast with Peanut Butter & Banana

Prep Time: 5 min, Serving: 1, Difficulty: Easy

Ingredients

- 1 tbsp peanut butter
- 1 slice sprouted-grain bread
- 1 medium banana, sliced

Instructions

1. Toast the bread.
2. Spread peanut butter on the bread and top it with banana slices.

14. Brussels Sprouts Salad with Crunchy Chickpeas

Prep Time: 10 min, Serving: 4, Difficulty: Easy

Ingredients

- 1 package shaved or shredded Brussels sprouts
- 4 cups chopped kale
- 1 medium avocado, quartered and pitted
- 1 cup chickpea snacks (roasted) with sea salt
- 1/2 cup Tahini Sauce with Garlic & Lemon

Instructions

1. Divide 4 single-serving lidded jars with Brussels sprouts and kale. Refrigerate for 4 days after sealing.
2. Refrigerate 2 tbsp tahini sauce in each of 4 small covered jars for 4 days.
3. Drizzle 1 part of tahini sauce over each salad just before serving and toss well to cover. 1/4 cup of roasted chickpeas & 1/4 avocado on top.

15. Avocado Egg Salad Sandwiches

Prep Time: 20 min, Serving: 2, Difficulty: Easy

Ingredients

- 2 leaves lettuce
- 1 ½ tsp lemon juice
- 4 slices whole-wheat sandwich bread, toasted
- 1 tsp avocado oil
- ⅛ tsp ground pepper
- 3 hard-boiled eggs, chopped
- ¼ cup finely chopped celery (about 1 stalk)
- 1 tbsp snipped fresh chives
- ½ ripe avocado
- ¼ tsp salt

Instructions

1. Scoop the avocado half's flesh into a medium mixing bowl. Add the lemon juice & oil and mash until the mixture is largely smooth. Next, stir in the chopped eggs, chives, celery, salt, & pepper until everything is well combined.
2. Divide the mixture between 2 toast pieces. Add a bit of lettuce and then another slice of bread to each.

16. Vegan Superfood Buddha Bowls

Prep Time: 15 min, Serving: 4, Difficulty: Easy

Ingredients

- 1 package cooked whole baby beets, sliced, refrigerated
- ¼ cup unsalted toasted sunflower seeds
- ½ cup hummus
- 1 avocado, sliced
- 2 tbsp lemon juice
- 1 (5 ounces) package baby kale
- 1 (8 ounces) pouch microwavable quinoa
- 1 cup shelled edamame, thawed, frozen

Instructions

1. Prepare quinoa as directed on the package; leave aside to cool.

2. In a small bowl, combine the hummus and lemon juice. Thin with water until the dressing reaches the desired consistency. Refrigerate the dressing in four small condiment jars with lids.

3. 4 single-serving jars with lids, divided baby kale Add 1/2 cup beets, 1/2 cup quinoa, 1/4 cup edamame, and 1 tbsp sunflower seeds to each bowl.

4. Top with 1/4 avocado and hummus dressing when ready to eat.

17. Chicken, Arugula & Butternut Squash Salad with Brussels Sprouts

Prep Time: 20 min, Serving: 6, Difficulty: Medium

Ingredients

- ½ cup very thinly sliced red onion
- 2 ¾ cups butternut squash (pre-cubed)
- 2 tsp Dijon mustard
- 2 ½ cups Brussels sprouts, halved
- 2 tbsp finely chopped shallot
- 1 tsp olive oil
- 2 tbsp white wine vinegar
- ¾ tsp salt, divided
- ¼ cup walnut oil or extra-virgin olive oil
- ⅛ tsp ground pepper
- 2 cups cooked chicken, cubed
- 1 package baby arugula
- 1 cup red grapes, halved

Instructions

1. Preheat the oven to 425 degrees Fahrenheit. Using cooking spray, coat a big rimmed baking sheet.

2. In a large mixing bowl, combine the squash, Brussels sprouts, 1 tsp olive oil, 1/4 tsp salt, and 1/8 tsp pepper. Arrange in a layer on the baking sheet that has been prepared. Roast

for 20 to 22 minutes, stirring once or twice until the veggies are soft.

3. In the reserved bowl, combine the grapes, onion, chicken, and arugula. Toss in the roasted veggies to mix.

4. In a small bowl, combine the walnut oil (or olive oil), vinegar, shallot, mustard, and 1/2 tsp salt and 1/4 tsp pepper. Pour the dressing over the salad & toss lightly to combine.

18. Red, White, and Blueberry Fruit Salad

Prep Time: 10 min, Serving: 8, Difficulty: Easy

Ingredients

- ½ cup white sugar
- 1-pint strawberries, hulled and quartered
- 4 bananas
- 1-pint blueberries
- 2 tbsp lemon juice

Instructions

1. In a mixing bowl, combine the strawberries and blueberries, season with sugar & lemon juice, and toss gently.

2. Refrigerate for at least 30 minutes or until completely cool. Slice the bananas and combine them with the berries about 30 minutes before serving.

19. Pan Seared Salmon

Prep Time: 10 min, Serving: 4, Difficulty: Easy

Ingredients

- ⅛ tsp salt
- 4 (6 ounce) fillets of salmon
- 4 slices lemon

- 2 tbsp olive oil
- 2 tbsp capers
- ⅛ tsp ground black pepper

Instructions

1. Preheat a big heavy skillet over heat for almost 3 minutes.
2. Using olive oil, coat fish. Turn the heat up to high in the skillet. 3 minutes of cooking Capers, salt, and pepper are added to the dish. Cook for almost 5 minutes, or until salmon is browned on the other side. When a fork easily flakes the salmon, it's ready.
3. Serve the salmon on separate dishes with lemon slices as a garnish.

20. Easy Roasted Broccoli

Prep Time: 10 min, Serving: 4, Difficulty: Easy

Ingredients

- 1 tbsp olive oil
- 14 ounces broccoli
- salt & ground black pepper to taste

Instructions

1. Preheat the oven to 400 degrees Fahrenheit.
2. Broccoli florets should be separated from the stalk. Slice the stalk into 1/4-inch segments after peeling it. In a mixing bowl, combine florets & stem pieces with olive oil; move to a baking sheet and season with salt and pepper.
3. Roast for 18 minutes in an oven and bake until broccoli is soft & lightly browned.

21. Tomato and Avocado Salad

Prep Time: 15 min, Serving: 4, Difficulty: Easy

Ingredients

- 1 tsp Dijon mustard
- 2 small tomatoes, each cut into 8 wedges
- ¼ cup extra-virgin olive oil
- ½ cup balsamic vinegar
- 1 pinch ground black pepper
- 1 avocado - peeled, pitted and sliced

Instructions

1. Whisk together the olive oil, mustard, pepper and balsamic vinegar in a small basin. Arrange the pieces of avocado & tomato alternately on a large serving plate or individual plates, as if they were spokes of a wheel.
2. Serve immediately with a thin drizzle of dressing.

22. Grilled Peppers

Prep Time: 15 min, Serving: 6, Difficulty: Easy

Ingredients

- 1 pinch dried oregano
- 3 green bell peppers, cut into large chunks
- ½ cup sliced jalapeno peppers
- 1 cup shredded mozzarella cheese

Instructions

1. Preheat the grill to medium-high. Lightly oil the grill grate once it's heated.
2. Place the peppers on the grill, inside out, with the insides facing down. Cook for 3 to 5 minutes, or until slightly charred.
3. Turn the peppers over and top with jalapeño slices. Add some mozzarella cheese and a pinch of oregano on the top. Remove to a platter and serve after the cheese has melted.

23. Mushrooms and Spinach Italian Style

Prep Time: 20 min, Serving: 4, Difficulty: Easy

Ingredients

- 4 tbsp olive oil
- chopped fresh parsley for garnish
- salt and freshly ground black pepper to taste
- 1 small onion, chopped
- ½ cup white wine
- 2 chopped cloves garlic
- 14 ounces mushrooms (fresh), sliced
- 2 tbsp balsamic vinegar
- 10 ounces spinach (clean & fresh), roughly chopped

Instructions

1. In a large pan, heat the olive oil over medium-high heat. In a skillet, sauté the onion and garlic until they begin to soften. Fry the mushrooms for 3 to 4 minutes, or until they begin to shrink. Toss in the spinach and cook for a few minutes, stirring regularly, or until the spinach has wilted.
2. Stir in the vinegar until it is completely absorbed, then add the white wine. Reduce to a low heat setting and continue to cook until the wine has been fully absorbed. Season to taste with salt and pepper, then top with fresh parsley. Serve immediately.

24. Turmeric Milk

Prep Time: 10 min, Serving: 1, Difficulty: Easy

Ingredients

- 1 (1 1/2 inch) piece fresh turmeric root, peeled and grated
- 1 pinch ground cinnamon
- 1 (1/2 inch) piece fresh ginger root, peeled and grated
- 1 tbsp honey
- 1 cup unsweetened almond milk
- 1 pinch ground turmeric

Instructions

1. In a mixing dish, combine the turmeric root, ginger root, and honey, crushing the turmeric & ginger as much as possible.
2. In a small saucepan, warm the almond milk. Reduce heat to low after little bubbles appear around the edges. Allow around 2 tbsp milk to soften the turmeric mixture and the honey to melt into a paste-like texture.
3. Mix the turmeric paste & milk; reduce to medium-low heat and simmer, constantly stirring, until well blended. For a smooth texture, use an immersion blender.
4. Fill a cup with turmeric tea and sprinkle with ground turmeric & cinnamon.

25. Cherry Coconut Smoothie

Prep Time: 10 min, Serving: 2, Difficulty: Easy

Ingredients
- 1 cup cherries, pitted
- 1 cup ice
- ½ cup almond milk
- ½ cup coconut water

Instructions
1. Blend almond milk, ice, cherries, and coconut water in a blender until it becomes smooth.
2. Serve and enjoy.

26. Homemade Melt-In-Your-Mouth Dark Chocolate (Paleo)

Prep Time: 10 min, Serving: 8, Difficulty: Easy

Ingredients

- ½ cup coconut oil
- ½ cup cocoa powder
- 3 tbsp honey
- ½ tsp vanilla extract

Instructions

1. In a saucepan over low heat, gently melt coconut oil. In a large mixing bowl, combine cocoa powder, honey, and vanilla extract.
2. Fill a candy mold or a pliable tray with the mixture. Refrigerate for 1 hour or until completely cooled.

27. Faux Fried Coconut Chicken with Honey Mustard

Prep Time: 20 min, Serving: 2, Difficulty: Easy

Ingredients:

- 1-½ cups almond flour
- 2 tbsp honey
- ¼ cup arrowroot powder
- ¼ cup Dijon mustard
- ½ cup shredded unsweetened coconut
- Dipping Sauce
- 2 tsp garlic powder
- 4 boneless, skinless chicken thighs or legs
- 2 tsp paprika
- 1 tsp garlic salt
- 2 large eggs

Instructions:

1. Preheat the oven to 400 degrees Fahrenheit. Brush the parchment paper with ghee or coconut oil and place it on a baking sheet.
2. Combine the arrowroot powder, almond flour, coconut, paprika, garlic powder, and garlic salt in a small bowl.
3. Whisk the eggs in a separate shallow basin.
4. After dipping each piece of chicken in the egg wash, evenly coat it with the flour mixture. Arrange on a baking sheet.
5. Bake for 14 to 20 minutes, or until a thermometer inserted in the thickest section reads 165°F and the juices flow clear, flipping once.
6. To prepare the dipping sauce, whisk together the honey and mustard in a small basin. With the dipping sauce, serve the chicken.

28. Walnut Crusted Salmon with Honey & Rosemary

Prep Time: 12 min, Serving: 3, Difficulty: Easy

Ingredients

- 2 salmon filets
- Pinch of salt
- 2 tbsp Dijon mustard
- 1 tsp dried or fresh rosemary
- 2 tbsp honey
- ⅓ cup chopped walnuts
- 1 clove garlic, finely minced
- ¼ tsp lemon zest
- 1 tsp lemon juice

Instructions:

1. Preheat the oven to 425 degrees Fahrenheit. Using parchment paper, line a big rimmed baking sheet. In a small bowl, combine garlic, mustard, lemon juice, lemon zest, honey, rosemary, and salt. In a separate small dish, combine the rosemary and walnuts.

2. Place the salmon skin-side down on the baking sheet. Apply the mustard mixture to the fish and then sprinkle the walnut mixture on top, pressing to adhere. Bake for 8 to 12 minutes, depending on thickness.

29. Citrus Salad and Ginger Yogurt

Prep Time: 10 min, Serving: 6, Difficulty: Easy

Ingredients

- 1 peeled pink grapefruit
- Additional dried cranberries
- 1/4 tsp ground cinnamon
- 2 big tangerines, peeled
- 1/4 cup golden brown sugar
- 3 navel oranges
- 2/3 cup minced crystallized ginger
- 1/2 cup cranberries, dried
- 1 container Greek yogurt
- 2 tbsp honey

Instructions

1. Grapefruit and tangerines should be cut into pieces. Grapefruit parts should be cut into thirds, while tangerine slices should be cut in half. In a deep serving bowl, combine the tangerines, grapefruit, and all juices. Remove all peel & white pith from oranges using a tiny sharp knife. Cut oranges into quarters after slicing them into 1/4-inch thick circles. In the same dish, combine all of the fluids and the oranges. Combine honey, 1/2 cup

dried cranberries, and cinnamon in a mixing bowl. Refrigerate for 1 hour after covering. In a dish, combine ginger and yogurt.

2. Place a spoonful of yogurt on top of the fruit. Brown sugar & dried cranberries are sprinkled on top.

30. Indian Spiced Carrot Soup with Ginger

Prep Time: 30 min, Serving: 8, Difficulty: Easy

Ingredients

- 1/2 tsp yellow mustard seeds
- 1 tsp coriander seeds
- 3 tbsp peanut oil
- 1/2 tsp curry powder
- 1 tbsp fresh ginger, minced peeled
- 2 cups chopped onions
- 1 1/2 pounds carrots, thinly sliced, peeled
- 1 1/2 tsp lime peel, finely grated
- 5 cups vegetable broth or low-salt chicken broth
- 2 tsp lime juice, fresh
- Plain yogurt

Instructions

1. In a spice mill, grind coriander & mustard seeds to a fine powder. In a heavy, big saucepan, heat the oil over medium-high heat. Stir in the curry powder and crushed seeds for 1 minute. Stir in the ginger for 1 minute.

2. Combine the following three ingredients in a mixing bowl.
   Season with salt & pepper and cook for 3 minutes, or until onions soften. Bring 5 cups broth to a boil. Reduce heat and cook, uncovered, for 30 minutes or until carrots are soft. Allow cooling slightly. In a blender,

purée in batches until smooth. Put the soup back in the pot. If the soup is too thick, add extra broth by 1/4 cupfuls. Season with salt & pepper after adding the lime juice. Allow cooling slightly. Chill uncovered until completely cold, then cover and refrigerate. Before serving, reheat the dish.

3. The soup should be ladled into bowls. Serve with a spoonful of yogurt on top.

31. Red Bell Pepper, Spinach, and Goat Cheese Salad with Oregano Dressing

Prep Time: 10 min, Serving: 4, Difficulty: Easy

Ingredients

- 1/3 cup chopped red onion
- 2 tbsp fresh lemon juice
- 3/4 cup crumbled soft fresh goat cheese
- 1 tbsp chopped fresh oregano
- 1 1/2 cups diced celery (about 3 stalks)
- 4 cups (packed) baby spinach leaves, coarsely chopped (about 4 ounces)
- 2 tbsp extra-virgin olive oil
- 1 1/2 large red bell peppers, diced

Instructions

1. In a large mixing bowl, combine the lemon juice, oil, and oregano. Season with salt & pepper to taste. Toss in the bell peppers, spinach, goat cheese, celery, and red onion with the dressing.
2. Serve the salad by dividing it among four plates.

32. Pan Seared Salmon on Baby Arugula

Prep Time: 8 min, Serving: 2, Difficulty: Easy

Ingredients

- 1 1/2 tbsp olive oil
- 2 center-cut salmon fillets (6 oz. each)
- 1 1/2 Tbsp fresh lemon juice
- Salt and freshly ground black pepper, to taste

For the salad:

- 3 cups baby arugula leaves
- 1 tbsp red-wine vinegar
- 2/3 cup grape or cherry tomatoes, halved
- 1 tbsp extra-virgin olive oil
- 1/4 cup thinly slivered red onion
- Salt and freshly ground black pepper, to taste

Instructions

1. In a small dish, put the fish fillets. Toss well with olive oil, lemon juice, pepper and salt. Allow 15 minutes for resting.
2. Cook the fish in a nonstick skillet, over medium-high heat for about 3 mins, shaking the pan & gently extracting the fish from the pan with a spatula.
3. Turn the heat down to medium. Cook for 3 to 4 minutes longer, covered until the fish is cooked through. The meat should be medium rare and the skin crisp.
4. In a separate bowl, mix the arugula, tomatoes, and onion. Season with salt & pepper and sprinkle with oil and vinegar just before serving. Toss thoroughly.

33. Arctic Char with Chinese Broccoli and Sweet Potato Purée

Prep time: 10 min, serving: 4, difficulty: easy

Ingredients

- 3 red-skinned sweet potatoes
- 2 tbsp vegetable oil, divided

- 1 tsp (or more) hot prepared Chinese mustard
- 4 5- to 6-ounce arctic char fillets
- 1 cup balsamic vinegar
- 2 tsp yellow mustard seeds
- 1 1/2 tsp soy sauce
- 1 pound Chinese broccoli
- 2 slices bacon, cut into 1-inch pieces

Instructions

1. Preheat the oven to 400 degrees Fahrenheit. Cover sweet potatoes in foil one at a time. Roast for 1 to 1 1/2 hours, or until tender. Allow cooling before peeling. Blend until smooth in a food processor. 3 cups puree, transferred to a microwave-safe dish. Add the mustard and mix well. Season with salt and pepper. Cover and set aside to cool. In a small pot, boil vinegar until it is reduced to a cup, approximately 8 minutes. Add the soy sauce and mix well. Remove the pan from the heat.
2. 1 minute in a saucepan of boiling salted water, cook broccoli till crisp-tender. Drain the water and put it aside. In a medium pan, cook bacon until crisp around the edges over medium heat. To drain, place on paper towels. Make the reduction and broccoli 2 hours ahead of time. Allow cooling to room temperature.
3. In a spice grinder, crush mustard seeds until they are finely ground. Season the fish with salt & pepper before serving. Over the top of the fish, sprinkle ground seeds. In a large skillet, heat 1 tablespoon of oil over medium-high heat. Cook until the fish is brown and almost opaque in the middle, approximately 3 minutes on each side, with the mustard side down.
4. Meanwhile, reheat the puree in the microwave until it is well cooked. Take a separate big pan, heat 1 tablespoon of oil.

Sauté the broccoli and bacon until they are cooked thoroughly. Salt & pepper to taste.

5. Arrange broccoli, fish, and purée on individual plates. Serve with a drizzle of balsamic reduction.

34. Roasted Salmon with Orange-Herb Sauce

Prep Time: 30 min, Serving: 6, difficulty: Medium

Ingredients

- 1 large orange, unpeeled, sliced
- Additional unpeeled orange slices
- 1 large onion, halved, thinly sliced
- 1 1/2 tbsp fresh lemon juice
- 1 1/2 tbsp olive oil
- 1/4 cup thinly sliced green onions
- 6 3-ounce skinless salmon fillets
- 3 tbsp chopped fresh dill
- 1/2 cup orange juice

Instructions

1. Preheat the oven to 400 degrees Fahrenheit. In a glass baking dish, arrange orange slices in a single layer. Onion slices should be placed on top. Drizzle some oil on top. Season to taste with salt and pepper. Roast for approximately 25 minutes, or until the onion is golden and soft. Remove the dish from the oven. Preheat the oven to 450 degrees Fahrenheit.
2. Slices of orange and onion should be pushed to the edge of the baking dish.
   Place the salmon in the dish's middle. 1 1/2 tablespoons dill, salt, and pepper Arrange orange and onion pieces on top of the salmon. Roast for approximately 8 minutes or until the fish is opaque in the middle.

3. In a separate dish, combine the lemon juice, green onions, orange juice, and the remaining 1 1/2 tablespoons dill.
4. Place the fish on a serving plate. Place the onion next to the roasted orange slices and toss them out. Serve the fish with an orange sauce. Add more orange slices as a garnish.

35. Carrots and Brussels Sprouts

Prep Time: 20 min, Serving: 4, Difficulty: Medium

Ingredients

- 2 tbsp chopped shallot (from 1 medium)
- 1 tbsp cider vinegar
- 3 tbsp divided unsalted butter
- 1 lb carrots, cut into 1/2-inch-thick pieces
- 1/3 cup water
- 1 lb Brussels sprouts, halved

Instructions

1. Cook shallot in 2 tbsp butter in a 12" heavy skillet over medium heat, turning periodically, until softened, 1 to 2 minutes. Add the Brussels sprouts, carrots, 3/4 teaspoon salt, 1/2 teaspoon pepper and cook, occasionally turn for 3 to 4 minutes, or until the veggies begin to brown.
2. Cover pan with water and simmer over medium-high heat for 5 to 8 minutes, or until veggies are cooked. Add the remaining tbsp butter, the vinegar, and season with salt and pepper to taste.

36. Chilled Red Bell Pepper and Habanero Soup

Prep Time: 30 min, Serving: 6, Difficulty: Medium

Ingredients

- 4 red bell peppers
- 2 chopped garlic cloves
- 1 3/4 cups reduced-sodium chicken broth
- 2 lb tomatoes
- 1/4 cup plus 2 tbsp extra-virgin olive oil, divided
- 1 sweet onion, chopped
- 6 fresh habanero chilies, finely chopped, seeds and stems discarded

Accompaniment:

- Crackers, flatbread, or bread

Instructions

1. Bell peppers should be roasted on racks of burners over high heat for 10 to 12 minutes, rotating with tongs until skins are browned. Wrap with plastic wrap and transfer to a bowl. Allow for 20 minutes of resting time. Remove the stems and seeds before peeling and splitting the fruit lengthwise.
2. Make a shallow X in the bottom of every tomato, then blanch for 20 seconds in boiling water before transferring to an ice bath. Next, remove the peel and finely slice the onion, saving the juices.
3. In a 3- to 4-quart heavy saucepan, cook chilies, garlic, 1 tsp salt, onion, and 1/4 tsp pepper in 2 tbsp oil over medium heat, occasionally stirring, until softened and light yellow, approximately 8 minutes.
   Add the tomatoes with broth, bell peppers, juices, and 1/4 teaspoon salt, and cook, covered, for 5 minutes, or until peppers are soft.
4. In a blender, puree the soup in two or three batches (take care when mixing hot liquids), dripping the remaining 1/4 cup oil into the first batch while the motor is running. For 10 to 15 minutes, cool soup in a metal dish put in an ice bath, stirring often. Season with salt and pepper.

37. Curried Chicken Salad with Spiced Chickpeas and Raita

Prep Time: 15 min, Serving: 4, Difficulty: Easy

Ingredients

For the curried chicken salad:

- 1 cup plain yogurt
- 1 medium onion, chopped (1 cup)
- 1 cup red grapes, halved
- 1 tbsp minced garlic
- 1 rotisserie chicken, meat coarsely shredded (3 to 4 cups)
- 1 tbsp minced peeled ginger
- 2 tbsp cilantro
- 2 tbsp vegetable oil
- 1 tbsp curry powder
- 1 tsp ground cumin
- 2 medium tomatoes, chopped (1 cup)

For chickpeas:

- 1/2 tsp turmeric
- 1/4 tsp cayenne
- 1 tbsp vegetable oil
- 1 (19-ounce) can chickpeas, rinsed, drained, and patted dry (2 cups)
- 1 tsp ground cumin
- For raita and topping:
- 2 tbsp chopped mint
- 1 cup plain yogurt
- 1 seedless cucumber, peeled, cored, and chopped (2 cups)
- 1/2 cup sliced almonds, toasted

Instructions

1. In a 10-inch heavy skillet, cook garlic, onion, and ginger in oil until softened, approximately 5 minutes, stirring periodically. Cook, stirring, for 2 minutes after adding the cumin, curry, and 1 1/2 teaspoon salt.

2. Cook, constantly stirring until the sauce has thickened, approximately 5 minutes over medium-high heat. Toss in the cilantro, yogurt, and chicken in a mixing bowl. Bring to room temperature before serving.

3. Heat the oil in a clean pan over medium heat until it shimmers, then cook the chickpeas for 1 minute while tossing constantly. Cook, tossing to coat, until cumin, cayenne, turmeric, and 1/4 teaspoon salt are aromatic, approximately 2 minutes. Bring to room temperature before serving.

4. Combine the mint, cucumber, yogurt, and 1/2 teaspoon salt in a mixing bowl.

5. Assemble the jars as follows:

6. Layer curried chickpeas, raita, chicken, and almonds on top of grapes in jars.

38. Beet Chips with Turmeric-Yogurt Dip

Prep Time: 22 min, Serving: 8, Difficulty: Easy

Ingredients

- 1/8 tsp ground red pepper
- 1 cup plain whole-milk Greek yogurt
- 3/4 tsp kosher salt
- 2 tbsp chopped fresh chives
- 1 tsp onion powder
- 1 tbsp extra-virgin olive oil
- 1 tsp ground turmeric
- 3 medium beets, peeled and sliced
- 2 tsp fresh lemon juice

Instructions

1. Paper towels should be used to line a big microwave-safe dish. Spread beet slices

on a towel-lined dish in batches and microwave on high for 3 mins or until crispy.

2. Stir together the yogurt and the other ingredients. Serve with beet chips as a dip.

39. Mighty Melon Green Tea Smoothie

Prep Time: 10 min, Serving: 2, Difficulty: Easy

Ingredients

- 1 pear, cored and cut into chunks
- 1 cup brewed green tea, chilled
- 4 fresh mint leaves, or more to taste
- 1 cup frozen pineapple chunks
- 1 cup cantaloupe chunks
- ½ cup plain Greek yogurt

Instructions

1. Combine pineapple, tea, pear, cantaloupe, mint leaves, and yogurt in a blender.
2. Mix until smooth and serve.

40. Grilled Tuna Steaks with Grape and Caper Salsa

Prep Time: 20 min, Serving: 4, Difficulty: Easy

Ingredients

- ¼ cup fresh lemon juice
- ⅓ cup capers, rinsed and drained
- 4 (8 ounces) tuna steaks
- 1 minced shallot
- 2 cups halved red seedless grapes
- 2 tbsp fresh parsley, chopped
- 1 tbsp olive oil
- black pepper and salt to taste

Instructions

1. Preheat an outside grill over medium-high heat and brush the grate lightly with oil.
2. In a bowl, combine the capers, grapes, parsley, shallot, and olive oil; season with salt and pepper to taste, and leave aside. Brush tuna steaks with lemon juice and place on a platter. To taste, season with salt and pepper.
3. Cook tuna steaks on a hot grill until the desired doneness is reached, approximately 2 to 3 minutes on each side for medium-rare. Toss with the grape & caper salsa before serving.

41. Turmeric Ginger C Boost Life Juice

Prep Time: 5 min, Serving: 1, Difficulty: Easy

Ingredients

- ½ lemon, peeled
- 2 Fuji apples, cored and sliced
- ½ tsp ground turmeric
- 1 orange, peeled and sectioned
- 1 (1 inch) piece fresh ginger

Instructions

1. Process orange, apples, ginger, and lemon through a juicer; mix in turmeric until evenly combined.
2. Serve and enjoy.

42. Salmon Avocado Salad

Prep Time: 20 min, Serving: 4, Difficulty: Easy

Ingredients

- 2 (6 ounce) fillets salmon
- 2 tbsp distilled white vinegar
- ¼ cup butter, melted and divided
- 1 fresh jalapeno pepper, chopped
- salt and pepper to taste
- 5 sprigs fresh cilantro, chopped
- 4 ounces fresh mushrooms, sliced
- 1 avocado - peeled, pitted, and cubed
- 12 grape tomatoes, halved
- 1-ounce feta cheese, crumbled
- 2 tbsp olive oil, divided
- 8 ounces leaf lettuce, torn into bite-size pieces

Instructions

1. Preheat the broiler in the oven. Aluminum foil should be used to line a baking pan. Brush the salmon with 2 tbsp melted butter before placing it on the foil. Salt & pepper to taste. Broil for 15 minutes, or until the fish flakes easily with a fork.
2. In a pan over medium heat, melt the rest of the butter and sauté the mushrooms until soft.
3. Toss the tomatoes in a dish with 1 tablespoon of olive oil. Salt & pepper to taste.
4. Toss the salmon, tomatoes, cilantro, mushrooms, avocado, lettuce, and jalapeño in a large mixing bowl. Drizzle the remaining olive oil & vinegar over the top.

To serve, season with salt & pepper and top with feta cheese.

43. Healthy Turmeric Chicken Stew

Prep Time: 15 min, Serving: 6, Difficulty: Easy

Ingredients

- 2 skinless, boneless chicken breasts, cubed
- 2 tsp ground turmeric
- 1 tbsp minced fresh ginger root
- ½ red onion, chopped
- 1 small eggplant, cubed
- 2 tbsp olive oil
- ½ cup low-sodium chicken broth
- 2 sweet potatoes, cubed
- 2 cloves garlic, minced

Instructions

1. In a large pan, heat the olive oil over medium-high heat. Cook, occasionally stirring, until the chicken is browned, approximately 5 minutes. Continue cooking until sweet potatoes & onion are transparent, about 2 to 3 minutes.
2. Cook for another minute, or until the eggplant, garlic, ginger, & turmeric are fragrant. Pour in the broth and cook, occasionally stirring, until the stew has thickened, approximately 20 minutes.

44. Tuna and Chickpea Salad

Prep Time: 10 min, Serving: 4, Difficulty: Easy

Ingredients

- ½ red onion, chopped
- 1 (2.25 ounce) can black olives, chopped

- 1 (5 ounces) can Italian tuna packed in olive oil, undrained
- salt and ground black pepper to taste
- 1 (16 ounces) can chickpeas (garbanzo beans), drained
- ¼ cup crumbled reduced-fat feta cheese or more to taste
- lemon, juiced
- ¼ cup chopped Italian (flat-leaf) parsley

Instructions

1. Stir the chickpeas, tuna, parsley, olives, feta cheese, red onion, and lemon juice together in a dish.
2. Season with pepper and salt.

45. Heirloom Salad including Tomatoes and Rosemary

Prep Time: 10 min, Serving: 4, Difficulty: Easy

Ingredients

- ¼ cup extra virgin olive oil
- 3 large heirloom tomatoes, quartered
- 2 tbsp rice wine vinegar
- 3 small heirloom tomatoes, quartered
- 1 sprig rosemary, fresh, finely chopped
- ground black pepper to taste
- Salt to taste
- ⅛ tsp dried oregano

Instructions

1. In a large mixing bowl, combine the rosemary, rice wine vinegar, olive oil, and oregano. Toss in the tiny and big tomatoes until they are equally covered.
2. Refrigerate for 10 to 15 minutes, covered and cooled. Salt & black pepper to taste. Before serving, toss once more.

46. Strawberry Spinach Salad

Prep Time: 10 min, Serving: 4, Difficulty: Easy

Ingredients

- 2 tbsp sesame seeds
- ¼ cup almonds, blanched and slivered
- 1 tbsp poppy seeds
- 1-quart strawberries - cleaned, hulled and sliced
- ½ cup white sugar
- 10 ounces fresh spinach - rinsed, dried and torn into bite-size pieces
- ½ cup olive oil
- 1 tbsp minced onion
- ¼ cup white vinegar, distilled
- ¼ tsp Worcestershire sauce
- ¼ tsp paprika

Instructions

1. Mix the poppy seeds, sesame seeds, olive oil, sugar, paprika, vinegar, onion, and Worcestershire sauce in a medium mixing bowl. Refrigerate for 1 hour, covered.
2. Mix the strawberries, spinach, and almonds in a large mixing bowl. Toss the salad with the dressing. Before serving, chill for 10 to 15 minutes.

47. Broiled Spanish Mackerel

Prep Time: 10 min, Serving: 6, Difficulty: Easy

Ingredients

- ½ tsp paprika
- 6 fillets Spanish mackerel fillets
- 12 slices lemon
- ground black pepper and salt to taste
- ¼ cup olive oil

Instructions

1. Position the oven rack approximately 6" from the source of heat and preheat the broiler. Grease a baking dish lightly.
2. Rub each mackerel fillet on both sides with olive oil and lay the skin side down in the baking dish. Season the paprika, salt, and pepper to taste on each fillet. Two lemon slices should be placed on top of each fillet.
3. Cook the fillets under the broiler for 5 to 7 minutes, or until the fish starts to flake. Serve right away.

48. Easy Roasted Broccoli and Bok Choy with Balsamic Glaze

Prep Time: 20 min, Serving: 4, Difficulty: Easy

Ingredients

- 1 lb baby bok choy (12-14 pieces)
- 1/2 lb broccoli (1/2 head)
- 2 tbsp olive oil
- ½ tsp garlic powder (or 1 clove finely minced)
- Salt and pepper
- Garnish: squeeze of lemon juice or sesame seeds

Instructions

1. 2 cups good balsamic vinegar and 1/2 cup brown sugar, heated. Bring to a gentle boil, then lower to medium-low heat and simmer, frequently stirring, for 8-10 minutes.
2. Preheat the oven to 450 degrees Fahrenheit. Bok choy should be sliced in half lengthwise after being sliced 1/2 inch off the ends. Remove any wilted or brown leaves with your fingers. Remove the stems from the broccoli and chop the florets in half or smaller pieces. In a large mixing bowl, combine broccoli florets & bok choy.

3. Set aside a baking sheet lined with foil. Drizzle the oil and spices over the broccoli & bok choy, and toss lightly to coat. Then roast for 6-8 minutes, or until slightly brown, in a single layer on a baking sheet.
4. Remove the dish from the oven. Place on a serving dish. Sprinkle with balsamic glaze & toasted sesame seeds, if preferred, as well as a squeeze of lemon.

49. My Big Fat Greek Salad

Prep Time: 20 min, Serving: 4, Difficulty: Easy

Ingredients

- 2 large English cucumbers
- 1 tsp minced fresh oregano, or to taste
- 1 pinch kosher salt
- 1 (4 ounces) package feta cheese, diced, divided
- 2 cups cherry tomatoes
- ⅓ cup olive oil, or to taste
- ¼ red onion
- ¼ cup red wine vinegar, or to taste
- ½ red bell pepper
- 1 pinch cayenne pepper, or to taste
- ½ cup pitted Kalamata olives
- ½ cup pitted green olives
- 2 tbsp minced fresh oregano
- salt and freshly ground black pepper to taste

Instructions

1. Using a channel knife, create a striped pattern by peeling off a few strips of cucumber skin. Cucumbers should be cut in half crosswise. Before slicing into 1/4- to 1/2-inch slices, divide each half into quarters. Toss with kosher salt in a colander and let aside for 15 minutes.
2. Meanwhile, halve the cherry tomatoes. Finally, cucumbers should be rinsed and

drained completely for another 10 to 15 minutes.

3. While the cucumbers are draining, finely slice the onion. Bell pepper should be cut into strips.

4. In a mixing dish, combine tomatoes, olives, cucumbers, bell pepper, onion, and 2 tablespoons oregano. Salt, black pepper, and cayenne pepper to taste. Toss in the vinegar and toss again. Drizzle some olive oil on top. Mix in 2/3 of the feta cheese and toss once more. Refrigerate for 60 minutes after wrapping in plastic wrap.

5. Toss the salad once more. Season with salt and pepper to taste. Sprinkle the remaining feta cheese over the top and finish with the oregano.

50. Spinach Salad with Chicken, Avocado, and Goat Cheese

Prep Time: 20 min, Serving: 4, Difficulty: Easy

Ingredients

Salad:

- 1 large avocado - peeled, pitted, and sliced
- ¼ cup pine nuts
- ⅓ cup crumbled goat cheese
- 8 cups chopped spinach
- ½ cup corn kernels
- 1 cup halved cherry tomatoes
- 1 ½ cups chopped cooked chicken

Salad Dressing:

- 1 tbsp Dijon mustard
- 3 tbsp white wine vinegar
- 2 tbsp extra-virgin olive oil
- 1 pinch salt and ground black pepper to taste

Instructions

1. In a small skillet, heat the oil over medium-high heat.
2. Then, 3 to 5 minutes in a heated pan, toast pine nuts until nicely browned and fragrant.
3. Toss spinach with tomatoes, pine nuts, avocado, corn kernels, chicken, and goat cheese in a big salad bowl.
4. In a small bowl, whisk together olive oil, white wine vinegar, and Dijon mustard until smooth; season with salt and pepper. Toss the salad gently in the dressing to coat it.

51 Fruit Salad with Red, White, and Blueberries

Ready in 40 min **Servings:** 8 **Difficulty:** Easy

Ingredients

- 1-pint strawberries
- 2 tbsp lemon juice
- 4 bananas
- 1-pint blueberries
- ½ cup white sugar

Instructions

1. In a mixing bowl, combine the strawberries and blueberries, season with sugar & lemon juice, and toss gently. Refrigerate for at least 30 minutes or until completely cool. Divide bananas into 3/4-inch slices and combine with the berries about 20 minutes before serving.

52 Seared Salmon in a Pan

Ready in 20 min **Servings:** 4 **Difficulty:** Easy

Ingredients

- ⅛ teaspoon salt
- ⅛ teaspoon ground black pepper
- 4 slices of lemon
- 4 fillets salmon
- 2 tbsp olive oil
- 2 tbsp capers

Instructions

1. Preheat a big heavy skillet for 3 minutes over medium heat.
2. Olive oil should be used to coat the salmon. Increase the heat to high in the skillet. 3 minutes in the oven Season with salt and pepper and capers. Cook for 5 minutes on the other side, or until browned. When a fork easily flakes the salmon, it's done.
3. Arrange the salmon on separate dishes and serve with lemon slices as a garnish.

53 Salad with Tomatoes and Avocados

Ready in 15 min **Servings:** 4 **Difficulty:** Easy

Ingredients

- ½ cup of balsamic vinegar
- 1 teaspoon of Dijon mustard
- ¼ cup virgin olive oil
- 2 small tomatoes
- 1 pinch black pepper
- 1 peeled avocado

Instructions

1. Whisk together all the mustard, balsamic vinegar, olive oil, and pepper in a small basin. Set the pieces of avocado & tomato alternately on a large serving plate or individual plates, as if they were spokes of a wheel. Serve immediately with a thin drizzle of dressing.

54 Broccoli Roasted with Ease

Ready in 30 min **Servings:** 4
Difficulty: Easy

Ingredients

- 14 ounces of broccoli
- salt and black pepper
- 1 tbsp of olive oil

Instructions

1. Preheat oven to 425 degrees Fahrenheit.
2. Step 2: Separate the florets from the stem of the broccoli. Slice the stalk into 1/4-inch segments after peeling it. In a mixing bowl, combine florets & stem portions with olive oil; move to a baking tray and season with salt.
3. Roast for 18 minutes in an oven and bake until broccoli is cooked & lightly browned

55 Peppers grilled

Ready in 15 min **Servings:** 6 **Difficulty:** Easy

Ingredients

- 1 pinch oregano
- 1 cup mozzarella cheese
- 3 green bell peppers
- ½ cup of sliced jalapeno peppers

Instructions

1. Preheat the grill to medium-high heat. Lightly oil the grill grate once it's heated.
2. Arrange the pepper slices on the grill so that the insides are facing down. Cook for 3 to 5 minutes, or until slightly charred.
3. Flip the peppers over and top with jalapeño slices. Add some mozzarella cheese and a pinch of oregano on the top. Remove to a platter and serve after the cheese has melted.

56 Italian Style Mushrooms with Spinach

Ready in 30 min **Servings:** 4 **Difficulty:** Easy

Ingredients

- 2 cloves garlic
- ½ cup of white wine
- salt and black pepper to taste
- chopped fresh parsley
- 4 tbsp olive oil
- 14 ounces sliced mushrooms
- 10 ounces fresh spinach
- 2 tbsp balsamic vinegar
- 1 small onion

Instructions

1. In a large pan, heat the olive oil over medium-high heat. In a skillet, sauté the onion and garlic until they begin to soften. Fry the mushrooms for 3 to 4 minutes, or till they begin to shrink. Toss within spinach and cook for a minute, stirring regularly, or until the spinach has wilted.
2. Stir in the vinegar until it is completely absorbed, then add the white wine. Reduce to a low heat setting and continue to cook till the wine has nearly fully absorbed. Season to taste with salt and pepper, then top with fresh parsley. Serve immediately.

57 Turmeric Milk

Ready in 15 min **Servings:** 1 **Difficulty:** Easy

Ingredients

- 1 cup almond milk
- 1 piece fresh turmeric root
- 1 piece fresh ginger root
- 1 tbsp honey
- 1 pinch ground cinnamon
- 1 pinch ground turmeric

Instructions

1. In a mixing bowl, combine the turmeric root, ginger root, and honey, smashing the turmeric & ginger as much as possible.
2. In a pan over medium heat, warm the almond milk. Medium heats after little bubbles appear around the edges. Allow around 2 tbsp of milk to soften the turmeric mixture and the honey to dissolve into such a paste-like consistency.
3. In a saucepan, combine the turmeric paste and milk; reduce to medium-low heat and simmer, constantly stirring, until entirely blended. For a smooth texture, use an immersion blender.

4. Fill a cup halfway with turmeric tea and sprinkle with ground turmeric & cinnamon.

58 Dark Chocolate Melt-In-Your-Mouth Homemade

Ready in 1 hr 10 min **Servings:** 8 **Difficulty:** Easy

Ingredients

- 3 tbsp honey
- ½ teaspoon of vanilla extract
- ½ cup of coconut oil
- ½ cup of cocoa powder

Instructions

1. In a pan with butter, gently melt coconut oil. In a large mixing bowl, combine cocoa powder, honey, & vanilla extract. Fill a candy mold or a pliable tray halfway with the mixture. Refrigerate for 1 hour or until completely cooled.

59 Tuna Steaks with Grape & Caper Salsa on the Grill

Ready in 25 min **Servings:** 4 **Difficulty:** Easy

Ingredients

- 1 shallot
- 4 tuna steaks
- ¼ cup lemon juice
- 2 tbsp chopped parsley
- 1 tbsp olive oil
- salt and black pepper
- 2 cups of red seedless grapes
- ⅓ cup of capers

Instructions

1. Preheat an outside grill over medium-high heat and brush the grate liberally with oil.

2. In a mixing bowl, combine the capers, parsley, grapes, shallot, & olive oil; season with salt and pepper to taste, and leave aside. Brush tuna steaks with lemon juice and place on a platter. To taste, season with salt.

3. Cook tuna steaks on a hot grill until the desired doneness is reached, about 2 to 3 minutes on each side for medium-rare. Toss with the grape & caper salsa before serving.

60 Smoothie with cherries and coconut

Ready in 10 min **Servings:** 2 **Difficulty:** Easy

Ingredients

- 1 cup cherries
- ½ cup of almond milk
- ½ cup of coconut water
- 1 cup of ice

Instructions

1. In a blender, combine cherries, almond milk, ice, & coconut water until smooth.

61 Smoothie with Mighty Melon and Green Tea

Ready in 10 min **Servings:** 2 **Difficulty:** Easy

Ingredients

- 1 cup of cantaloupe chunks
- 1 pear
- ½ cup plain yogurt
- 1 cup chilled green tea
- 1 cup pineapple chunks
- 4 fresh mint leaves

Instructions

1. In a blender, combine the tea, cantaloupe, pineapple, yogurt, pear, and mint leaves. Blend until completely smooth.

62 Life Juice with Turmeric and Ginger

Ready in 5 min **Servings:** 1 **Difficulty:** Easy

Ingredients

- ½ lemon
- 1 piece ginger
- ½ teaspoon turmeric
- 2 Fuji apples
- 1 orange

Instructions

1. Using a juicer, juice the apples, orange, lemon, & ginger; whisk in the turmeric until it is uniformly distributed.

63 Turmeric Chicken Stew

Ready in 43 min **Servings:** 6 **Difficulty:** Easy

Ingredients

- ½ red onion
- 2 teaspoons turmeric
- ½ cup chicken broth
- 1 small eggplant
- 2 cloves garlic
- 2 tbsp olive oil
- 2 chicken breasts
- 2 sweet potatoes
- 1 tbsp minced ginger root

Instructions

1. In a large pan, heat the olive oil over medium-high heat. Cook, occasionally stirring, until the chicken is browned and so no longer pink, mostly in the middle, approximately 5 minutes. Continue cooking until sweet potatoes & onion are transparent, about 2 to 3 minutes. Cook for another minute, or until the eggplant, garlic, ginger, & turmeric are aromatic. Pour in the broth and cook, stirring periodically, until the stew has thickened, approximately 20 minutes.

64 Salad with Salmon and Avocado

Ready in 35 min **Servings:** 4 **Difficulty:** Easy

Ingredients

- salt and pepper
- 4 ounces fresh mushrooms
- 2 fillets salmon
- ¼ cup butter
- 8 ounces leaf lettuce
- 1 avocado
- 12 grape tomatoes
- 2 tbsp olive oil
- 2 tbsp distilled white vinegar
- 1 ounce feta cheese
- 5 sprigs of fresh cilantro
- 1 fresh jalapeno pepper

Instructions

1. Preheat the broiler in the oven. Aluminum foil should be used to line a baking pan. Brush the salmon with 2 tbsp of butter before placing it on the foil. Salt & pepper to taste. Broil for 15 minutes or until the salmon flakes easily with a fork.
2. In a pan over medium heat, melt the leftover butter and sauté the mushrooms until soft.
3. Toss the tomatoes with 1 tbsp oil in a mixing basin. Salt & pepper to taste.
4. Toss the mushrooms, lettuce, avocado, tomatoes, cilantro, salmon, and jalapeño in a

large mixing bowl. Drizzle the remaining olive oil and vinegar over the top. To serve, sprinkle with salt and black pepper and top with feta cheese.

65 Chickpea salad & Tuna

Ready in 10 min **Servings:** 4 **Difficulty:** Easy

Ingredients
- 1 can of black olives
- salt and black pepper
- ¼ cup Italian parsley
- 1 can Italian tuna in olive oil
- 1 can chickpeas
- ¼ cup cheese,
- ½ red onion
- Lemon juice

Instructions

1. In a mixing bowl, combine the tuna, olives, chickpeas, red onion, lemon juice, parsley, & feta cheese. Salt & pepper to taste.

66 Salad of Heirloom Tomatoes with Rosemary

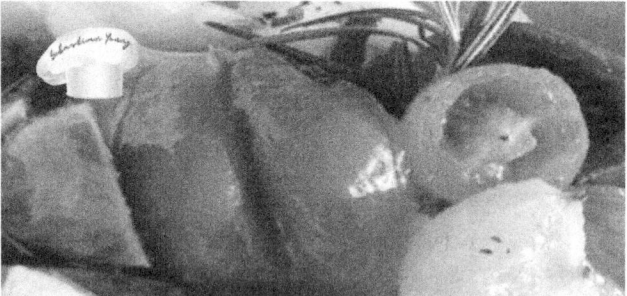

Ready in 20 min **Servings:** 4 **Difficulty:** Easy

Ingredients
- 1 sprig of fresh rosemary
- ⅛ teaspoon oregano
- ¼ cup virgin olive oil
- 2 tbsp rice wine vinegar
- 3 heirloom tomatoes
- 3 heirloom tomatoes
- Salt & black pepper

Instructions

1. In a large mixing bowl, combine the olive oil, rosemary, rice wine vinegar, & oregano. Toss in the tiny and big tomatoes until they are equally covered. Refrigerate for 10 to 15 minutes, covered and cooled. Salt & black pepper to taste. Before serving, toss one more.

67 Salad with strawberries and spinach

Ready in 1 hr 10 min **Servings:** 4 **Difficulty:** Easy

Ingredients
- ½ cup of white sugar
- ½ cup of olive oil
- ¼ cup distilled vinegar
- 2 tbsp sesame seeds
- 1 tbsp poppy seeds
- ¼ teaspoon paprika
- 10 ounces spinach
- 1-quart strawberries
- ¼ teaspoon of Worcestershire sauce
- 1 tbsp minced onion
- ¼ cup almonds

Instructions

1. Combine the sesame seeds, sugar, olive oil, poppy seeds, vinegar, Worcestershire sauce, paprika, and onion in a medium mixing bowl. Refrigerate for one hour, covered.
2. Combine the spinach, strawberries, and almonds in a large mixing basin. Toss the salad with the dressing. Before serving, chill for 10 to 15 minutes.

68 Spanish Mackerel, broiled

Ready in 15 min **Servings:** 6 **Difficulty:** Easy

Ingredients

- ½ teaspoon of paprika
- salt and black pepper
- 12 slices of lemon
- 6 fillets Spanish mackerel fillets
- ¼ cup of olive oil

Instructions

1. Place the oven rack approximately 6 inches from the heat source and preheat the broiler. Lubricate a baking dish lightly.
2. Rub each mackerel fillet on both sides with olive oil and lay the skin side down in the baking dish. Season the paprika, salt, & pepper to taste on each fillet. Two lemon slices should be placed on top of each fillet.
3. Broil the fillets for 5 to 7 minutes, just until the fish just starts to flake. Serve right away.

69 Big Fat Greek Salad

Ready in 1 hr 10 min **Servings:** 4 **Difficulty:** Easy

Ingredients

- 2 cups of cherry tomatoes
- ¼ red onion
- ½ red bell pepper
- 2 large cucumbers
- 1 pinch of salt
- 2 tbsp minced oregano
- salt and black pepper
- 1 pinch cayenne pepper
- ½ cup pitted Kalamata olives
- ½ cup green olives
- 1 package feta cheese
- 1 teaspoon oregano

- ¼ cup of red wine vinegar
- ⅓ cup olive oil

Instructions

1. Using only a channel knife, create a striped pattern by peeling off just a few strips of cucumbers skin. Cucumbers should be cut in half crosswise. Before chopping into 1/4- to 1/2-inch slices, divide each half into quarters. Toss with kosher salt in a colander and set aside for 15 minutes.
2. Meanwhile, halve the cherry tomatoes. Cucumbers should be rinsed and drained completely for another 10 to 15 minutes.
3. While the cucumbers are draining, finely slice the onion. Bell pepper should be cut into strips. Slice strips in diamond-shaped pieces by turning the knife diagonally. Kalamata and green olives, sliced
4. In a mixing dish, combine the cucumbers, bell pepper, onion, olives, tomatoes, & 2 teaspoons oregano. Salt, black pepper & cayenne pepper to taste. Toss in the vinegar and toss again. Drizzle some olive oil on top. Mix in 2/3 of the feta cheese & toss once more. Refrigerate for 60 minutes after wrapping in plastic wrap.
5. Toss the salad one more. Season with salt and pepper to taste. Sprinkle the remaining feta cheese over the top and finish with the oregano.

70 Salad with Chicken, Avocado, & Goat Cheese on Spinach

Ready in 20 min **Servings:** 4 **Difficulty:** Easy

Ingredients

- 1 cup cherry tomatoes
- 1 ½ cups cooked chicken
- ¼ cup nuts
- 8 cups spinach

- ⅓ cup goat cheese
- 1 avocado
- ½ cup of corn kernels

Dressing of Salad
- 3 tbsp white wine vinegar
- 2 tbsp extra-virgin olive oil
- 1 tbsp Dijon mustard
- 1 pinch salt and black pepper

Instructions

1. In a small skillet, heat the oil over medium-high heat. 3 to 5 minutes in a heated pan, toast pine nuts until lightly browned & aromatic.
2. Toss spinach with pine nuts, tomatoes, avocado, corn kernels, chicken, & goat cheese in a large salad dish.
3. In a small bowl, whisk together olive oil, white wine vinegar, & Dijon mustard until smooth; add salt and pepper. Toss the salad gently in the dressing to coat it.

71 Sandwich with Smashed Chickpea Avocado Salad & Cranberries + Lemon

Ready in 5 min **Servings:** 2 **Difficulty:** Easy

Ingredients
- 2 teaspoon lemon juice
- 1/4 cup cranberries
- salt & pepper
- 1 - 15 oz can chickpeas
- 1 ripe avocado

Instructions

1. Using a fork, mash chickpeas in a medium bowl. Add in the avocado and crush it with a fork until it is smooth but still has a few lumpy chunks.

2. Add the cranberries and lemon juice. To taste, season with salt. Keep refrigerated until ready to use (best within 1-2 days).
3. To serve, toast the bread and spread 1/2 of the chickpea avocado salad on one piece. If preferred, garnish with arugula, red onion, or spinach. Top with the second toasted slice, now cut in half & enjoy!

72 Salmon Patties with Butternut Squash

Ready in 40 min **Servings:** 10 Patties
Difficulty: Easy
Ingredients
- 1/2 C. Butternut Squash
- 24 oz Canned Salmon
- 4 Eggs
- ¼ Coconut Flour
- 1/4 Green Onion
- 1 tbsp Coconut Aminos
- 2 teaspoon Dijon Mustard
- 1 teaspoon Garlic Powder
- Salt & Pepper

Instructions

1. Preheat oven to 375 ° F. Using parchment paper or a silicone mat, line a baking sheet.
2. Combine all ingredients in a large mixing basin and stir until well blended.
3. Divide the mixture into ten portions that are about equal in size. Each portion should be rolled into a ball but then pressed into a 1-inch-thick patty on the baking sheet. Rep till all of the concoction has been consumed.
4. Preheat oven to 350°F and bake patties for 25-30 min, or until firm.
5. Optional Step: Brown the patty in a pan with 1 tbsp of coconut oil over medium heat.

73 Sweet Potato Fries

Ready in 30 min **Servings:** 5 **Difficulty:**
Easy

Ingredients

- 3 Sweet Potatoes
- Garlic Powder
- Salt and black pepper
- 2 tbsp Avocado Oil

Instructions

1. Sweet potatoes should be peeled and sliced into 1/4-½ inch thick fries.
2. Optional Step: To eliminate the starch, soak the fries in a dish of ice water for approximately 30 minutes. Rinse the fries and pat them dry.
3. Combine the fries, paprika, garlic powder, black pepper, & oil in a large mixing basin. Toss until the oil and spices are well distributed among the fries. Arrange the fries on the baking pan in an equal layer.
4. Fries should be baked for 15 minutes. Fries should be flipped. Bake for a further 10-15 minutes, or until the edges are gently browned.
5. Add the sea salt after the fries are done. Enjoy.

74 No Mayo Mediterranean Tuna Salad

Ready in 20 min **Servings:** 6 **Difficulty:**
Easy

Ingredients

- 1/2 red onion
- 1 cup of roasted red peppers
- 1/2 cup of pepperoncini
- 2 cans Albacore Tuna
- 1/4 cup feta cheese
- olives
- 1/3 cup parsley
- Sundried tomatoes
- 1 14.5 ounces can chickpeas
- 1/2 avocado
- Pinch of fine sea salt
- Pinch of black pepper
- 1 cucumber
- 2 teaspoons capers
- 1 teaspoon lemon juice
- 1 teaspoon dried parsley
- Red Wine Vinaigrette
- 2 tbsp olive oil
- Pinch of salt
- Pinch of black pepper
- 2 tbsp red wine vinegar
- 1 teaspoon oregano, dried

Instructions

1. Mix all of the salad components in a large mixing basin.
2. Whisk together the dressing ingredients in a small dish.
3. Toss the ingredients in the dressing to mix.
4. Taste and adjust the seasonings as needed!
5. End up serving over a salad, over a sandwich, with spaghetti, lettuce wraps, or half an avocado.

75 Greek Salad Chicken Wrap

Ready in 45 min **Servings:** 4 **Difficulty:**
Easy

Ingredients
For Greek Salad

- 4 cups romaine
- 1/3 cup cherry tomatoes
- 1/4 cup red onion

- 1/2 cup cucumber slices
- 4 tbsp kalamata olives
- 1/2 cup cheese
- 1 tbsp red wine vinegar
- 1 tbsp olive oil
- fresh lemon wedges
- 4 whole wheats
- 1/2 cup of prepared hummus

For chicken
- 2 chicken breasts
- 1 1/2 teaspoons olive oil

Few shakes of the following per chicken breast
- garlic powder
- lemon pepper
- dried oregano

Instructions

1. Preheat the oven to 375 ° F for the chicken. Spray a baking pan with cooking spray and line it with foil. Season 2 bone-in chicken breasts with salt, pepper, dried oregano, and lemon pepper and place on top.
2. Drizzle 1 1/2 tbsp of olive oil over the chicken and bake about 35-40 minutes, or until cooked through. Use right away or save the leftovers for such a wrap. This amount of chicken will make four big wraps.
3. To create the salad, cut the romaine lettuce and set it in a bowl. Cherry tomatoes, olives, red onion, cucumbers, and feta cheese are sprinkled over the top. Add a couple of shakes of dry oregano on top. Drizzle with vinegar & olive oil to finish. Squeeze a juicy lemon over everything (1 large wedge is fine). Stir in the spices and taste to see if they need to be adjusted.
4. To prepare the wrap, put 2 tbsp of hummus on your preferred wrap. Top with chicken pieces and a hearty helping of Greek salad. Wrap, roll and eat.

76 Avocado Sauced Grilled Salmon Taco Wraps

Ready in 20 min **Servings:** 4 **Difficulty:** Easy

Ingredients
- 1/4 cup Avocado Sauce
- 1 head of butter lettuce
- 1 orange
- 2 cups pre-packaged coleslaw mix
- 1 lime juice
- 2 tbsp Seasoning Salt
- 2 fresh salmon filets
- 2 tbsp olive oil

Instructions

1. Make the Everyday Seasoning Salt & Avocado Sauce ahead of time to save time
2. Season salmon with Seasoning Salt liberally. Drizzle just slight olive oil over each fillet to help it stick together.
3. Preheat the grill to normal high heat. Grill the salmon for 5 to 8 minutes on each side, rotating once. Cook until the fillets are easy to flake but still juicy. Remove the steaks from the grill and put them aside to cool.
4. Mix Cole slaw mix with chopped cilantro leaves & 1 lime juice in a small mixing dish. season with salt to taste
5. Rinse the butter lettuce leaves and dry them in a salad spinner or with paper towels. To make lettuce wrap tacos, use the nicest cup-shaped leaves.
6. Cooled salmon fillets should be broken apart. Place salmon slices into lettuce wrap tacos and top with Coleslaw dressing.
7. Add a hearty dab of Avocado Sauce to each lettuce wrap taco.

77 Glowing Spiced Lentil Soup

Ready in 20 min **Servings:** 7 Cups
Difficulty: Easy

Ingredients

- 2 garlic cloves
- 2 teaspoons turmeric
- 1 1/2 teaspoons cumin
- 1/2 teaspoon cinnamon
- 1 1/2 tbsp virgin olive oil
- 2 cups onion
- 1/4 teaspoon cardamom
- 3/4 cup uncooked red lentils
- 3 1/2 cups low-sodium vegetable broth
- 1 can diced tomatoes
- 1 can full-fat coconut milk
- 1/2 teaspoon fine sea salt
- Black pepper
- 1 spinach
- 2 teaspoons lime juice
- Red pepper flakes

Instructions

1. Combine the oil, onion, & garlic in a big saucepan. Add a bit of salt, stir, and cook for 4 to 5 minutes over medium heat until the onion softens.
2. Combine the turmeric, cumin, cinnamon, & cardamom in a large mixing bowl. Cook for another minute or so until aromatic.
3. Add the chopped tomatoes, coconut milk, red lentils, broth, salt, & pepper to taste. Taste and season with red pepper flakes. To blend, stir everything together. Raise the heat to high & bring the mixture to a low boil.
4. Reduce heat to medium-high and continue to cook, uncovered, for 18 to 22 minutes, or until the lentils remain bubbly and soft.
5. Remove the pan from the heat and whisk in the spinach once it has wilted. To taste, add

the lime juice. If desired, season with extra salt and pepper. Garnish with toasted bread & lime wedges, ladled into bowls

78 Bowls of Turkey Taco Meal Prep

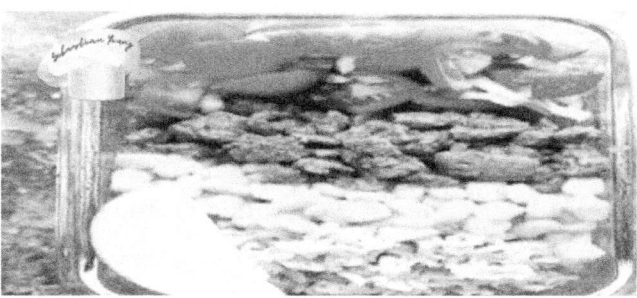

Ready in 1 hr 10 min **Servings:** 4 **Difficulty:** Easy

Ingredients
For Rice

- ⅛ teaspoon of salt
- 1 lime
- ¾ cup brown rice

Turkey

- ¾ lb. lean ground turkey
- 2 tbsp homemade taco seasoning
- ⅔ cup of water

Salsa

- ¼ cup red onion
- ½ lime juice
- 1 pint cherry tomatoes
- 1 chopped jalapeno
- ⅛ teaspoon of salt

Other

- 12 oz can corn kernels
- ½ cup mozzarella

Instructions

1. Brown rice should be cooked according to package guidelines, with lime zest and salt added to the cooking water. Allow cooling gently before dividing into portions.
2. Cook until the turkey is no longer pink in a medium skillet over medium heat, splitting

it up with a spatula (approximately 10 minutes).
3. The taco seasoning should be sprinkled over cooked meat before adding the water. Stir and cook for a few minutes or until the sauce has thickened.
4. Remove from the heat and set aside to cool gently before serving.
5. Toss together all of the salsa ingredients.
6. Divide the ingredients equally among four 2-cup size meal prep containers to make the lunch bowls.

79 Pasta with Golden Sun-Dried Tomatoes and Red Lentils

Ready in 40 min **Servings:** 6 **Difficulty:** Easy

Ingredients
- 6 cloves garlic
- 1 tbsp dried basil
- 1 tbsp dried oregano
- 1/4 cup virgin olive oil
- 1 sweet onion
- 2 teaspoons turmeric
- salt and pepper
- 1 tbsp apple cider vinegar
- 1 box red lentil pasta
- 1 can fire-roasted tomatoes
- 1/2 cup oil-packed sun-dried tomatoes
- 2 large spinach
- grated parmesan, nutritional yeast, seeds for topping

Instructions

1. In a large saucepan over medium heat, heat the olive oil. When the oil begins to shimmer, add the onion & simmer for 5-10 minutes, or until tender and caramelized. Garlic, basil, turmeric, salt, oregano, and pepper are added. Cook for 1 minute or until the mixture is aromatic.
   Slowly pour in the tomatoes and their juices, smashing the tomatoes with the back of a wooden spoon as you go. Toss in the sun-dried tomatoes & balsamic vinegar. Simmer for 10-15 minutes, or until the sauce has somewhat reduced. You may purée the sauce in a blender if desired.
2. Cook for another five minutes after adding the spinach.
3. Now, put a large pot of salted water to such a boil & cook the pasta until al dente, as directed on the box. Drain.
4. Toss the pasta with a liberal quantity of sauce in each bowl. Cheese, nuts, and herbs may be added as desired.

80 Glow getter Roasted Carrots Butternut Squash Soup

Ready in 40 min **Servings:** 4 **Difficulty:** Easy

Ingredients
- ½ cup shallots
- 2 tbsp avocado oil
- 4 cup of vegetable stock
- 1 teaspoon salt
- Black pepper
- 1 can coconut milk
- 1-pound carrots
- 1 butternut squash
- 1 tbsp fresh ginger

For Garnishing
- Roasted chickpeas
- Coconut milk
- Cilantro

Instructions

1. Preheat the oven to 400 ° F.
2. On a parchment-lined baking sheet, place the carrots, butternut squash, and sliced shallots.
3. Splash with avocado oil & season with salt and pepper.
4. Toss lightly to coat.
5. Roast carrots and squash for 30 min, or until fork-tender.
6. Transfer to a blender with vegetable stock, coconut milk, ginger, salt, and pepper after cooling it somewhat. If you have a smaller blender, you may need to do it in two batches.
7. Blend until smooth and creamy, adding more stock or water if necessary to thin.
8. Garnish with roasted chickpeas, fresh cilantro, and a drizzle of coconut milk.

81 Chickpea and Vegetable Coconut Curry

Ready in 30 min **Servings:** 4 **Difficulty:** Easy

Ingredients
- 1 tbsp virgin olive oil
- Steamed rice
- 1 red onion
- 3 garlic cloves
- 2 teaspoons of chili powder
- ¼ cup chopped cilantro
- 1 red bell pepper
- 1 tbsp ginger
- 4 scallions
- 1 small cauliflower
- 1 teaspoon coriander
- 3 tbsp red curry paste
- 14-ounce coconut milk
- 1 lime
- One can chickpeas
- 1½ cups of frozen peas
- Kosher salt & black pepper

Instructions

1. Heat the oil in a pan saucepan over medium heat. Cook, occasionally stirring, until the onion & bell pepper is almost cooked, approximately 5 minutes. Add the garlic and ginger and cook for 1 minute, or until fragrant.
2. Stir in the cauliflower & toss thoroughly. Cook, constantly stirring, until the chili powder, coriander, and red curry paste begins to caramelize, approximately 1 minute.
3. Add the coconut milk & bring the liquid to a low boil over medium heat. Cover the skillet and continue to cook for another 8 to 10 minutes until the cauliflower is soft.
4. Remove the cover and mix thoroughly to incorporate the lime juice and the curry. Return the mixture to a simmer; add salt and pepper, and add the chickpeas and peas.
5. If preferred, serve with rice. 1 tbsp cilantro & 1 tbsp scallions should be garnished on each serving.

82 Egg and Veggie Breakfast Bowl

Ready in 35 min **Servings:** 4 **Difficulty:** Easy

Ingredients
- 1-pound sprouts
- 1-pound potatoes
- 1½ tbsp olive oil
- 2 cups of arugula
- 4 eggs
- 2 tbsp harissa
- 3 tbsp apple cider vinegar

Instructions

1. Preheat oven to 400 ° ° F. Using parchment paper, line a baking sheet.
2. Remove the Brussels sprouts from their stalks and cut them in half.
3. Cut the sweet potatoes into cubes.
4. Place the brussels sprouts & sweet potatoes on a baking pan and spread them out evenly. Season with salt after drizzling the olive oil equally over veggies.
5. Roast for 17 to 20 minutes, until it's golden brown and soft.
6. Combine the harissa, olive oil, and cider vinegar in a small bowl.
7. Cook the eggs in a poaching or frying pan. (Need some assistance? Here's how to poach something, and here's how to fried something.)
8. To serve, split the brussels sprouts & sweet potatoes amongst four dishes and top with 12 cup arugula and 1 egg in each. 2 tbsp of harissa vinaigrette drizzled over each bowl

83 Apple Slaw & Kale Broccoli

Ready in 25 min **Servings:** 6 **Difficulty:** Easy

Ingredients
- 1/2 cup cranberries
- 1-2 granny apples
- 2-3 tbsp goat cheese
- 2 bunches of kale
- 2 cups of shredded broccoli
- 1/2 cup of sunflower seeds
- 1/2 cup of slivered almonds
- 1 avocado peeled

Instructions

1. Mix all of the ingredients in a serving dish.

2. Toss with a vinaigrette made with Orange Muscat Champagne.

84 Champagne Vinaigrette with Orange Muscat

Ready in 25 min **Servings:** 4 **Difficulty:** Easy

Ingredients
- 1 teaspoon Pure Maple Syrup
- 1 teaspoon Dijon Mustard
- Sprinkle of sea salt and pepper
- Lime juice
- 4 teaspoon Olive Oil
- 2 teaspoon Champagne Vinegar

Instructions

1. Mix all components in a glass jar
2. Place the lid on the jar and jiggle vigorously
3. Drizzle dressing over salad

85 Salmon with a Walnut-Rosemary Crusted

Ready in 20 min **Servings:** 4 **Difficulty:** Easy

Ingredients
- 3 tbsp chopped walnuts
- 1 teaspoon extra-virgin olive oil
- 1 skinless salmon fillet
- Olive oil cooking spray
- Chopped parsley & lemon wedges
- 1 teaspoon of lemon juice
- 1 teaspoon of chopped rosemary
- ½ teaspoon of honey
- ½ teaspoon of salt
- ¼ teaspoon red pepper

- 3 tbsp breadcrumbs
- 2 teaspoons of Dijon mustard
- 1 clove garlic
- ¼ teaspoon of lemon zest

Instructions

1. Heat the oven to 425 ° F. Using parchment paper, line a large covered baking sheet.
2. In a small mixing bowl, lemon zest, mix mustard, garlic, lemon juice, rosemary, salt, honey, and crushed red pepper. In a separate small bowl, combine the panko, walnuts, and oil.
3. Place the fish on the baking sheet that has been prepared. Apply the mustard mixture to the fish and then top with panko mixture, pushing it in to adhere. Coat lightly with cooking spray.
4. Bake for 8 to 12 mins, depending on thickness, till its fish flakes easily with only a fork.
5. Garnish with parsley and, if preferred, serve with lemon wedges.

86 Latte with Matcha Green Tea

Ready in 10 min **Servings: 1 Difficulty:** Easy

Ingredients
- 1 cup milk, low-fat
- 1 teaspoon of honey
- ¼ cup of boiling water
- 1 teaspoon powder of matcha tea

Instructions

1. In a blender, combine hot water and matcha powder until frothy. Bring the milk and honey to a near-boiling temperature. Whisk the milk vigorously until it becomes foamy. Fill a cup halfway with milk, then halfway with tea.

87 Spicy Cranberry Relish on Roasted Salmon

Ready in 30 min **Servings: 8 Difficulty:** Easy

Ingredients
- 1 peeled Granny Smith apple
- 1 finely diced stalk celery
- 1 shallot
- 1 seeded serrano pepper
- 1 tbsp of balsamic vinegar
- 1 ½ teaspoon of salt
- ½ teaspoon of cracked black peppercorns
- 1 lemon zest
- 2 cups of frozen cranberries
- 2 tbsp of extra-virgin olive oil
- 2 teaspoons of Dijon mustard
- 2 ½ pounds of skin-on salmon fillet

Instructions

1. Preheat the oven to 400 ° F. Using parchment paper, line a wide baking sheet.
2. Arrange the salmon on the pan that has been prepared. With a fork or a pestle and mortar, mash the garlic, One teaspoon salt, peppercorns, and lemon zest into a pulp. 1 tbsp of oil & mustard should be added to a small bowl. Apply to the salmon. Bake for 15 minutes or until the meat flakes readily with a fork.
3. Meanwhile, in a food processor, finely chop the cranberries, shallot, and serrano.
4. Add the apple, celery, vinegar, 1 tbsp parsley, the remaining 1 tbsp oil, and 1/2 teaspoon salt to a medium mixing bowl.
5. Toss the leftover 1 tbsp of parsley on top of the salmon & garnish with the relish & lemon wedges.

88 Lentil Soup

Ready in 40 min **Servings:** 6 **Difficulty:** Easy

Ingredients

- 1 cup of turnip, chopped
- 3 radishes
- ¼ cup parsley leaves
- 1 tbsp fresh thyme, chopped
- 6 cups vegetable broth
- 2 tbsp extra-virgin olive oil
- 1 cup onion, chopped
- 1 cup of carrots, chopped
- 2 cups of brown lentils
- 5 cups of spinach
- 1 ½ tbsp balsamic vinegar
- ¾ teaspoon of salt

Instructions

1. On a programmed pressure multicooker, choose the Sauté setting. Allow for preheating on the High-temperature setting. Heat 1 tbsp of oil in the cooker until it shimmers. Simmer, sometimes stirring, until the onion is soft, approximately 5 minutes. Add the onion, carrots, turnip, & thyme; cook, occasionally stirring, till the onion is cooked, approximately 5 minutes. Combine the broth, lentils, and salt in a mixing bowl.
2. Press the Cancel button. Cover the pot with the lid and secure it. The pressure release handle should be in the Sealing position. Choose the Manual/Pressure Cook option. Set the timer for 10 minutes on high pressure.
3. Before removing the lid from the cooker, gently switch the steam release lever to Venting and let the steam completely escape (the float valve will drop; this will take approximately 5 minutes). Combine the spinach and vinegar in a mixing bowl.

4. In a small bowl, toss the radishes & parsley with the other 1 tbsp oil. Distribute the soup into 6 dishes and sprinkle with the radish combination.

89 Pecans with Spices

Ready in 1 hr 40 min **Servings:** 20 **Difficulty:** Easy

Ingredients

- ½ teaspoon of salt
- ¼ teaspoon allspice
- ¼ teaspoon cloves
- 1 tbsp water
- 6 tbsp sugar
- Pinch of pepper
- 4 cups of pecan halves
- ¼ teaspoon of nutmeg
- Pinch of cinnamon

Instructions

1. Preheat the oven to 275 ° F. Using parchment paper, prepare a rimmed baking sheet.
2. In a large mixing bowl, whisk together the egg white, sugar, salt, water, allspice, cloves, cinnamon, nutmeg, and cayenne.
3. Stir in the pecans until they are uniformly coated. On the prepared pan, distribute in a single layer.
4. Preheat oven to 350°F and bake for 30 mins. Bake for another 30 minutes, rotating the dish from back to front, till the nuts are crunchy & dry to the touch. Allow 20 minutes for the pan to cool fully. Before serving, separate the pieces.

90 Curry Soup with Roasted Cauliflower and Potatoes

Ready in 1 hr 30 min **Servings:** 8 **Difficulty:** Easy

Ingredients

- 2 teaspoons of lime zest
- 2 tbsp lime juice
- 3 cups peeled russet potatoes
- 3 cups peeled sweet potatoes
- 1 can coconut milk
- 1 ½ teaspoon of grated ginger
- 1 fresh red chili pepper
- Chopped cilantro
- 3 cloves garlic
- 1 can tomato sauce
- ¾ teaspoon pepper
- ⅛ teaspoon cayenne pepper
- 4 cups vegetable broth
- 1 ¼ teaspoons of salt
- 1 small cauliflower
- 2 tbsp virgin olive oil
- 2 teaspoons of ground coriander
- 2 teaspoons of ground cumin
- 1 ½ teaspoon of ground cinnamon
- 1 chopped onion
- 1 cup of carrot
- 1 ½ teaspoon of ground turmeric

Instructions

1. Preheat the oven to 450 ° F.
2. In a small bowl, mix coriander, turmeric, cumin, cinnamon, salt, pepper, and cayenne. In a large mixing basin, combine the cauliflower with 1 tbsp of the oil, then add two tbsp of mixture & toss again. On a baking tray, spread inside a single layer. Then Roast cauliflower for 15 to 20 minutes, or even the edges are browned. Remove from the equation.
3. Meanwhile, in a large saucepan over medium-high heat, heat and cook 1 tbsp oil. Cook, often turning, until the onion and carrot begin to brown, 4 minutes. Reduce heat to low and cook, often turning, for 3 to 4 minutes, until the onions are tender. Combine the garlic, ginger, chili, and the remaining spice combination in a mixing bowl. Cook for another minute, stirring constantly.
4. Boil for 1 minute after adding the tomato sauce and scraping off any browned pieces. Combine the broth, potatoes, lime zest, sweet potatoes, and juice in a large mixing bowl. Bring to a boil, covered, over high heat. Reduce the heat to maintain a moderate simmer and cook, partly covered and stirring periodically, for 35 to 40 minutes, or until the veggies are soft.
5. Combine the coconut milk and roasted cauliflower in a mixing bowl. Return to low heat to finish heating.

91 Smoothie Bowl with Berries and Almonds

Ready in 10 min **Servings:** 1 **Difficulty:** Easy

Ingredients

- ½ cup plain almond milk
- 5 tbsp sliced almonds
- ¼ teaspoon of ground cinnamon
- ⅔ cup raspberries
- ⅛ teaspoon of vanilla extract
- ¼ cup blueberries
- ½ cup banana
- ⅛ teaspoon of ground cardamom
- 1 tbsp coconut flakes

Instructions

1. In a blender, puree the banana, raspberries, almond milk, 3 tbsp almonds, cardamom, cinnamon, and vanilla until smooth.
2. Toss the blueberries, remaining 2 tbsp of almonds, and coconut into a bowl with the smoothie.

92 Chamomile Herbal Health Tonic

Ready in 20 min **Servings:** 4 **Difficulty:** Easy

Ingredients

- 2 teaspoons ginger
- 4 slices of lemon
- 4 cups of boiling water
- 6 bags of chamomile tea
- 2 sprigs of rosemary
- 2-4 teaspoons honey

Instructions

1. In a large heatproof dish, combine honey, boiling water, ginger, tea bags, lemon, and rosemary. Steep for 20 mins, stirring once in a while. Using a fine-mesh strainer, strain the liquid, pushing just on tea bags to extract as much liquid as possible.

93 Salmon with Miso and Maple

Ready in 15 min **Servings:** 8 **Difficulty:** Easy

Ingredients

- ¼ cup of white miso
- 2 lemons
- 2 limes
- 1 skin-on salmon fillet
- Sliced scallions
- ¼ teaspoon of ground pepper
- Pinch of cayenne pepper
- 2 tbsp extra-virgin olive oil
- 2 tbsp maple syrup

Instructions

1. Preheat the broiler to high and place the rack in the top third of the oven. Using foil, line a large covered baking sheet.
2. Juice In a small dish, combines 1 lemon & 1 lime. Miso, maple syrup, pepper, oil, and cayenne pepper are whisked together. Pour the miso mixture on top of the salmon, skin-side down, in the prepared pan. Cut the leftover lemon and lime in halves and place cut-sides up around the fish.
3. Broil the salmon for 12 minutes or until it flakes easily with a fork. Served with lemon and orange halves on top, and scallions on the side, if preferred.

94 Green Smoothie Bowl with Almonds and Matcha

Ready in 10 min **Servings:** 1 **Difficulty:** Easy

Ingredients

- ½ cup sliced banana
- ½ cup almond milk
- 5 tbsp slivered almonds
- ½ cup peaches
- 1 teaspoon maple syrup
- ½ ripe kiwi
- 1 cup spinach
- 1 ½ teaspoon matcha tea powder

Instructions

1. In a blender, puree almond milk, peaches, the banana, 3 tbsp almonds, matcha, spinach, and maple syrup until smooth.
2. Transfer the smoothie to a bowl and top with the leftover 2 tbsp slivered almonds and kiwi.

95 Bagna Cauda with Salmon and Fall Vegetables

Ready in 40 min **Servings:** 4 **Difficulty:** Easy

Ingredients

- 1-pound potatoes, and sweet potato and cut into 1/2-inch-thick wedges
- 1 bunch trimmed broccolini
- 1 tablespoon virgin olive oil
- ½ teaspoon salt
- 1 pound salmon
- 2 medium heads of Belgian endive and leaves separated
- ½ small head of radicchio and cut into 1/2-inch-thick wedges

Bagna Cauda

- ⅓ cup virgin oil
- 2 tbsp vinegar
- 1 tbsp butter
- 2 cloves of garlic
- 8 fillets, anchovy

Instructions

1. Preheat the oven to 425 ° F. Using cooking spray, cover a large rimmed baking tray.
2. In a large mixing bowl, combine the potatoes & broccolini with 1 tbsp oil and 1/4 teaspoon salt. Place the potatoes on the baking sheet that has been prepared. Roast the potatoes for 15 minutes, turning halfway through.
3. Press the potatoes to a baking sheets edge. Season the salmon with the extra 1/4 teaspoon salt and place it in the center of the pan. Arrange the broccolini in a circular pattern around the fish. Roast for 6 to 10 minutes, or until the veggies are tender, as well as salmon, is just done through.
4. In the meanwhile, make the bagna cauda: In a small saucepan, heat the oil and garlic over medium-low heat till the garlic is aromatic, approximately 2 minutes. Lightly smash the anchovies until they break apart. Cook, often stirring, for another 2 mins over very low heat with vinegar and butter.
5. Arrange the salmon, potatoes, and broccolini on a plate with the fennel, endive, and radicchio. If desired, garnish with the saved fennel fronds. For dipping or drizzling, serve with bagna cauda.

96 Green Salad with Beets and Edamame

Ready in 15 min **Servings:** 1 **Difficulty:** Easy

Ingredients

- ½ medium raw beet
- 1 tbsp plus 1 1/2 teaspoons vinegar
- 2 teaspoons olive oil
- Ground pepper to taste
- 2 cups salad greens, mixed
- 1 cup of shelled edamame
- 1 tbsp cilantro, chopped

Instructions

1. On a big dish, arrange the greens, edamame, and beet. In a small bowl, combine the vinegar, cilantro, oil, salt, and pepper. Drizzle the dressing over the salad & serve.

97 Salad of Purple Fruits

Ready in 15 min **Servings:** 8 **Difficulty:** Easy

Ingredients

- 2 cups plums
- 2 cups of seedless black grapes
- 1 cup of Lime Yogurt for Fruit Salad Dressing
- 2 cups of halved blueberries
- 2 tbsp chopped basil, purple

Instructions

1. In a large mixing bowl, mix grapes, blueberries, plums, and basil. If preferred, serve with a yogurt dressing.

98 Cup of Noodles in Miso Soup with Shrimp and Green Tea Soba

Ready in 25 min **Servings:** 3 **Difficulty:** Easy

Ingredients

- 3 cups of hot water
- 3 teaspoons of rice vinegar, unseasoned
- 1 ½ cups of sliced snow peas
- 9 ounces shrimp, peeled and cooked
- 4 tbsp of white miso
- 6 teaspoons of mirin
- 3 tbsp scallions, thinly sliced
- 1 dried kombu
- 1 ½ teaspoons wakame, dried
- 1 1/2 cups green tea soba noodles, dried

Instructions

1. In three 1 1/2-pint canning jars, combine 1 tablespoon & 1 teaspoon miso, 1 teaspoon vinegar, and 2 teaspoon mirin. Each jar should include 3 ounces shrimp, 1/2 cup snow peas, 1/2 teaspoon wakame, and 1/2 cup noodles. 1 tablespoon scallions on top of each. Place piece of kombu between the components & the jar's side. Put it in the fridge for three days if covered.

2. To prepare each jar, follow these steps: To dissolve the miso, add 1 cup of extremely hot water to the container, cover, and shake vigorously. Uncover and microwave for 2 to 3 minutes on High, in 1-minute increments, until boiling. Remove the kombu and throw it away. To ensure the miso is completely dissolved, give it a good stir. Allow resting for a few mins before serving.

99 Avocado Chickpea Salad Sandwich with Lemon and Cranberries

Ready in 10 min **Servings:** 2 **Difficulty:** Easy

Ingredients

- 15 oz drained and rinsed chickpeas
- 2 tsp squeezed lemon fresh juice
- 1 ripe avocado
- 1/4 cup of dried cranberries
- 4 slices of whole grain bread
- Fresh salt & pepper for taste
- Toppings: Red onion, Arugula or spinach

Instructions

1. Mix chickpeas with a fork in a medium pan. Add in the avocado and crush it with a fork until it is smooth but still has some chunky pieces.
2. Combine the cranberries and lemon juice in a mixing bowl. To taste, season with salt & pepper. Keep refrigerated until ready to use.
3. Toast the bread and put 1/2 of the chickpea avocado salad on one piece when ready to serve. If preferred, garnish with arugula, red onion, or spinach. Top with the second toasted slice, then cut in halfway and enjoy.

100 Wild Rice and Buddha Bowl with Avocado, Kale and Orange

Ready in 40 min **Servings:** 2 **Difficulty:** Easy

Ingredients

- 1 cup of wild rice
- 1 minced garlic clove
- 3 cups of water or vegetable broth
- 2 tbsp of rice vinegar
- 1 tbsp of chopped fresh mint
- 2 tbsp extra-virgin olive oil
- Salt & freshly black ground pepper

For dressing

- 1 roughly chopped of bunch kale
- 1 tsp of rice vinegar
- 2 tbsp of olive oil
- 1 orange and cut into segments
- ¼ cup of pomegranate seeds
- ¼ cup of pumpkin seeds
- 2 hard-boiled eggs
- ½ sliced avocado
- Salt & freshly black ground pepper

Instructions

1. Start making the rice, mix the rice, broth (or water, if using), and garlic in a medium saucepan. Over medium-high heat, bring the liquid to a simmer.
2. Reduce heat to low and continue to cook until the rice is cooked and all of the liquid has been evaporated, about 15 - 17 minutes.
3. Allow 5-10 minutes for the rice to cool before tossing it with the vinegar, olive oil, mint, salt & pepper.
4. Toppings: Toss kale with vinegar and olive oil in a medium bowl. Divide the rice into two dishes and top with kale in equal quantities.
5. Add 2 tbsp pomegranate seeds, half of the orange slices, half of avocado slices, 2 tsp pumpkin seeds, and then a hard-boiled egg to each of the bowls. Using salt & pepper, season the egg. Serve right away.

101 Chickpea & Vegetable Coconut Curry

Ready in 30 min **Servings:** 2 **Difficulty:** Easy

Ingredients

- 1 tbsp olive oil extra-virgin
- 1 thinly sliced, red pepper
- 3 minced garlic cloves
- 1 thinly sliced red onion
- 1 tbsp minced fresh ginger
- 2 tbsp chili powder
- 1 cauliflower small, cut into small pieces
- 1 tsp ground coriander
- 3 tbsp paste of red curry
- 1 halved lime
- One 14-ounce coconut milk
- 1½ cups peas
- Salt & freshly black pepper
- Steamed rice (optional) for serving
- ¼ cup fresh cilantro chopped
- 4 thinly sliced scallions

Instructions

1. Heat the olive oil in a big saucepan over medium heat. Cook, occasionally stirring, until the onion & bell pepper is almost tender, approximately 5 minutes. Add the garlic and ginger and cook for 1 minute, or until fragrant.

2. Mix in the cauliflower until everything is nicely combined. Cook, constantly stirring, until the chili powder, coriander, and red curry paste begins to caramelize about 1 minute.

3. Over medium-low heat, add in the coconut milk & bring the mixture to a simmer. Cover the skillet and continue to cook for another 8 to 10 minutes, or when the cauliflower is soft.

4. Remove the cover and mix in the lime juice until everything is properly combined. Return the mixture to a simmer, season with pepper and salt, and add the chickpeas and peas.

5. If preferred, serve with rice. 1 tbsp scallions and 1 tbsp cilantro should be garnished on each serving.

102 White Turkey with Avocado

Ready in 20 min **Servings:** 8 **Difficulty:** Easy

Ingredients

- 2 tbsp olive oil extra-virgin
- 1 diced onion
- 1 pound ground turkey
- 4 minced garlic cloves
- Salt & black pepper
- 1 tsp cayenne pepper
- 2 tsp of ground cumin
- 1 tsp of ground coriander
- 4 cups broth chicken
- One 15-ounce can of corn kernels, white beans
- 1 diced avocado

Instructions

1. Heat the olive oil in a big saucepan over medium heat. Add onion and cook for 6 to 8 minutes, or until transparent. Cook for another minute, or until the garlic is aromatic.
2. Cook for 5 to 7 minutes, or until the turkey is browned and thoroughly cooked. Season with salt & pepper, then add the cumin, coriander, and cayenne, and simmer for 1 to 2 minutes, until fragrant.
3. Add the broth and combine well. Over medium heat, bring the soup to a simmer. Reduce heat to low and cook for 30 to 35 minutes, or until a nice flavor emerges.
4. Boil for 2 to 3 minutes after adding the corn and beans.
5. Ladle the chili into bowls & top with 1-2 tbsp avocado to serve.
6. Serve right away.

Chapter 4: Dinner Recipes

11. Slow Cooker Turkey Chili

Prep Time: 10 min, Serving: 10, Difficulty: Easy

Ingredients

- 1 tbsp olive oil
- 30 ounces canned black beans, rinsed and drained
- Salt and black pepper, to taste
- 1 lb 99% lean ground turkey
- 1 tbsp cumin
- 1 medium onion, diced
- 2 tbsp chili powder
- 1 red pepper, seeded, stemmed, and chopped
- 1 cup frozen corn
- 1 yellow pepper, chopped
- 16-ounce jar tamed jalapeno peppers (deli-sliced), drained
- 30 ounces tomato sauce
- 30 ounces canned red kidney beans, rinsed and drained
- 30 ounces petite diced tomatoes
- Optional toppings: shredded cheese, green onions, sour cream/Greek yogurt, avocado

Instructions

1. Take a pan, heat the oil over medium-low heat. Cook the turkey in the pan until it is brown. Place the turkey in the slow cooker.
2. Add the peppers, onion, diced tomatoes, tomato sauce, jalapenos, beans, chili powder, corn, and cumin. Season to taste with salt & pepper.
3. Cook for 4 hrs (high) or low for 6 hrs, covered. If preferred, serve with additional toppings.

2. Baked Tilapia Recipe with Pecan Rosemary Topping

Prep Time: 15 min, Serving: 4, Difficulty: Easy

Ingredients

- 1/3 cup chopped raw pecans
- 4 4 ounces each tilapia fillets
- 1/3 cup whole-wheat panko breadcrumbs
- 1 egg white
- 2 tsp chopped fresh rosemary
- 1 1/2 tsp olive oil
- 1/2 tsp coconut palm sugar or brown sugar
- 1/8 tsp salt
- 1 pinch cayenne pepper

Instructions

1. Preheat the oven to 350 degrees Fahrenheit.
2. Combine breadcrumbs, pecans, coconut palm sugar, rosemary, cayenne pepper, and salt in a small baking dish. Toss in the olive oil to coat the pecan mixture.
3. Bake for 7 to 8 minutes, or until the pecan mixture is lightly browned.
4. Raise the temperature to 400 degrees F. Using cooking spray, coat a big glass baking dish.
5. Mix the egg white in a small dish. Working with one tilapia at a time, gently cover each side of the fish with the egg white & then the pecan mixture. Put the fillets in the baking dish that has been prepared.
6. The leftover pecan mixture should be pressed into the tops of the tilapia fillets.
7. Bake for approximately 10 minutes. Serve the food.

3. Italian Stuffed Red Peppers

Prep Time: 20 min, Serving: 6, Difficulty: Easy

Ingredients

- 1 lb Lean ground meat
- 1/2 cup shredded mozzarella
- 3 Red bell peppers
- 1/2 cups Parmesan cheese
- 2 cups Marinara
- 1 (10 oz) pkg frozen spinach
- 1 tsp Italian seasoning
- 1 tsp Garlic powder
- 1/2 tsp Salt

Instructions

1. Preheat the oven to 450 degrees Fahrenheit. Coat a baking sheet with nonstick cooking spray and line it with foil.
2. Remove the stem from red peppers by washing them and cutting around them.
3. Remove the seeds & ribs from inside the peppers by cutting them in half lengthwise. Place peppers on a baking sheet.
4. In a large nonstick skillet, brown ground turkey over medium-high heat. While the turkey is cooking, stir it and break it up. Add the sauce & seasonings to a pan when the turkey is nearly done cooking. Cook, occasionally stirring, until the turkey is fully cooked. Spinach should be thawed and squeezed dry. Stir in the frozen spinach and

parmesan until everything is completely incorporated in the skillet with the turkey.
5. Fill each pepper with 1/2 cup of the turkey mixture.
6. Distribute the cheese among the peppers.
7. Bake for 20 to 30 minutes, or until the cheese has melted and become a light golden brown color.
8. Remove from the oven, set aside to cool, then eat!!!

4. One pan lemon herb salmon and zucchini

Prep Time: 15 min, Serving: 4, Difficulty: Easy

Ingredients

- 2 tbsp olive oil
- 4 zucchini, chopped
- Kosher salt and freshly ground black pepper, to taste

For the salmon
- 1/2 tsp dried oregano
- 2 tbsp brown sugar, packed
- 2 tbsp freshly chopped parsley leaves
- 2 tbsp freshly squeezed lemon juice
- 4 (5-ounce) salmon fillets
- 1 tbsp Dijon mustard
- Kosher salt and freshly ground black pepper, to taste
- 2 cloves garlic, minced
- 1/4 tsp dried rosemary
- 1/2 tsp dried dill
- 1/4 tsp dried thyme

Instructions

1. Preheat the oven to 400 degrees F. Coat a baking sheet with light oil.
2. Brown sugar, Dijon, lemon juice, dill, garlic, thyme, oregano, and rosemary in a small

bowl; season with salt and pepper to taste. Remove from the equation.

3. Place the zucchini in a layer on the baking sheet that has been prepared. Season with salt and pepper to taste after drizzling with olive oil. Brush each salmon fillet with the herb mixture and arrange in a single layer.

4. Cook until the salmon flakes with a fork, approximately 16-18 minutes, in the oven.

5. Serve immediately with parsley on top, if preferred.

5. Spicy Sweet Potato Black Bean Burgers with avocado-cilantro crema + sprouts

Prep Time: 55 min, Serving: 6, Difficulty: Medium

Ingredients

- 1/2 cup quinoa
- Sprouts
- 1 can black beans, rinsed and drained
- 6 whole-grain hamburger buns
- 1 large sweet potato
- olive oil or coconut oil for cooking
- 1/2 cup diced red onion
- salt and pepper, to taste
- 2 cloves garlic, minced
- 1/4 cup gluten-free oat flour
- 1/2 cup chopped cilantro
- 2 tsp spicy Cajun seasoning
- 1/2 jalapeno, seeded and diced
- 1 tsp cumin

For Avocado-Cilantro Crema:

- 1/2 large ripe avocado, diced
- salt, to taste
- 1/4 cup low-fat sour cream or plain Greek yogurt

- 2 tbsp chopped cilantro
- 1 tsp lime juice
- dash of hot sauce, if desired

Instructions

1. In a mesh sieve, rinse the quinoa with cold water. Bring a cup of water to a boil in a medium saucepan. Bring the mixture to a boil with the quinoa. Cover, lower the heat to low, cook for 15 minutes, or until the quinoa has soaked all of the liquid. Remove quinoa from heat and fluff with a fork; transfer to a large mixing bowl and put aside to cool for 10 minutes. There should be roughly 1 1/2 cups of quinoa.

2. Poke the sweet potato many times with a fork, then microwave for 3-4 minutes, or until soft and well cooked. If you overcook the sweet potato, it will become hard. Alternatively, you may bake the sweet potatoes in the oven for 30 minutes at 400 degrees F. When the meat is done cooking and cooled, remove the skin.

3. Add cooked sweet potato, beans, cilantro, red onion, cumin, garlic, and Cajun spice to a food processor bowl and pulse until nearly smooth, scraping down the sides of the machine as needed.

4. Combine the mixture with the cooked quinoa in a mixing bowl. Season with salt and pepper to taste, as well as extra Cajun spice if desired.

5. Mix in a little amount of oat bran/oat flour, just enough to form patties.

6. Refrigerate for 30 minutes to assist burgers in sticking together.
Divide into 6 patties (approximately 1/2 cup each) and lay on parchment paper on a baking sheet.

7. Place diced avocado, sour cream, lime juice, and cilantro in a food processor bowl. Blend until completely smooth.

8. Season with salt to taste. Refrigerate till ready to serve the burgers.
9. Preheat the skillet to medium-high. Spray a pan with cooking spray made from coconut, olive, or canola oil. Place in a skillet and cook 3-4 minutes every side, or until lightly browned. Buns, sprouts, crema, and preferred toppings are served on the side.

6. Turkey & Quinoa Stuffed Peppers

Prep Time: 10 min, Serving: 2, Difficulty: Easy

Ingredients

- 3 large yellow peppers
- 1 cup dry quinoa
    - lb extra lean ground turkey
- 1 cup chicken broth
- 1 cup diced mushrooms
- 1 cup (1 8oz can) tomato sauce
- 1/4 cup diced sweet onion
- 1 cup chopped fresh spinach
- 2 tsp minced garlic

Instructions

1. Cook the veggies in a skillet with some butter or olive oil while the quinoa cooks.
2. Add the ground turkey & garlic to the veggies after approximately 5 minutes. Cook on a medium heat setting. Add the tomato sauce & nearly half of the chicken broth after the turkey is almost cooked. Allow to heat until the turkey is thoroughly cooked and part of the liquid has evaporated.
3. Preheat the oven to 400 degrees Fahrenheit.
4. Prepare your bell peppers while the turkey mixture simmers. Remove the stalk and seeds from the peppers after washing them and cutting them in half. Place the sliced bell peppers in a 9x13 baking pan that has been sprayed with cooking spray (open side up).

5. When the quinoa is done, combine it with the turkey and veggies in the pan. Combine all ingredients in a mixing bowl. Then, put the mixture inside each bell pepper. Make sure they're right, nice, and full! If you choose to use cheese, sprinkle just enough over the top to cover the mixture (too much cheese will make the oven dirty!). Pour the remaining chicken broth into the pan's bottom. Yellow peppers filled with turkey and quinoa
6. Cover with foil & bake for 30-35 minutes at 400 degrees F. Serve hot and enjoy!

7. Greek Roasted Fish with Vegetables

Prep Time: 35 min, Serving: 4, Difficulty: Medium

Ingredients

- ½ tsp sea salt
- 2 medium red, yellow or orange sweet peppers, cut into rings
- 1 pound fingerling potatoes, halved lengthwise
- 1 lemon
- 2 tbsp olive oil
- ¼ cup finely snipped fresh oregano or 1 tbsp dried oregano, crushed
- 5 garlic cloves, coarsely chopped
- ¼ cup pitted kalamata olives, halved
- ½ tsp freshly ground black pepper
- 1 ½ cups chopped fresh parsley (1 bunch)
- 4 5 to 6-ounce fresh or frozen skinless salmon fillets
- 2 cups cherry tomatoes

Instructions

1. Preheat the oven to 425 degrees Fahrenheit. In a large mixing bowl, place the potatoes. Toss with 1 tbsp oil, garlic, and 1/8 tsp salt and black pepper; stir to coat. Cover with foil

and transfer to a baking pan. 30 minutes of roasting.

2. In the meanwhile, defrost any frozen fish. Sweet peppers, parsley, tomatoes, oregano, olives, and 1/8 teaspoon salt & black pepper all go into the same dish. Drizzle the leftover 1 tbsp oil over the top and toss to coat.

3. Rinse the salmon and pat it dry. Add the remaining 1/4 teaspoon salt and black pepper to taste. Top potatoes with the sweet pepper mixture and fish. Roast for another 10 minutes, uncovered, or until fish flakes easily.

4. Lemon zest should be removed. Lemon juice should be squeezed over the fish and veggies. Add a dash of zest.

8. Mediterranean Chicken Quinoa Bowl

Prep Time: 15 min, Serving: 4, Difficulty: Easy

Ingredients

- 1 tsp paprika
- ½ tsp ground cumin
- 1 pound boneless, skinless chicken breasts, trimmed
- 1 cup diced cucumber
- ¼ tsp salt
- ¼ cup finely chopped red onion
- 1 7-ounce jar red peppers (roasted), rinsed
- 2 tbsp finely chopped fresh parsley
- ¼ tsp ground pepper
- ¼ cup crumbled feta cheese
- ¼ cup almonds (slivered)
- ¼ cup pitted Kalamata olives, chopped
- 4 tbsp olive oil (extra-virgin), divided
- 2 cups cooked quinoa
- 1 small crushed clove garlic
- ¼ tsp crushed red pepper (Optional)

Instructions

1. Preheat the broiler to high and place a rack in the top third of the oven. Using foil, line a baking sheet.

2. Season the chicken with salt and pepper before placing it on the baking sheet. Broil, rotating once, for 14 to 18 minutes. Using a clean cutting board, slice or shred the chicken.

3. In a tiny food processor, combine peppers, almonds, 2 tablespoons oil, garlic, paprika, cumin, and crushed red pepper (if using). Puree until the mixture is pretty smooth.

4. In a medium mixing bowl, combine the quinoa, olives, red onion, and the remaining 2 tablespoons oil.

5. To serve, split the quinoa mixture into four bowls and top evenly with cucumber, chicken, and red pepper sauce. Garnish with feta cheese and parsley.

9. Kale & Avocado Salad with Blueberries & Edamame

Prep Time: 20 min, Serving: 4, Difficulty: Easy

Ingredients

- ½ cup crumbled goat cheese (2 ounces)
- 6 cups coarsely chopped and stemmed curly kale
- 1 tsp salt
- 1 diced avocado
- 1 tsp Dijon mustard
- 1 ½ tsp honey
- 1 cup yellow cherry tomatoes, halved
- 1 tbsp minced chives
- 1 cup shelled edamame (cooked)
- 3 tbsp lemon juice
- ¼ cup sliced almonds, toasted
- 1 cup blueberries
- ¼ cup olive oil

Instructions

1. In a large mixing bowl, massage the kale leaves with your hands to soften them. Avocado, tomatoes, blueberries, almonds, edamame, and goat cheese are all good additions.
2. In a small dish or jar with a tight-fitting lid, combine the lemon juice, oil, chives, mustard, honey, and salt. Well whisked or shaken
3. Toss the salad with the vinaigrette to mix the flavors.

10. Skillet Lemon Chicken & Potatoes with Kale

Prep Time: 30 min, Serving: 4, Difficulty: Medium

Ingredients

- ½ cup low-sodium chicken broth
- 3 tbsp extra-virgin olive oil, divided
- 6 cups baby kale
- 1 pound boneless, skinless chicken thighs, trimmed
- 1 tbsp chopped fresh tarragon
- ½ tsp salt, divided
- 4 cloves garlic, minced
- ½ tsp ground pepper, divided
- 1 lb Yukon Gold potatoes, cut lengthwise
- 1 big lemon, cut & seeds removed

Instructions

1. Preheat the oven to 400 degrees Fahrenheit.
2. In a large cast-iron pan, heat 1 tablespoon of oil over medium-high heat. Season the chicken with a quarter teaspoon of salt and pepper. Cook for 5 minutes total, flipping once, until brown on both sides. Place on a plate to rest.

3. Toss in the remainder 2 tbsp oil, the potatoes, and 1/4 teaspoon salt and pepper. Cook the potatoes for 3 minutes until golden. Combine the lemon, broth, tarragon, and garlic in a mixing bowl.
4. Toss the chicken back into the pan.
5. Preheat the oven to 350°F. Roast for 15 minutes. Stir in the kale and roast for 3 to 4 minutes, or until it has wilted.

11. Spinach Salad with White Beans, Roasted Sweet Potatoes, and Basil

Prep Time: 20 min, Serving: 2, Difficulty: Medium

Ingredients

- 1 tbsp finely chopped shallot
- 1 sweet potato (12 ounces), peeled and diced (1/2-inch)
- ⅓ cup chopped pecans, toasted
- 5 tbsp extra-virgin olive oil, divided
- 1 cup chopped red bell pepper
- ½ tsp ground pepper, divided
- 2 cups shredded cabbage
- ¼ tsp salt, divided
- 1 can of low-sodium cannellini beans, rinsed
- ½ cup packed fresh basil leaves
- 10 cups baby spinach
- 3 tbsp cider vinegar
- 2 tsp whole-grain mustard

Instructions

1. Preheat the oven to 425 degrees Fahrenheit.
2. In a large mixing dish, combine sweet potatoes, 1 tablespoon oil, 1/4 teaspoon pepper, and 1/8 teaspoon salt. Roast, tossing once, until soft, 15 to 18 minutes on a wide-rimmed baking sheet. Allow at least 10 mins for cooling.

3. In a little food processor, combine basil, the remainder 1/4 cup oil, shallot, vinegar, mustard, and the remainder 1/8 teaspoon salt & 1/4 teaspoon pepper. Process until the mixture is largely smooth. Transfer to a large mixing bowl. Combine the cabbage, spinach, beans, pecans, bell pepper, and cooled sweet potatoes in a large mixing bowl. Toss to coat evenly.

12. Roasted Salmon with Greens & Smoky Chickpeas

Prep Time: 40 min, Serving: 4, Difficulty: Medium

Ingredients

- ¼ cup chopped fresh chives or dill
- ½ tsp divided ground pepper
- 2 tbsp extra-virgin olive oil, divided
- 1 ¼ pounds sliced wild salmon
- 1 tbsp smoked paprika
- ¼ cup water
- ½ tsp salt, divided, plus a pinch
- 10 cups chopped kale
- 1 can no-salt-added chickpeas, rinsed
- ⅓ cup buttermilk
- ¼ cup mayonnaise
- ¼ tsp garlic powder

Instructions

1. Preheat oven to 425 degrees F, with racks in the top third and center.
2. In a medium mixing dish, combine 1 tablespoon oil, paprika, and 1/4 teaspoon salt. Toss the chickpeas with the paprika mixture after fully drying them. Place on a baking sheet to cool. Bake the chickpeas for 30 minutes on the top rack, stirring twice.
3. Meanwhile, in a blender, mix the mayonnaise, buttermilk, 1/4 teaspoon

pepper, herbs, and garlic powder until smooth. Remove from the equation.
4. In a large skillet, heat the remaining 1 tbsp oil over medium heat. Cook, stirring occasionally, for 2 mins after adding the greens. Cook, occasionally stirring, until the kale is soft, approximately 5 minutes longer.
5. Remove the pan from the heat and add a pinch of salt.
6. Take the chickpeas out of the oven and place them on 1 side of the pan. Season the opposite side of the salmon with the remainder 1/4 teaspoon of salt and pepper. Bake for 5 to 8 minutes, or until the fish is just cooked through.
7. Serve the salmon with the greens and chickpeas, drizzling the remaining dressing on top and garnishing with extra herbs if wanted.

13. Jason Mraz's Guacamole

Prep Time: 20 min, Serving: 12, Difficulty: Medium

Ingredients

- ¼ cup lime or lemon juice
- 4 ripe avocados
- Hot sauce, cayenne pepper, finely diced fresh jalapeños or chipotle powder to taste
- ½ cup chopped fresh cilantro
- Ground pepper to taste
- ⅓ cup finely chopped red onion
- 1 tbsp extra-virgin olive oil
- ½ tsp fine sea salt

Instructions

1. In a medium mixing bowl, mash the avocados. Next, stir in the onion, cilantro, lime (or lemon) juice, salt, oil, and pepper.
2. If desired, season with jalapenos, spicy sauce, cayenne, or chipotle.

14. Celeriac & Walnut Tacos

Prep Time: 25 min, Serving: 4, Difficulty: Easy

Ingredients

- ¼ tsp salt plus a pinch, divided
- ⅛ tsp onion powder
- ½ cup walnuts
- 1 ripe avocado, sliced
- 2 tbsp corn oil
- 8 corn tortillas, warmed
- 1 clove garlic, finely chopped
- 1 tbsp lime juice
- 1 tsp chili powder
- ½ cup julienned peeled jicama or radish
- 8 ounces celeriac (celery root), peeled and cut into 1-inch pieces
- ½ cup water
- ¼ tsp crushed red pepper
- ¾ tsp ground cumin
- ⅛ tsp dried oregano
- ½ cup fresh salsa or pico de gallo
- ¼ cup fresh cilantro

Instructions

1. Take a medium pan, over medium heat, toast walnuts for approximately 2 minutes, or until fragrant. Coarsely chop in a food processor. Place in a small mixing basin.
2. In a food processor, pulse celeriac until it is thinly sliced into 1/4-inch pieces.
3. In a medium-sized pan, heat the oil. Cook, stirring periodically, for approximately 5 minutes, or until the celeriac is soft. Cook for 30 seconds, constantly stirring, after adding the walnuts and garlic. Cook for 30 seconds, constantly stirring, with chili powder, crushed red pepper, cumin, onion powder, 1/4 teaspoon salt, and oregano. 1 to 2 minutes after adding water, simmer until it is largely absorbed but still saucy. Remove from the heat and cover with a towel to keep warm.
4. Mix the jicama with the remaining sprinkle of salt and lime juice.
5. Serve the celeriac mixture with jicama, avocado, salsa, and cilantro in tortillas.

15. Vegan Coconut Chickpea Curry

Prep Time: 20 min, Serving: 4, Difficulty: Easy

Ingredients

- 2 cups precooked brown rice, heated according to package
- 1 cup chopped onion
- 4 cups baby spinach
- 1 cup bell pepper, diced
- ½ cup vegetable broth
- 1 medium zucchini, sliced and halved
- 2 tsp avocado oil or canola oil
- 1 ½ cups coconut curry sauce
- 1 can chickpeas, rinsed drained and

Instructions

1. In a large skillet, heat the oil over medium-high heat. Cook, often turning, until the onion, pepper, and zucchini begin to brown, about 5 to 6 minutes.
2. Stir in the chickpeas, sauce, and broth, and bring to a boil. Reduce the heat to and cook for 4 to 6 minutes, or until the veggies are soft. Just before serving, add the spinach. Over rice, if desired.

16. Basil Pesto Pasta with Grilled Vegetables

Prep Time: 45 min, Serving: 4, Difficulty: Medium

Ingredients

- ¼ cup grated Parmesan cheese
- ⅓ cup low-sodium canned cannellini beans, rinsed
- ¼ cup chopped toasted walnuts
- 2 cups zucchini "noodles" (6 oz.)
- 1 clove garlic, minced
- ¼ tsp ground pepper, divided
- 2 medium bell peppers (orange, red, or yellow), quartered
- ¼ cup extra-virgin olive oil
- ½ tsp salt, divided
- 4 ounces whole-wheat penne pasta
- 2 cups fresh basil leaves
- 5 scallions, trimmed
- 3 portobello mushroom caps, stemmed, gills removed
- 1 medium yellow summer squash

Instructions

1. Preheat the grill to medium-high temperature. A big pot of water should be brought to a boil. In a food processor, mix Parmesan, basil, garlic, walnuts, 1/4 teaspoon salt, and 1/8 teaspoon pepper until finely chopped. Pour 1/4 cup oil slowly through the feed tube and process until the mixture is smooth. Place in a medium mixing bowl and put aside.
2. In a large mixing bowl, combine the bell peppers, portobellos, scallions, squash, and the remaining 2 tbsp oil, 1/4 tsp salt, and 1/8 tsp pepper to coat.
3. Grates on the barbecue should be oiled. Grill the veggies for 8 minutes on each side, or until cooked and faintly browned. Remove the steaks from the grill and cut coarsely.
4. Cook the pasta as directed on the packet. During the final 2 minutes of cooking, add zucchini to the pasta. Before draining the pasta, save 1/2 cup of the water. Then, in a large mixing basin, drain the spaghetti and zoodles.
5. 1/4 cup saved pasta water is whisked into the pesto. Next, toss the pasta in the sauce, adding additional saved pasta water if necessary to loosen it up. Finally, toss in the grilled veggies and beans, making sure they're fully coated.

17. Mediterranean Chicken with Orzo Salad

Prep Time: 40 min, Serving: 4, Difficulty: Medium

Ingredients

- 1 tsp lemon zest
- ¼ cup crumbled feta cheese
- 1 clove garlic, grated
- ½ tsp ground pepper, divided
- ¼ cup chopped red onion
- 2 tsp chopped fresh oregano
- ¾ cup orzo (whole-wheat)
- 2 tbsp lemon juice
- 2 tbsp chopped Kalamata olives
- 3 tbsp extra-virgin olive oil, divided
- ½ tsp salt, divided
- 2 cups baby spinach (thinly sliced)
- 1 cup cucumber (chopped)

- 2 skinless, boneless chicken breasts (8 ounces each), halved
- 1 cup tomato (chopped)

Instructions

1. Preheat the oven to 425 degrees Fahrenheit.
2. 1 tbsp oil, lemon zest, and 1/4 tsp salt and pepper on the chicken. In a baking dish combine all of the ingredients. Bake for 25 to 30 minutes, or until an instant-read thermometer inserted in the thickest section registers 165 degrees F.
3. Meanwhile, in a medium bowl over high heat, bring a quart of water to a boil. Cook for 8 mins after adding the orzo. Cook for a further minute after adding the spinach. Rinse with cold water after draining. Drain completely and place in a large mixing bowl. Cucumber, tomato, onion, feta, and olives are all good additions. To blend, stir everything together.
4. In a small dish, combine the remaining 2 tablespoons of oil, oregano, garlic, lemon juice, and the remaining 1/4 teaspoon salt and pepper. All except 1 tbsp of the dressing should be mixed into the orzo mixture. Serve with the salad and the leftover dressing drizzled over the chicken.

18. Quinoa Power Salad

Prep Time: 20 min, Serving: 2, Difficulty: Easy

Ingredients

- 1 medium sweet potato, peeled and cut into 1/2-inch-thick wedges
- ½ red onion, cut into 1/4-inch-thick wedges
- 1 tbsp cider vinegar
- 1 tbsp pure maple syrup
- 4 cups baby greens, such as kale spinach or arugula, dried and washed
- ½ tsp garlic powder

- ½ cup red quinoa (cooked), cooled
- 8 ounces chicken tenders
- 1 tbsp sunflower seeds (unsalted), toasted
- ¼ tsp salt, divided
- 2 tbsp extra-virgin olive oil, divided
- 1 tbsp shallot (finely chopped)
- 2 tbsp whole-grain mustard, divided

Instructions

1. Preheat the oven to 425 degrees Fahrenheit. In a larger bowl, toss sweet potato & onion with 1 tablespoon oil, garlic powder, and 1/8 teaspoon salt. Roast for 15 minutes when spread out on a big rimmed baking sheet.
2. Meanwhile, combine the chicken and 1 tablespoon mustard in a mixing basin and toss to combine. Remove the veggies from the oven after 15 minutes of roasting and toss. In the same pan, add the chicken. Return to the oven and roast for another 10 minutes or until the veggies start to brown & the chicken is cooked through. Allow cooling after removing from the oven.
3. In a large mixing bowl, whisk together shallot, maple syrup, vinegar, 1 tbsp oil, 1 tbsp mustard, and 1/8 tsp salt.
4. After the chicken has cooled, slice it and combine it with the dressing in a mixing bowl. Next, combine the baby greens, quinoa, and roasted veggies in a bowl. Finally, mix with the dressing and a few sunflower seeds on top.

19. Quinoa, Chicken & Broccoli Salad with Roasted Lemon Dressing

Prep Time: 35 min, Serving: 4, Difficulty: Medium

Ingredients

- ¾ cup chopped walnuts, toasted
- 1 cup low-sodium chicken broth
- 2 cups arugula
- ½ cup quinoa
- 1 tbsp Dijon mustard
- 2 small lemons, thinly sliced and seeded
- 8 ounces broccoli with stems (about 1 medium head)
- 1 (8 ounces) boneless, skinless chicken breast, trimmed
- ½ cup chopped fresh mint
- 4 tbsp extra-virgin olive oil, divided
- ½ cup dried cranberries
- ⅛ tsp salt plus 1/4 tsp, divided
- ¼ cup red-wine vinegar

Instructions

1. Preheat the oven to 425 degrees Fahrenheit.
2. On the side of a rimmed baking sheet, place the chicken. Drizzle 1 tbsp oil over the top and season with 1/8 tsp salt. 10 minutes of roasting. Put lemon slices on the baking sheet's opposite side. Roast for 7 to 9 minutes longer, rotating once until a thermometer is put into the thickest part of the chicken registers 160°F, and the lemons are browned.
3. Meanwhile, in a small saucepan, bring broth & quinoa to a boil. Reduce the heat to maintain a low simmer, cover, and cook for approximately 15 minutes, or until the liquid has been absorbed. Remove from heat and set aside for 10 minutes, covered.
4. Remove the florets from the stalks of broccoli. The stems should be trimmed, peeled, and thinly sliced, and the florets should be chopped into bite-size pieces.
5. Half of the lemon segments should be chopped. Combine the remainder 3 tbsp oil, 1/4 tsp salt, and vinegar in a large mixing bowl.
6. Chicken should be shredded. Toss together the chicken, remaining lemon slices, broccoli, quinoa, arugula, walnuts, cranberries, and mint with the dressing.

20. Spicy Shrimp Tacos

Prep Time: 20 min, Serving: 4, Difficulty: Easy

Ingredients
- ⅛ tsp salt
- 2 tbsp chopped fresh cilantro
- 4 tbsp extra-virgin olive oil, divided
- ½ cup pico de gallo
- 1 pound peeled, deveined large shrimp
- 1 avocado, sliced
- 1 tbsp Shrimp seasoning
- 8 (6 inches) corn tortillas, warmed
- 1 ½ cups thinly sliced red cabbage
- 2 tbsp lime juice

Instructions
1. In a large skillet, heat 2 tablespoons of oil over high heat. Season shrimp equally with salt and shrimp seasoning. Cook, occasionally stirring, until the shrimp are opaque, for 3 to 4 minutes. Place on a plate to cool.
2. In a medium mixing bowl, combine the cabbage, cilantro, lime juice, and the remaining 2 tablespoons of oil.
3. Warm the tortillas and split the shrimp among them. Serve with the avocado, cabbage mixture, and pico de gallo on the side.

21. Walnut-Rosemary Crusted Salmon

Prep Time: 10 min, Serving: 4, Difficulty: Easy

Ingredients

- ½ tsp honey
- ½ tsp kosher salt
- ¼ tsp crushed red pepper
- 2 tsp Dijon mustard
- Chopped fresh parsley and lemon wedges for garnish
- 1 clove garlic, minced
- Olive oil cooking spray
- ¼ tsp lemon zest
- 1 (1 pound) skinless salmon fillet, fresh or frozen
- 1 tsp lemon juice
- 1 tsp extra-virgin olive oil
- 1 tsp chopped fresh rosemary
- 3 tbsp finely chopped walnuts
- 3 tbsp panko breadcrumbs

Instructions

1. Preheat the oven to 425 degrees Fahrenheit. Using parchment paper, line a big rimmed baking sheet.
2. In a small bowl, combine garlic, mustard, lemon juice, lemon zest, honey, salt, rosemary, and crushed red pepper. In a separate small bowl, combine the panko, walnuts, and oil.
3. Place the salmon on the baking sheet that has been prepared. Apply the mustard mixture to the fish and then top with the panko mixture, pushing it in to adhere. Coat lightly with cooking spray.
4. Bake for 8 to 12 minutes, depending on thickness until the salmon flakes easily with a fork.
5. If preferred, garnish with parsley & serve with lemon wedges.

22. Panzanella with Tomatoes & Grilled Corn

Prep Time: 30 min, Serving: 6, Difficulty: Medium

Ingredients

- 1 cup red onion, thinly sliced
- ¼ tsp ground pepper
- ½ tsp kosher salt
- 2 tbsp lemon juice
- 2 cloves garlic, minced
- 3 tbsp red-wine vinegar
- 3 ears corn, remove the husks
- 1 cup torn fresh basil leaves
- 8 ounces sourdough bread (crusty)
- 8 tbsp extra-virgin olive oil, divided
- 1 pound tomatoes, cut into 1-inch pieces

Instructions

1. Preheat a gas grill to medium heat, create a charcoal grill fire, or start a campfire & let it burn down to 400 degrees F.
2. In a large mixing bowl, combine the onion, vinegar, and lemon juice. Set aside, stirring every now and again.
3. Meanwhile, cook corn for 8 to 10 minutes, occasionally turning, until soft and slightly browned. Allow cooling slightly before removing the kernels from the cobs and placing them in the bowl with the onion.
4. 2 tbsp oil, brushed or drizzled over both sides of the bread Grill the bread until both sides are nicely toasted, 2 to 3 minutes each side, rotating once halfway through.
5. Add the toasted bread to the bowl by tearing or cutting it into 1-inch chunks. Stir in the remaining 6 tablespoons of oil, basil, tomatoes, salt, garlic, and pepper. Serve right away.

23. Chicken, Quinoa & Sweet Potato Casserole

Prep Time: 15 min, Serving: 8, Difficulty: Easy

Ingredients

- ¼ cup fresh cilantro
- 3 tbsp water
- ½ cup crumbled queso fresco
- 4 cups peeled sweet potatoes, cubed
- ⅛ tsp cayenne pepper
- 1 ½ pound skinless, boneless chicken thighs
- ½ tsp ground cinnamon
- 2 cups chopped seeded poblano chilies
- 1 tbsp canola oil
- 1 tsp ground cumin
- ½ cup thinly sliced shallots
- 1 tsp kosher salt
- 2 tbsp minced garlic
- ⅓ cup dry white wine
- 2 cups unsalted chicken broth
- 1 ½ cups multi-colored quinoa

Instructions

1. Preheat the oven to 400 degrees Fahrenheit.
2. In a microwave-safe bowl, combine sweet potatoes and water. Cover with plastic wrap and a fork puncture a few holes in the top. 4 minutes on high in the microwave
3. Meanwhile, in a large pan over medium-high heat, heat the oil. Cook until the chicken is browned on both sides, about 4 to 5 minutes on each side. Allow the chicken to rest for 5 minutes on a clean chopping board.
4. Then, using a 1-inch strip cutter, cut the cake into 1-inch strips.
5. Cook, turning periodically until the shallots become lightly browned, approximately 2 minutes, with the shallots, poblanos, and garlic in the pan over medium-high heat.

Combine the quinoa, broth, salt wine, cinnamon, cumin, and cayenne pepper in a large mixing bowl. Bring the water to a boil. Take the pan off the heat and add the sweet potatoes & chicken.

6. Fill a broiler-proof baking dish halfway with the mixture. Wrap foil around the dish. Preheat oven to 350°F and bake for 20 minutes.
7. Remove from the oven and turn the heat up to broil. Remove the lid from the dish and top with cheese. 5 minutes at 8" from the heat source, broil until golden brown. Garnish with chopped cilantro. Allow 5 minutes to cool before serving.

24. Citrus Vinaigrette

Prep Time: 10 min, Serving: 8, Difficulty: Easy

Ingredients

- ¼ cup organic canola oil or avocado oil
- ½ tsp ground pepper
- ¼ cup extra-virgin olive oil
- ½ tsp salt
- ½ small shallot, quartered
- 2 tsp Dijon mustard
- ¼ cup orange juice, preferably freshly squeezed
- 1 tsp orange zest
- 2 tbsp lemon juice

Instructions

1. In a blender or small food processor, combine orange zest, shallot, lemon juice, orange juice, salt, mustard, and pepper. (Alternatively, mix all of the ingredients in a jar and mix with an immersion blender.)
2. Blend in the olive and canola (or avocado) oils until smooth.

25. Chicken Massaman Curry with Turmeric Brown Rice

Prep Time: 40 min, Serving: 4, Difficulty: Medium

Ingredients

- ¼ tsp salt
- 2 tbsp canola oil, divided
- 3 tbsp chopped fresh cilantro or parsley
- 3 cloves garlic, finely chopped
- 1 tbsp lime juice
- 2 tbsp finely chopped fresh ginger, divided
- 4 cups broccoli florets
- 1 ¾ cups brown basmati rice
- 1 tbsp brown sugar
- 1 ½ tsp ground turmeric
- 2 tbsp Thai red curry paste
- 2 ¼ cups rice milk(unsweetened), divided
- 1 medium bell pepper, diced
- 1 pound skinless, boneless chicken thighs, cut and trimmed into bite-size pieces
- 1 ¼ cups water

Instructions

1. In a medium saucepan, heat 1 tablespoon of oil over medium heat. Cook, stirring periodically, for 1 minute, or until garlic & 1 tbsp ginger are fragrant. Cook, stirring periodically, for 2 minutes after adding the rice and turmeric. Bring 1 cup rice milk, 1 cup water, and 1 teaspoon salt to a boil at high heat.

2. Reduce to low heat, cover, cook for 35 minutes, or until the rice is cooked and the liquid has been absorbed.

3. Take a large skillet, heat 1 tbsp oil over medium heat. Cook, occasionally tossing until the chicken is browned, about 5 to 7 minutes. Cook, constantly stirring, for 1 minute after adding the bell pepper, curry paste, and the remainder 1 tbsp ginger. Return to a slow boil over high heat with the remaining 1 1/4 cup rice milk & brown sugar. Reduce heat to a low simmer, cover, and cook for 3 to 5 minutes, or until broccoli is tender. Add the lime juice and mix well. Serve the curry over rice and garnish with cilantro.

26. Mediterranean Cod with Roasted Tomatoes

Prep Time: 15 min, Serving: 4, Difficulty: Easy

Ingredients

- 4 (4 ounces) fresh or frozen skinless cod fillets, 3/4- to 1-inch thick
- 2 tsp snipped fresh oregano
- 2 tsp capers
- 1 tsp snipped fresh thyme
- 2 tbsp sliced pitted ripe olives
- ½ tsp salt
- 1 tbsp olive oil
- ¼ tsp garlic powder
- 2 cloves garlic, sliced
- ¼ tsp paprika
- 3 cups cherry tomatoes
- ¼ tsp black pepper
- Fresh oregano or thyme leaves
- Nonstick cooking spray

Instructions

1. Preheat the oven to 450 degrees Fahrenheit.
2. If the fish is frozen, thaw it first. Then, clean the fish by rinsing it and patting it dry with paper towels. Combine snipped thyme, snipped oregano, garlic powder, salt, black pepper, and paprika in a small bowl. Half of the oregano mixture should be sprinkled on both sides of every fish fillet.

3. Foil-line a 15x10x1-inch baking tray. Spray the foil with nonstick cooking spray. Place the fish on one of the foil-lined pan's sides. To the opposite side of the foil-lined pan, add the tomatoes and garlic pieces. Combine the rest of the oregano mixture with the oil. Toss the tomatoes in the oil mixture to coat them. Bake for 8 to 12 minutes, stirring once, or until fish flakes easily when checked with a fork. In a large mixing bowl, combine the olives and capers with the cooked tomato mixture.

4. Using four serving dishes, equally distribute the fish & roasted tomato combination. Fresh oregano or thyme leaves may be used as a garnish.

27. Slow-Cooker Mediterranean Stew

Prep Time: 15 min, Serving: 6, Difficulty: Easy

Ingredients

- 2 (14 ounces) cans of no-salt-added fire-roasted diced tomatoes
- 6 lemon wedges (optional)
- 3 cups low-sodium vegetable broth
- Fresh basil leaves, torn if large
- 1 cup coarsely chopped onion
- 3 tbsp extra-virgin olive oil
- ¾ cup chopped carrot
- 1 tbsp lemon juice
- 4 cloves garlic, minced
- 1 bunch lacinato kale, stemmed and chopped (about 8 cups)
- 1 tsp dried oregano
- 1 (15 ounces) can no-salt-added chickpeas, rinsed, divided
- ¾ tsp salt
- ½ tsp crushed red pepper
- ¼ tsp ground pepper

Instructions

1. In a 4-quart slow cooker, combine broth, tomatoes, carrot, onion, oregano, garlic, crushed red pepper, salt, and pepper. Cook on low heat for 6 hours, covered.

2. In a small dish, pour 1/4 cup of the slow cooker's cooking liquid. 2 tbsp chickpeas, mashed until smooth with a fork

3. In the slow cooker, combine the lemon juice, greens, mashed chickpeas, and the remaining whole chickpeas. To blend, stir everything together. Cover and cook on low for 30 minutes, or until the kale is cooked.

4. Pour the stew into 6 dishes and sprinkle with oil. Serve with basil as a garnish. If desired, garnish with lemon slices.

28. Greek Stuffed Portobello Mushrooms

Prep Time: 15 min, Serving: 4, Difficulty: Easy

Ingredients

- 4 portobello mushrooms (about 14 ounces), wiped clean, stems and gills removed
- 3 tbsp extra-virgin olive oil, divided
- 1 tbsp chopped fresh oregano
- 1 clove garlic, minced
- 2 tbsp pitted and sliced Kalamata olives
- ½ tsp ground pepper, divided
- ⅓ cup crumbled feta cheese
- ¼ tsp salt

- 1 cup chopped spinach
- ½ cup quartered cherry tomatoes

Instructions

1. Preheat the oven to 400 degrees Fahrenheit.
2. In a small bowl, combine 2 tablespoons oil, garlic, 1/4 teaspoon pepper, and salt. Apply the oil mixture all over the mushrooms using a silicone brush. Place on a big rimmed baking sheet & bake for 8 to 10 minutes, or until the mushrooms are largely tender.
3. Add oregano, tomatoes, spinach, olives, feta, & the rest of the 1 tbsp oil in a medium mixing bowl. Remove the mushrooms from the oven after they have softened and fill with the mixture of spinach. Bake for approximately 10 minutes, or until the tomatoes have wilted.

29. Mediterranean Ravioli with Artichokes & Olives

Prep Time: 15 min, Serving: 4, Difficulty: Easy

Ingredients

- 2 (8 ounce) packages frozen or refrigerated spinach-and-ricotta ravioli
- ¼ cup chopped fresh basil
- ½ cup oil-packed sun-dried tomatoes, drained (2 tbsp oil reserved)
- 3 tbsp toasted pine nuts
- 1 package quartered artichoke hearts (frozen), thawed
- 1 can cannellini beans (no-salt-added), rinsed
- ¼ cup sliced Kalamata olives

Instructions

1. A big pot of water should be brought to a boil. Cook ravioli as directed on the box. Set aside after draining and tossing with 1 tbsp reserved oil.
2. Take a large nonstick skillet, heat 1 tbsp oil over medium heat. Sauté for 2 to 3 minutes, or until artichokes and beans are cooked through.
3. Combine the sun-dried tomatoes, ravioli, pine nuts, olives, and basil in a mixing bowl.

30. Provençal Baked Fish with Roasted Potatoes & Mushrooms

Prep Time: 15 min, Serving: 4, Difficulty: Easy

Ingredients

- 1 pound Yukon Gold or red potatoes, cubed
- Fresh thyme for garnish
- 1 pound mushrooms, trimmed and sliced
- 1 tsp herbes de Provence
- 2 tbsp extra-virgin olive oil, divided
- 4 tbsp lemon juice
- ¼ tsp salt
- ¼ tsp ground pepper
- 2 cloves garlic, peeled and sliced
- 14 ounces halibut, grouper or cod fillet, cut into 4 portions

Instructions

1. Preheat the oven to 425 degrees Fahrenheit.
2. In a large mixing bowl, combine mushrooms, potatoes, 1 tablespoon oil, salt, & pepper. Fill a 9x13-inch baking dish with the mixture. Roast for 30 to 40 minutes or until the veggies are barely tender.
3. Stir in the veggies, followed by the garlic. Arrange the fish on top.

4. Drizzle with the remainder 1 tbsp. oil and lemon juice. Herbes de Provence should be sprinkled on top. Bake for 10 to 15 minutes, or until the salmon is opaque in the middle and flakes readily. If desired, garnish with thyme.

31. Sheet-Pan Mediterranean Chicken, Brussels Sprouts & Gnocchi

Prep Time: 20 min, Serving: 4, Difficulty: Easy

Ingredients

- 1 tbsp red wine vinegar
- 2 tbsp chopped fresh oregano, divided
- 1 cup halved cherry tomatoes
- 2 large cloves garlic, minced, divided
- 4 boneless, skinless chicken thighs, trimmed
- ½ tsp ground pepper, divided
- 1 cup sliced red onion
- ¼ tsp salt, divided
- 1 pound Brussels sprouts, trimmed and quartered
- 4 tbsp extra-virgin olive oil, divided
- 1 (16 ounces) package shelf-stable gnocchi

Instructions

1. Preheat the oven to 450 degrees Fahrenheit.
2. In a large mixing bowl, combine 2 tablespoons of oil, 1 tablespoon oregano, half of the garlic, 1/4 teaspoon pepper, and 1/8 teaspoon salt. Toss in the Brussels sprouts, gnocchi, and onion to coat. Place on a broad-rimmed baking sheet and spread out evenly.
3. In a large mixing bowl, combine 1 tablespoon oil, the remaining 1 tablespoon oregano, the remaining garlic, and the remaining 1/4 teaspoon pepper and 1/8

teaspoon salt. Toss in the chicken to coat. Place the chicken in the vegetable mixture and tuck it in. 10 minutes of roasting

4. Remove the pan from the oven & toss in the tomatoes. Continue roasting for another 10 minutes. In a mixing bowl, combine the vegetable combination, vinegar, and the remainder 1 tbsp oil.

32. Vegan Pesto Spaghetti Squash with Mushrooms & Sun-Dried Tomatoes

Prep Time: 30 min, Serving: 4, Difficulty: Easy

Ingredients

- 1 3-pound spaghetti squash,
- ½ tsp ground pepper
- 4 tbsp divided extra-virgin olive oil
- 2 tsp nutritional yeast
- 8 ounces cremini mushrooms, sliced
- 3 tbsp lemon juice
- ½ cup julienned sun-dried tomatoes
- ⅓ cup unsalted raw cashews
- ½ tsp salt, divided
- 1 cup packed fresh basil leaves
- 2 cloves garlic, coarsely chopped

Instructions

1. Cut-side down, place squash halves in a dish with 2 tbsp water. Microwave on High for 10 to 14 minutes, uncovered, until soft.
2. Preheat the oven to 400 degrees F and bake for 40 to 50 minutes, or until the potatoes are soft.
3. Meanwhile, in a large pan, heat 1 tbsp oil over medium heat. Add the mushrooms, tomatoes, and 1/4 teaspoon salt; simmer.

Occasionally turning, for 5 to 6 minutes, or until the mushrooms are tender and beginning to brown. Remove the pan from the heat.

4. In a food processor, combine basil, the remaining 3 tablespoons oil, garlic, cashews, lemon juice, nutritional yeast, and the remaining 1/4 teaspoon salt and pepper. Process until the mixture is largely smooth.

5. Remove the squash covering from the shells into a colander with a fork. To remove some of the liquid, softly press on the skin. Squash should be divided among four plates. Place a dollop of basil pesto on top of each dish of the mushroom mixture.

33. Simple Grilled Salmon & Vegetables

Prep Time: 25 min, Serving: 4, Difficulty: Easy

Ingredients

- ½ tsp ground pepper
- 1 zucchini, sliced lengthwise
- 1 lemon, cut into 4 wedges
- 2 orange, yellow or red bell peppers, halved, trimmed & seeded
- ¼ cup thinly sliced fresh basil
- 1 red onion, sliced into 1" wedges
- 1 tbsp olive oil (extra-virgin)
- ½ tsp salt, divided
- 1 ¼ pounds salmon fillet, cut into 4 portions

Instructions

1. Preheat the grill to medium-high temperature.
2. Oil the zucchini, peppers, and onion, and season with 1/4 teaspoon salt. Season the salmon with the remaining 1/4 teaspoon salt and pepper.

3. Place the veggies and salmon slices on the grill, skin-side down. Cook the veggies for 4 to 6 minutes on each side, flipping once or twice, till just tender & grill marks appear. Cook the salmon for 8 to 10 minutes, without turning it, until it flakes if checked with a fork.

4. When the veggies are cool enough, roughly chop them and combine them in a large mixing basin. If preferred, remove the skin of the salmon fillets and serve with the veggies. Serve with 1 tablespoon basil and a lemon wedge on top of each plate.

34. Goat Cheese Pizza

Prep Time: 25 min, Serving: 2, Difficulty: Easy

Ingredients

- 2 ounces cooked turkey or chicken breast, shredded
- 1 (7 inch) whole-wheat pizza crust
- 2 tbsp snipped fresh basil
- 1 tsp olive oil
- ¼ cup crumbled goat cheese (1 ounce)
- 1 cup fresh baby spinach
- 1 roma tomato, sliced
- ¼ cup red onion, thinly sliced

Instructions

1. Using a brush, coat the pizza dough with oil. Spinach, red onion, turkey, tomato, and goat cheese go on top. Bake according to the instructions on the crust package.
2. Sprinkle with basil before serving.

35. Slow-Cooker Mediterranean Chicken & Chickpea Soup

Prep Time: 20 min, Serving: 6, Difficulty: Easy

Ingredients

- ¼ cup chopped fresh parsley or cilantro
- 4 cups water
- ½ tsp salt
- 1 large yellow onion, finely chopped
- ¼ cup halved pitted oil-cured olives
- 1 can no-salt-added diced tomatoes, preferably fire-roasted
- 1 can artichoke hearts, quartered and drained
- 2 tbsp tomato paste
- 2 lb bone-in chicken thighs, trimmed, skin removed
- 4 cloves garlic, finely chopped
- ¼ tsp ground pepper
- 1 bay leaf
- ¼ tsp cayenne pepper
- 4 tsp ground cumin
- 1½ cups dried chickpeas, soaked overnight
- 4 tsp paprika

Instructions

1. Place chickpeas in a 6-quart slow cooker, drained. Stir together 4 cups water, onion, tomatoes and juice, tomato paste, garlic, bay leaf, cumin, paprika, cayenne, and ground pepper. Toss in the chicken.
2. Cook on low for about 8 hrs or high for about 4 hrs, covered.
3. Allow the chicken to cool slightly on a clean chopping board. Bay leaf should be discarded. Stir together the artichokes, olives, and salt in the slow cooker. Remove the bones from the chicken and shred them.

Add the chicken to the broth and mix well. Serve with parsley on top (or cilantro).

36. Romesco Sauce with Whole-Grain Pasta & Parmesan

Prep Time: 20 min, Serving: 8, Difficulty: Easy

Ingredients

- 2 large red bell peppers
- ¼ cup grated Parmesan cheese
- ½ of a (28 ounce) can no-salt-added whole peeled plum tomatoes (1 1/3 cups)
- 12 ounces dried whole-grain pasta
- ½ cup whole almonds, toasted
- ½ tsp smoked paprika
- 3 tbsp olive oil
- ½ tsp kosher salt
- 2 tbsp chopped fresh Italian parsley plus more for garnish
- 2 cloves garlic
- 1 tbsp sherry vinegar
- 1 tbsp honey

Instructions

1. Preheat the oven to 400 degrees Fahrenheit. A baking sheet should be lightly oiled. Remove the stems, seeds, and membranes from bell peppers by cutting them in half lengthwise. Put the pepper halves, sliced sides up, on the baking sheet that has been prepared. Roast for 45 minutes until peppers are tender and the skins easily peel away. Wrap the peppers in plastic wrap and place them in a bowl. Allow for 30 minutes of cooling time or until cold enough to handle. The skins should be peeled off and discarded.

2. In a blender or food processor, mix the tomatoes, roasted peppers, oil, almonds, 2 tablespoons parsley, honey, sherry vinegar, salt, garlic, and smoked paprika. Blend or process until almost smooth, covered.

3. In a medium pot, pour the sauce. Bring to a boil, then turn off the heat. Cook for 20 minutes.

4. Meanwhile, cook the pasta as directed on the box; drain. Pour the sauce over the spaghetti and top with Parmesan cheese. Garnish with more parsley, if preferred.

37. Farfalle with Tuna, Lemon, and Fennel

Prep Time: 15 min, Serving: 4, Difficulty: Easy

Ingredients

- 6 ounces whole-grain farfalle pasta, dried
- 1 can solid white tuna
- 1 cup thinly sliced fennel
- 1 Olive oil
- ½ tsp crushed red pepper
- ¼ tsp salt
- 2 cloves garlic, minced
- 2 (14.5 ounce) cans diced tomatoes (no-salt-added), undrained
- 2 tbsp snipped Italian (flat-leaf) parsley (fresh)
- 1 tsp lemon peel, finely shredded

Instructions

1. Drain pasta and cook according to package instructions, avoiding salt. Return the spaghetti to the pan and cover to keep it heated. Meanwhile, drain the tuna and set aside the oil. If required, add another tbsp of olive oil to make a total of 3 tbsp. set aside the flakes of tuna.

2. Heat the 3 tbsp of saved oil in a medium saucepan over medium heat. Cook, stirring periodically, for 3 minutes after adding the fennel. Add the garlic, crushed red pepper, salt and simmer, constantly stirring, for approximately 1 minute, or until the garlic is golden.

3. Toss in the tomatoes. Bring to a boil, then turn off the heat. Cook, uncovered, for 5–6 minutes, or until the mixture thickens. Stir in the tuna and continue to cook, uncovered, for another minute or until the tuna is well heated.

4. Pour the tuna mixture over the noodles and toss to incorporate. Parsley & lemon peel should be sprinkled on top of each dish.

38. Slow-Cooker Pasta e Fagioli Soup Freezer Pack

Prep Time: 15 min, Serving: 6, Difficulty: Easy

Ingredients

- 2 cups chopped onions
- 4 tsp dried Italian seasoning
- ½ cup grated Parmigiano-Reggiano cheese
- 1 cup chopped carrots
- 2 tbsp best-quality extra-virgin olive oil
- 1 cup chopped celery
- 4 tbsp chopped fresh basil, divided (Optional)
- 1 lb cooked Chicken Thighs, diced
- 4 cups baby spinach
- 4 cups whole-wheat rotini pasta (cooked)
- 1 (15 ounces) can no-salt-added white beans, rinsed
- 6 cups chicken broth (reduced-sodium)
- ¼ tsp salt

Instructions

1. In a big sealable plastic bag, combine the onions, carrots, and celery. In a separate bag, combine cooled cooked chicken & cooked pasta. Freeze for up to five days after sealing both bags. Before starting, defrost the bags overnight in the refrigerator.
2. Fill a large slow cooker halfway with the vegetable mixture. Combine the broth, Italian seasoning, and salt in a large mixing bowl. Cook on low heat for 7 1/4 hours, covered.
3. Add the defrosted chicken & pasta, along with the beans, spinach, and 2 tablespoons basil, if using. Cook for another 45 minutes. Into bowls, ladle the soup. Sprinkle a little oil into every bowl and top with the remaining 2 tablespoons basil, if preferred.

39. Guacamole Chopped Salad

Prep Time: 20 min, Serving: 4, Difficulty: Easy

Ingredients

- 1 tbsp chopped pickled jalapeño pepper
- 2 tbsp lime juice
- ¼ cup slivered red onion
- 1 clove garlic, grated
- 1 cup grape tomatoes, quartered
- ¼ tsp salt
- 2 ripe avocados, diced
- ¼ tsp ground pepper
- 2 tbsp corn oil or avocado oil
- 4 cups chopped romaine lettuce

Instructions

1. Whisk lime juice, oil, salt, garlic and pepper in a big bowl.
2. Add avocado, romaine, onion, tomatoes and jalapeño; mix gently to coat.

40. Greek Salad with Edamame

Prep Time: 20 min, Serving: 4, Difficulty: Easy

Ingredients

- ¼ cup slivered red onion
- 3 tbsp extra-virgin olive oil
- ¼ cup sliced Kalamata olives
- ¼ tsp salt
- ¼ cup slivered fresh basil
- ¼ tsp ground pepper
- ½ cup crumbled feta cheese
- 8 cups chopped romaine (about 2 romaine hearts)
- ½ European cucumber, sliced
- 16 ounces frozen shelled edamame (about 3 cups), thawed
- ¼ cup red-wine vinegar
- 1 cup halved cherry or grape tomatoes

Instructions

1. Whisk oil, vinegar, pepper and salt in a big bowl.
2. Add edamame, romaine, cucumber, tomatoes, basil, feta, onion and olives; toss to coat.

41. Honey Walnut Shrimp

Prep Time: 15 min, Serving: 4, Difficulty: Easy

Ingredients

- 2 cups hot cooked brown rice or white rice (Optional)
- 2 tbsp light brown sugar
- ½ cup sliced scallions
- ½ cup walnuts, coarsely chopped
- ¼ tsp salt
- 1 pound jumbo peeled, deveined raw shrimp
- ½ tsp ground pepper
- 1 tbsp honey
- 1 tbsp lemon juice
- 2 tbsp extra-virgin olive oil, divided
- 2 tbsp water
- 2 ½ tbsp mayonnaise

Instructions

1. In a big nonstick skillet over medium heat, bring water and brown sugar to a boil; boil until the sugar is fully dissolved, approximately 2 minutes. Cook, often stirring, for approximately 2 minutes, or until the sugar is brown & caramelized. On a parchment paper-lined dish, evenly distribute the walnuts. Wipe the pan clean.
2. In a mixing dish, combine the shrimp, honey, and 1 tablespoon of oil. Bring the skillet back up to medium-high heat. Cook, occasionally tossing, for approximately 4 minutes, or until the shrimp are thoroughly browned and cooked through. Remove the pan from the heat. In a small dish, combine lemon juice, mayonnaise, salt, pepper, and the remaining 1 tbsp oil; toss to coat the shrimp mixture in the pan. Add the caramelized walnuts and onions on top. Serve with rice if preferred.

42. Mushroom Shawarma with Yogurt-Tahini Sauce

Prep Time: 15 min, Serving: 4, Difficulty: Easy

Ingredients

- 1 pound portobello mushrooms, gills removed, stemmed, halved and sliced
- 1 medium red onion, halved and sliced
- 3 tbsp extra-virgin olive oil
- ½ cup cilantro leaves
- 1 ½ tsp ground cumin, divided
- 1 cup chopped tomatoes
- 1 tsp ground coriander
- 1 cup chopped romaine lettuce
- ½ tsp garlic powder
- 4 pitas, warmed
- ½ tsp smoked paprika
- 1 tbsp lemon juice
- ½ tsp chipotle chile powder
- 2 tbsp tahini
- ½ tsp salt plus 1/8 tsp, divided
- ½ cup low-fat plain Greek yogurt

Instructions

1. Preheat the oven to 425 degrees Fahrenheit. In a large mixing bowl, combine the cumin, oil, garlic powder, coriander, chile powder, smoked paprika, and 1/2 teaspoon salt. Stir in the mushrooms and onion until everything is thoroughly coated. Transfer to a big rimmed baking sheet & roast, turning once or twice, for approximately 20 minutes, or until the veggies are soft.
2. In a small bowl, mix yogurt, lemon juice, tahini, and the remaining 1/2 teaspoon cumin and 1/8 teaspoon salt.
3. Spread the yogurt sauce over the pitas, then layer the lettuce, mushroom mixture, tomatoes, & cilantro on top.

43. Cucumber & Avocado salad

Prep Time: 20 min, Serving: 4, Difficulty: Easy

Ingredients

- 1 ripe avocado, halved, pitted and sliced crosswise
- 3 tbsp fresh lime juice
- 1 English cucumber, thinly sliced
- 3 tbsp extra-virgin olive oil
- ½ tsp salt
- 1 tbsp thinly sliced fresh mint
- 1 medium shallot, thinly sliced crosswise and separated into rings
- 1 tbsp thinly sliced fresh basil

Instructions

1. Mix shallot rings & lime juice in a big bowl and set aside for almost 10 minutes to soften. Combine the oil, mint, basil, and salt in a mixing bowl. Stir in the cucumber and toss to coat. Allow the cucumber to marinate in the dressing for approximately 10 minutes, stirring regularly.
2. Move the cucumber to a dish using a slotted spoon and top with the avocado. Sprinkle the dressing over the salad and toss to combine. Serve right away.

44. Ginger-Tahini Salmon and Vegetables (Oven-Baked)

Prep Time: 25 min, Serving: 4, Difficulty: Medium

Ingredients

- 1 large sweet potato cubed (about 12 oz.)
- 2 tbsp chopped fresh chives
- 1 pound white button or cremini mushrooms, cut into 1-inch pieces (6 cups)
- 2 tsp rice vinegar
- 2 tbsp olive oil, divided
- ½ tsp salt, divided
- 1 ½ tsp finely grated fresh ginger
- 1 pound green beans, trimmed
- 2 tbsp reduced-sodium soy sauce
- 1 ¼ pounds salmon
- 1 tbsp plus 2 tsp. tahini
- 1 tbsp plus 1 tsp. honey

Instructions

1. Preheat the oven to 350°F and place a big rimmed baking sheet inside. One rack should be in the center of the oven, and the other should be approximately 6" from the broiler. Preheat the oven to 425 degrees Fahrenheit.
2. In a large mixing bowl, mix mushrooms, sweet potato, 1 tablespoon oil, and 1/4 teaspoon salt; toss to coat.
3. Preheat the oven to 350°F. Remove the baking sheet from the oven. Arrange the vegetable mixture in an equal layer on the pan and roast, turning once, for approximately 20 minutes, or until the sweet potatoes begin to brown.
4. Mix green beans with the remainder 1 tbsp oil & 1/4 tsp salt in the meanwhile. In a small bowl, combine the honey, tahini, soy sauce, and ginger.
5. Take the pan out of the oven. Put the green beans on one side and the mushrooms & sweet potatoes on the other. Place the salmon in the center, if necessary, resting it on top of the veggies. Half of the tahini sauce should be spread on top of the fish. Roast for another 8 to 10 minutes, or until the fish flakes. Preheat the broiler to high; transfer the pan to the top shelf and broil for 3 minutes, or until the salmon is glazed.

6. Drizzle the leftover tahini sauce over the veggies and fish after stirring in the vinegar. If preferred, garnish with chives before serving.

45. Peanut Zucchini Noodle Salad with Chicken

Prep Time: 30 min, Serving: 4, Difficulty: Medium

Ingredients

- 3 cups spiralized red cabbage (about 1/2 small head)
- 4 cups spiralized zucchini (1 large)
- 1 ½ tbsp fish sauce
- 1 tsp hot sauce, such as Sriracha
- 1 tsp grated garlic
- ¾ cup creamy natural peanut butter
- ¼ cup chopped unsalted roasted peanuts
- ¾ cup hot water
- 2 cups shredded rotisserie chicken (8 ounces)
- ¼ cup lime juice
- ½ cup chopped fresh cilantro
- 2 tbsp light brown sugar
- 1 cup spiralized carrot (1 large)
- 2 tbsp reduced-sodium tamari or soy sauce

Instructions

1. In a blender, combine the lime juice, peanut butter, tamari (or soy sauce), brown sugar, spicy sauce, fish sauce, and garlic. Pulse until the mixture is completely smooth.
2. In a large mixing bowl, combine the cabbage, zucchini, cilantro, and carrot. Toss to coat with 1 cup of the dressing (save the remainder for later use). Chicken and peanuts go on top of the salad. Serve right away.

46. Everything Bagel Avocado Toast

Prep Time: 5 min, Serving: 1, Difficulty: Easy

Ingredients

- Pinch of flaky sea salt (such as Maldon)
- 2 tsp everything bagel seasoning
- 1 slice whole-grain bread, toasted
- ¼ medium avocado, mashed

Instructions

1. Spread avocado on the toast.
2. Top with salt and seasoning.
3. Serve and enjoy.

47. Tomato, Cucumber & White-Bean Salad with Basil Vinaigrette

Prep Time: 25 min, Serving: 4, Difficulty: Easy

Ingredients

- ½ cup packed fresh basil leaves
- ½ cucumber halved lengthwise and sliced (1 cup)
- ¼ cup extra-virgin olive oil
- 1 cup halved cherry or grape tomatoes
- 3 tbsp red wine vinegar
- 1 (15 ounces) can low-sodium cannellini beans, rinsed
- 1 tbsp finely chopped shallot
- 10 cups mixed salad greens
- 2 tsp Dijon mustard
- 1 tsp honey
- ¼ tsp salt
- ¼ tsp ground pepper

Instructions

1. Place honey, basil, vinegar, oil, mustard, shallot, salt & pepper in a food processor.

2. Process until the mixture is largely smooth.
3. Place in a large mixing bowl. Combine the greens, beans, tomatoes, and cucumber in a large mixing bowl. Toss to coat evenly.

48. Pesto Pasta Salad

Prep Time: 20 min, Serving: 5, Difficulty: Easy

Ingredients

- 8 ounces whole-wheat fusilli (about 3 cups)
- 1 cup quartered cherry tomatoes
- 1 cup small broccoli florets
- ½ tsp ground pepper
- 2 cups packed fresh basil leaves
- ¾ tsp salt
- ¼ cup pine nuts, toasted
- 1 large clove garlic, quartered
- ¼ cup grated Parmesan cheese
- 2 tbsp lemon juice
- 2 tbsp mayonnaise
- 2 tbsp extra-virgin olive oil

Instructions

1. A big pot of water should be brought to a boil. Stir in broccoli one minute before the pasta is done. Cook for 1 minute before draining and rinsing under cold running water to end the cooking process.
2. In a little food processor, combine pine nuts, basil, mayonnaise, Parmesan, lemon juice, oil, salt, garlic, and pepper. Process until the mixture is practically smooth. Place in a large mixing basin. Toss in the broccoli, pasta, and tomatoes. Toss to coat evenly.

49. Slow-Cooker Mediterranean Stew

Prep Time: 15 min, Serving: 6, Difficulty: Easy

Ingredients

- 2 (14 ounce) cans no-salt-added fire-roasted diced tomatoes
- 6 lemon wedges (Optional)
- 3 cups low-sodium vegetable broth
- Fresh basil leaves, torn if large
- 1 cup coarsely chopped onion
- 3 tbsp extra-virgin olive oil
- ¾ cup chopped carrot
- 1 tbsp lemon juice
- 4 cloves garlic, minced
- 1 bunch lacinato kale, stemmed and chopped (about 8 cups)
- 1 tsp dried oregano
- 1 (15 ounce) can no-salt-added chickpeas, rinsed, divided
- ¾ tsp salt
- ½ tsp crushed red pepper
- ¼ tsp ground pepper

Instructions

1. In a 4-quart slow cooker, combine broth, tomatoes, carrot, onion, oregano, garlic, crushed red pepper, salt, and pepper. Cook on low heat for 6 hours, covered.
2. In a small dish, pour 1/4 cup of the slow cooker's cooking liquid. 2 tbsp chickpeas, mashed until smooth with a fork
3. In the slow cooker, combine the lemon juice, greens, mashed chickpeas, and the remaining whole chickpeas. To blend, stir everything together. Cover and cook on Low for 30 minutes, or until the kale is cooked.
4. Pour the stew into 6 dishes and sprinkle with oil. Serve with basil as a garnish. If desired, garnish with lemon slices.

50. Greek Stuffed Portobello Mushrooms

Prep Time: 15 min, Serving: 4, Difficulty: Easy

Ingredients

- 4 portobello mushrooms (about 14 ounces), wiped clean, stems and gills removed
- 3 tbsp extra-virgin olive oil, divided
- 1 tbsp chopped fresh oregano
- 1 clove garlic, minced
- 2 tbsp pitted and sliced Kalamata olives
- ½ tsp ground pepper, divided
- ⅓ cup crumbled feta cheese
- ¼ tsp salt
- 1 cup chopped spinach
- ½ cup quartered cherry tomatoes

Instructions

1. Preheat the oven to 400 degrees Fahrenheit.
2. In a small bowl, combine 2 tablespoons of oil, garlic, 1/4 teaspoon pepper, and salt. Apply the oil mixture all over the mushrooms using a silicone brush. Place on a big rimmed baking sheet & bake for 8 to 10 minutes, or until the mushrooms are largely tender.
3. Add oregano, tomatoes, spinach, olives, feta, and the rest of the 1 tbsp oil in a medium bowl. Remove the mushrooms from the oven after they have softened and fill with the mixture of spinach. Bake for approximately 10 minutes, or until the tomatoes have wilted.

51 Chicken & Snap Pea Stir-Fry

Ready in 20 min **Servings:** 4 **Difficulty:** Easy

Ingredients

- 2 tbsp vegetable oil
- 2 tbsp Sriracha (optional)
- 1 bunch of thinly sliced scallions
- 2 cloves of minced garlic
- 1 thinly sliced red bell pepper
- 2 tbsp sesame seeds, plus more for finishing
- 2½ cups snap peas
- 1¼ cups thinly sliced boneless skinless chicken breast
- Freshly ground black pepper and Salt
- 2 tbsp rice vinegar
- 3 tbsp soy sauce or tamari
- 3 tbsp chopped fresh cilantro, plus more for finishing

Instructions

1. Heat the oil in a pan saute pan over medium heat. Saute the green onion and garlic for 1 minute or until aromatic. Saute the snap peas & the bell pepper for 2 to 3 minutes, or until just tender.
2. Add chicken and cook for 4 to 5 minutes, or until browned and thoroughly cooked, and even the veggies are soft.
3. Toss together the rice vinegar, soy sauce, Sriracha (if using), and sesame seeds. Allow 1 to 2 minutes for the mixture to boil.
4. Mix inside the cilantro, and then top with a sprinkling of sesame seeds and more cilantro. Serve right away.

52 Greek Turkey Burgers alongside Tzatziki Sauce

Ready in 1 hr 10 min **Servings:** 4 **Difficulty:** Easy

Ingredients
Turkey Burgers

- 1 tbsp extra-virgin olive oil
- 1 egg
- 1 minced sweet onion
- ½ cup fresh parsley chopped
- 1 pound ground turkey
- ½ teaspoon of oregano
- ¼ teaspoon of red pepper flakes
- ¾ cup of bread crumbs
- 2 minced garlic cloves
- Freshly ground black pepper & salt

Tzatziki Sauce

- ½ diced European cucumber
- 1 tbsp extra-virgin olive oil
- 2 tbsp lemon juice
- 1 pinch garlic powder
- 1 cup Greek yogurt
- Freshly ground black pepper & salt
- ¼ cup fresh parsley, chopped

Burger Toppings

- ½ sliced red onion
- 4 hamburger buns, whole-wheat
- 2 sliced tomatoes
- 8 Boston lettuce leaves

Instructions

1. **To Make Turkey Burgers:** Heat oil in a small pan over medium heat. Cook for 3 to 4 minutes, or until the onion is soft. 1 minute later, add the garlic and cook until fragrant. Allow solidifying at room temperature before serving.

2. Combine the cooled onion mixture, egg, herbs, oregano, red pepper flakes, and ground turkey in a medium mixing dish. Mix in the bread crumbs, seasoning with salt and pepper as needed.

3. Preheat oven to 375 degrees Fahrenheit. Assemble the meat mixture into four equal-sized patties. Spray a big oven-safe skillet using nonstick cooking spray and heat it over medium-high heat.

4. In a pan, saute the patties from each side until nicely browned, about 4 to 5 minutes on each side. Transfer the pan to the oven and cook for another 15 to 17 minutes, or when the burgers are thoroughly cooked through.

5. **To Make Tzatziki Sauce:** Combine the yogurt, cucumber, olive oil, lime juice, and garlic powder in a medium mixing bowl. Season to taste using salt and pepper, and then add the parsley.

6. **Assemble the toppings:** Arrange all burgers on bottom half of a bun, top with approximately a quarter cup of tzatziki, 2 lettuce leaves, 2 tomato slices, & the top half of the bread. Serve right away.

53 Easy One-Pan Ratatouille

Ready in 1 hr 30 min **Servings:** 4 **Difficulty:** Easy

Ingredients

- 2 tbsp thyme leaves
- 5 tbsp olive oil
- 2 sprigs oregano
- 1 thickly sliced small eggplant
- 1 thickly sliced medium red onion
- 2 smashed garlic cloves
- 2 thickly sliced medium summer squash
- 2 thickly sliced medium zucchini
- 3 thickly sliced medium tomatoes
- Freshly ground black pepper & Salt
- 2 halved small red bell peppers
- 1 cup tomato sauce

Instructions

1. Preheat oven to 375 degrees Fahrenheit. On a baking sheet, set four individual baking pans or one 9-inch rectangular baking dish.
2. Heat the oil and garlic in a small saucepan over medium-low heat. Cook for 1 minute or until aromatic. Remove the saucepan from the heat and soak the oregano for 15 minutes. Garlic and oregano should be removed and discarded.
3. Put 2 teaspoons olive oil into each tiny baking dish's base (or 2 tbsp on the base of the larger baking dish).
4. In the bottom of each baking dish, place 2 tbsp tomato puree (or 14 cups in the bigger baking dish).
5. In the prepared baking plates, arrange the onion, eggplant, summer squash, pepper, zucchini and tomato. Don't stress about being flawless or matching the slices; just make sure they're all packed in securely.
6. Drizzle the remaining oil equally over the top, and then apply the remaining tomato sauce on top. Season with salt & pepper and a sprig of thyme.
7. Roast for 25 to 30 minutes, or until soft and starting to brown on the top and edges. Allow five to ten minutes to cool before serving.

54 Hula Ginger vinaigrette with Seared Ahi Tuna Poke Salad & Wonton Crisps

Ready in 25 min Servings: 4 Difficulty: Easy

Ingredients
Seared Ahi Tuna Poke
- 1/4 cup honey
- 1/4 cup of soy sauce
- 2 ahi tuna steaks
- 2 tbsp white and black sesame seeds toasted
- 1 teaspoon corn starch
- 1 teaspoon of chili garlic sauce
- 1/4 cup pineapple juice
- 20 square wonton wrappers cut into strips (to make this gluten-free, use corn tortillas)

Salad
- 1/2 cup fresh cilantro
- 1 cup fresh pineapple diced
- 1 sliced avocado
- 1 jalapeno or red chili sliced
- 4-8 cup spring greens

Hula Ginger Vinaigrette
- 1/2 cup toasted sesame oil or hot chili sesame oil
- 2 tbsp pineapple juice
- 2 tbsp rice vinegar
- 1/4 cup of soy sauce
- 1 teaspoon of chili garlic sauce or more to taste
- 1 lime zested & juiced
- 2 teaspoon grated fresh ginger
- 1 clove garlic minced or grated
- 1 tbsp tahini
- black and white sesame seeds toasted

Instructions

1. Bake oven at 400 degrees Fahrenheit.
2. Organize the wonton strips on an oiled baking sheet in such a thin layer (or as well you can arrange them). Using a spray of olive oil and then a generous amount of sea salt, coat the wontons. Bake for 5-10 minutes in a preheated oven, keeping an eye on them to ensure they don't burn. When they're a light golden hue and crisp, they're done. Remove the baking sheet from the microwave and put it aside.

3. Whisk with 1/4 cup of soy sauce & 1 teaspoon cornstarch in a small sauce saucepan until smooth. 1 teaspoon of chili garlic sauce, 1/4 cup pineapple juice, 1/4 cup of honey. Bring the saucepan to a boil on the stovetop over medium heat. Reduce the heat to low and cook for 3-4 minutes, or until the sauce thickens enough to cover the slotted spoon. Turn off the heat.

4. Heat the sesame oil in a big cast iron pan over high heat. In a pan, brown the tuna steaks for 1-2 minutes before flipping and brushing the browned side with soy sauce mixture. Take the steaks out from the pan after another minute or two of searing and coating it with the leftover soy sauce mixture. Cut the slices into strips.

5. In a mixing bowl, mix the cilantro, spring greens, avocado, pineapple chunks, and jalapeno (or red chili).

6. Make the vinaigrette in a separate small bowl. Mix the hot chili sesame oil, fresh ginger and garlic, soy sauce, pineapple juice, tahini, rice vinegar, chili garlic sauce, 1 teaspoon lime zest and juice, 1-2 teaspoons sesame seeds, black and white.

7. Arrange the greens on individual plates. Tuna, avocado slices, and wonton chips go on top. Drizzle the vinaigrette over the salad. Get your hands dirty!

55 Chicken marinated in Balsamic Vinegar, Brussels sprouts, Cranberries, and Pumpkin Seeds

Ready in 20 min **Servings:** 4 **Difficulty:** Easy

Ingredients
- about 15 to 20 trimmed and halved lengthwise Brussels sprouts
- about 1 1/4 pounds diced into bite-sized pieces boneless skinless chicken breast
- 1 peeled and diced small-large shallot
- 3 tbsp olive oil
- for seasoning to taste, salt and pepper
- 1/2 cup sun-dried tomatoes (not oil-packed)
- 1/2 cup dried cranberries
- 1/4 cup balsamic vinegar
- 1/2 cup pumpkin seeds candied or roasted
- 2 tbsp honey

Instructions

1. Heat 2 tbsp of olive oil in a large pan over medium-high heat, then add Brussels sprouts cut side down and cook for 5 minutes until it's seared and softly golden brown.

2. Flip the sprouts and place them on one side of the grill. If you have to stack these on top of one another, that's ok.

3. Add the remaining 1 tbsp of olive oil (if required, add more) to the uncovered side of the plate and add the chicken, shallots, salt and pepper to taste, and cook for 4 to 5 minutes, or until chicken is 80 to 90% cooked through; toss and turn the chicken regularly.

4. Pour the balsamic vinegar and honey evenly over the top and whisk to mix.

5. Lower the heat to medium-low and continue to cook for 2 to 3 minutes, or until the meat is cooked through and the sprouts are crisp-tender.

6. Toss in the sun-dried tomatoes, cranberries, and pumpkin seeds, and mix well. Serve right away. The dish is best served warm and fresh, but it may be stored in an airtight container in the refrigerator for up to five days or frozen for up to three months.

56 Pineapple Fried Rice

Ready in 30 min **Servings:** 4 **Difficulty:** Easy

Ingredients

- 3 cups cooked brown rice
- 1/2 cup frozen peas
- 2 cups pineapple diced
- 1/2 cup diced ham
- 1/4 teaspoon white pepper
- 2 green sliced onions
- 3 tbsp soy sauce
- 1 tbsp sesame oil
- 1/2 teaspoon ginger powder
- 2 tbsp olive oil
- 2 cloves garlic, minced
- 1 diced onion
- 2 peeled and grated carrots
- 1/2 cup frozen corn

Instructions

1. Combine sesame oil, soy sauce, ginger powder, and white pepper in a small bowl; leave aside.
2. In a large frying pan or wok, heat the olive oil on medium-high heat. Add the onion and ginger to the skillet and cook, often stirring, for 3-4 minutes, or until onions are translucent. Stir in the carrots, corn, peas, and simmer, frequently stirring, for 3-4 minutes, or until the veggies are soft.
3. Combine the pineapple, ham, rice, green onions, and soy sauce combination in a large mixing bowl. Cook, stirring continually, for approximately 2 minutes, or until well cooked.
4. Serve right away.

57 Baked Sesame-Ginger Salmon in Parchment

Ready in 30 min **Servings:** 4 **Difficulty:** Easy

Ingredients

- 1 teaspoon sesame oil
- 2 tbsp honey
- 2 tbsp soy sauce
- 2 tbsp grated fresh ginger
- Pinch of red pepper flakes
- 2 large zucchini, thinly sliced & halved lengthwise
- Four 6-ounce skinless salmon fillets
- 1 red onion, thinly sliced & halved
- 1 quartered lime
- 1 teaspoon garlic powder
- 4 teaspoons sesame seeds

Instructions

1. Preheat oven to 350 degrees Fahrenheit. Prepare four parchment sheets (around 15 by 17 inches). To produce a crease, wrap each piece in half, then unfold and put it aside.
2. Combine the sesame oil, soy sauce, garlic, ginger powder, honey, and red pepper flakes in a small bowl.
3. Assemble the parchment packs one by one. Put a quarter of zucchini in an equal layer on one side of a sheet of paper & top with the quarter of the red onion. Squeeze one lime segment over the veggies liberally.
4. Top the veggies with a salmon fillet. Brush the soy sauce mixture thoroughly over the fish and sprinkle with one teaspoon of sesame seeds.
5. To thoroughly seal the package, wrap the blank side of the paper over the fish and then wrap the two sides inward toward the fish, forming multiple creases.

6. Use the remaining paper and ingredients to repeat the process. Place the prepared packets on a baking tray and bake for 16 to 18 minutes, or until the salmon is thoroughly cooked.

7. To serve, either takes the fish and vegetables from the packet and place them on plates or cut holes in the top of the paper and serve the fish and vegetables in the paper. Serve right away.

58 Mediterranean roast chicken with turmeric & fennel

Ready in 1 hr **Servings:** 4-6 **Difficulty:** Easy
Ingredients

- ½ cup extra virgin olive oil
- Salt and Pepper
- ½ cup dry white wine
- ½ cup orange juice
- 1 lime juice
- 2 tbsp yellow mustard
- 1 tbsp garlic powder
- ¾ tbsp ground turmeric spice
- 1 teaspoon ground coriander
- 1 large sliced into half-moons sweet onion
- 3 tbsp brown sugar
- 1 large sliced fennel bulb
- 6 pieces bone-in, skin-on chicken (chicken legs or breasts)
- 2 Oranges sliced unpeeled
- 1 thinly sliced lime
- 1 teaspoon sweet paprika

Instructions
1. Make the marinade first. Combine the first six ingredients in a large mixing bowl or deep dish: white wine, olive oil, orange juice, mustard, lime juice, and brown sugar.
2. Combine the spices in a small bowl: garlic powder, turmeric, paprika, coriander, salt & pepper. Half of the spice mix should now be added to the liquid marinade. To blend, stir everything together.

3. Press the fillets dry and season thoroughly with the remaining spice mixture. Peel the chicken wings slightly & rub part of the spice mixture beneath the skin.

4. Combine the marinated chicken and the other marinade ingredients in a large mixing dish. Incorporate the meat well into the marinade. Cover and marinate for 1-2 hours (skip the marination if you do not have time).

5. Preheat to 475 degrees F when ready. Transfer the chicken, including the marinade and the rest of the ingredients, to a large baking sheet and arrange everything in one layer. Make sure the skin of the bird is facing up. If desired, season with a pinch of salt and additional brown sugar.

6. Grill for 45 mins or until chicken is fully done and the skin has browned attractively. The internal temperature of the chicken must be 170 degrees F.

59 One-Pan Eggs with Tomatoes & Asparagus

Ready in 30 min **Servings:** 4 **Difficulty:** Easy

Ingredients
- 1 pint cherry tomatoes
- 2 pounds asparagus
- 2 tbsp olive oil
- 4 eggs
- Salt and pepper
- 2 teaspoons chopped fresh thyme

Instructions

1. Preheat oven to 400 ° degrees Fahrenheit. Using nonstick cooking spray, grease a baking sheet.
2. Organize the asparagus & cherry tomatoes on the baking tray in an equal layer.

Pour the olive oil over veggies and season to taste with thyme, salt, and pepper.

3. Roast for 10 to 12 minutes, or until the asparagus is almost soft and the tomatoes are wrinkled.

4. Scatter the eggs over the asparagus and sprinkle with salt.

5. Bake for another 8 mins until the egg whites get set; however, the yolks are mostly jiggly.

6. Arrange the asparagus, tomatoes, and eggs on four dishes to serve.

60 Citrus Salad with Sweet Potato Bulgur

Ready in 1 hr **Servings:** 6 **Difficulty:** Easy

Ingredients

- Black pepper for taste
- 1/2 cup finely chopped mint
- 1 cup finely chopped parsley
- 1/4 cup finely chopped red onion
- 2 tbsp orange zest
- 1 tbsp avocado oil
- 2 teaspoons maple syrup
- Coarse salt and freshly ground black pepper
- 1/4 cup olive oil
- 1/4 cup freshly squeezed orange juice
- 1 tbsp red wine vinegar
- 1 small clove garlic
- 1/2 teaspoon salt
- 2 tbsp lemon juice
- 2 medium-sized sweet potatoes, peeled and cubed
- 1 1/4 cups bulgur wheat

Instructions

1. Oven preheated to 425 degrees Fahrenheit. Combine the sweet potatoes, cooking oil, syrup, a big teaspoon of coarse salt, and a couple of grinds of pepper in a mixing bowl. Place the potatoes on a baking sheet coated with parchment paper and bake for 35-40 minutes until it's very soft and lightly caramelized, stirring halfway through.

2. Boil 3 1/2 cups water while the potatoes are roasting. Reduce the heat to a low and add the bulgur. Cook, stirring periodically, for 8 minutes. Take the bulgur off the heat, cover it, and set it aside for 10 minutes. Drain the bulgur and fluff it with a fork to remove any extra water.

3. Combine the olive oil, salt, orange juice, red wine vinegar, lemon juice, garlic, and pepper in a mixing bowl and whisk to combine.

4. When the potatoes are done, combine them in a large mixing dish with the cooked bulgur, mint, orange zest, parsley and red onion. Toss in the dressing. Toss everything together until fully combined, then taste and adjust spices as required. Serve the food.

61 Citrus Salad with Sweet Potato Bulgur

Ready in 30 min **Servings:** 4 **Difficulty:** Easy

Ingredients

- 1 White Onion
- 3 Carrots
- 3 cloves minced garlic
- 1 inch finely grated Piece of Fresh Ginger
- 1 tbsp Lemon Juice
- 2 inch finely grated Piece of fresh Turmeric
- Black Sesame Seeds
- Canned Coconut Milk
- 4 cups (950ml) Vegetable Stock

Instructions

1. Thinly slice the ginger and turmeric, then chop the onion as well as carrot into tiny bits

2. In the bottommost of a deep stockpot, heat a little olive oil and saute onion for 3 minutes, or until transparent, next mix the minced turmeric, ginger and garlic, and cook for another minute.
3. Add the chopped carrots and continue to cook for the next 2 minutes. Now mix the veggie stock and boil for another 20-25 minutes, or until the carrots are tender and cooked through.
4. Mix the soup with a stick blender until smooth, or transfer to an upright blender and blend. Garnish with a splash of buttermilk and some black sesame seeds after adding the lemon juice.

62 Roasted Salmon in a Single Pan with Potatoes and Romaine

Ready in 40 min **Servings:** 4 **Difficulty:** Easy

Ingredients
- 4 tbsp extra-virgin olive oil, divided
- 1 teaspoon lemon juice
- Kosher salt and freshly ground black pepper for taste
- 1 pound baby Yukon Gold potatoes
- 1 tbsp unsalted melted butter
- ¼ teaspoon paprika
- 2 hearts romaine lettuce
- Four 6-ounce salmon fillets

Instructions

1. Preheat oven to 400 ° degrees Fahrenheit.
2. Mix the potatoes with 2 tbsp olive oil in a medium mixing basin; spread out in a thin layer on a baking tray. 15 minutes in the oven, until the potatoes are slightly browned and fork-tender.
3. In the meantime, chop the romaine hearts in half and drizzle with 3 tbsp olive oil and lemon juice. Salt & pepper to taste. Remove from the equation.
4. Brush the melted butter over the salmon fillets using a pastry brush. Season each fillet to taste with paprika, salt, and pepper.
5. Set the romaine hearts, salmon, and potatoes on the baking sheet. Continue roasting for another 5 to 7 minutes or until the lettuce is soft and also the fish is done through. Divide the potatoes, romaine, and salmon across four dishes to serve.

63 Peppers stuffed with ground turkey and sweet potatoes

Ready in 1 hr **Servings:** 4 **Difficulty:** Easy

Ingredients
- 1 tbsp virgin olive oil
- 2 cups of grass-fed turkey
- 2 cloves minced garlic
- ½ cup of homemade tomato sauce
- red pepper to taste
- salt and pepper
- 1⅔ cups of diced sweet potatoes
- 2 large bell peppers, cut in half
- feta cheese garnish
- ½ cup diced onions
- fresh parsley for garnish

Instructions
1. Preheat the oven to 350 degrees Fahrenheit.
2. Heat the olive oil in a pan over medium-high heat.
3. Stir in the garlic and ground turkey. Cook for approximately 10 minutes, until the chicken, is no longer pink, stirring periodically. As the meat cooks, be careful to split it up with a wooden spoon.
4. Stir in the onions and sauté until golden brown.

5. Put the sweet potatoes and simmer, covered, until they are soft. It takes roughly 8 minutes to complete.
6. Don't forget to stir now and again. Toss in the tomato sauce, crushed red pepper, salt, and freshly ground black pepper to taste. When cook the sweet potatoes, add extra olive oil or a splash of water if required.
7. Place the peppers in a prepared baking dish, cavity side up.
8. Stuff each half of bell pepper with both the chopped turkey-sweet potato mixture.
9. Bake for 30 mins, uncovered, and when the peppers are tender and cooked.
10. Remove the dish from the oven and top with feta cheese and parsley.

64 Smoky Chickpeas & Greens with Roasted Salmon

Ready in 40 min **Servings:** 4 **Difficulty:** Easy

Ingredients
- ¼ teaspoon of garlic powder
- 2 tbsp of virgin olive oil
- ½ teaspoon of salt, divided, plus a pinch
- 1 tbsp of smoked paprika
- ⅓ cup of buttermilk
- ¼ cup of mayonnaise
- ¼ cup of chopped fresh chives & dill, and garnish
- ½ teaspoon of ground pepper, divided
- 10 cups of chopped kale
- 1 (15 ounces) can rinsed chickpeas
- 1 ¼ pounds of wild salmon, and cut into 4 portions
- ¼ cup of water

Instructions
1. Preheat oven to 425 degrees F, with racks in the top third and center.
2. In a medium mixing dish, mix 1 tablespoon oil, paprika, and 1/4 teaspoon salt. Toss the chickpeas with the paprika mixture after fully drying them. Place on a baking tray to cool. Bake the chickpeas for 30 minutes on the top rack, stirring twice.
3. Meanwhile, in a blender, mix the buttermilk, mayonnaise, herbs, 1/4 teaspoon pepper, and garlic powder until smooth. Remove from the equation.
4. In a large skillet, heat and cook 1 tablespoon of oil over medium heat. Cook, stirring periodically, for 2 minutes after adding the kale. Cook, occasionally stirring, until the kale is soft, approximately 5 minutes longer. Remove the pan from the heat and add a little salt.
5. Take the chickpeas out of the oven and place them on one side of the pan. Season, the salmon with the leftover 1/4 teaspoon salt and pepper on the opposite side. Bake for 5 to 8 minutes, or until salmon is just done through.
6. Pour the reserved dressing over the salmon and serve with the greens and chickpeas.

65 Quinoa Bowl with Mediterranean Chicken

Ready in 30 min **Servings:** 4 **Difficulty:** Easy

Ingredients

- 1 pound trimmed boneless chicken breasts
- 2 tbsp of finely chopped parsley
- ¼ teaspoon of ground pepper
- 1 7-ounce jar of roasted red peppers
- ¼ cup of slivered almonds
- ¼ teaspoon of salt
- 4 tbsp of virgin olive oil
- 1 small crushed clove garlic
- ½ teaspoon of ground cumin
- ¼ teaspoon of crushed red pepper
- 2 cups cooked quinoa
- 1 teaspoon of paprika
- ¼ cup chopped of pitted Kalamata olives
- 1 cup of diced cucumber
- ¼ cup of crumbled feta cheese
- ¼ cup of finely chopped red onion

Instructions

1. Preheat the broiler to high and place a rack in the top third of the oven. Using foil, cover a rimmed baking sheet.
2. Season the chicken using salt and pepper before placing it on the baking sheet. Broil, rotating once, for 14 to 18 minutes, until an instant-read input signal in the thickest section registers 165 degrees F. Using a cutting board, shred or slice the chicken.
3. In a tiny food processor, combine the peppers, almonds, 2 tbsp oil, paprika, cumin, garlic, and red pepper. Puree until the mixture is pretty smooth.
4. In a medium mixing bowl, combine the quinoa, olives, red onion, and the remaining 2 tbsp oil.
5. To assemble, distribute the quinoa combination among four bowls and top evenly with cucumber, chicken, and red pepper sauce. Garnish with feta cheese and parsley.

66 Salad with Tomatoes, Cucumbers, and White Beans with Basil Vinaigrette

Ready in 25 min **Servings:** 4 **Difficulty:** Easy

Ingredients

- ¼ cup of virgin olive oil
- ½ cup fresh basil leaves
- 3 tbsp of vinegar
- 1 tbsp of finely chopped shallot
- 1 teaspoon of honey
- ¼ teaspoon of salt
- 2 teaspoons of Dijon mustard
- ¼ teaspoon of ground pepper
- 1 (15 ounces) can rinse cannellini beans, low-sodium
- 10 cups mixed green salad
- 1 cup halved grape of tomatoes or cherry
- ½ cucumber, sliced & halved lengthwise

Instructions

1. In a tiny food processor, combine basil, vinegar, oil, shallot, honey mustard, salt, and pepper. Process until the mixture is largely smooth. Place in a large mixing basin. Combine the greens, beans, tomatoes, and cucumber in a large mixing bowl. Toss to coat evenly.

67 Pasta Salad with Pesto

Ready in 20 min **Servings:** 5 **Difficulty:** Easy

Ingredients

- 1 cup small of broccoli florets
- 8 ounces 3 cups of whole-wheat fusilli
- ¼ cup of toasted pine nuts
- 2 tbsp of mayonnaise
- ¼ cup of grated Parmesan cheese
- 2 tbsp virgin olive oil
- 2 tbsp of lemon juice
- 1 large quartered clove garlic
- ¾ teaspoon of salt
- 1 cup quartered tomatoes
- 2 cups fresh basil leaves
- ½ teaspoon of ground pepper

Instructions

1. A big pot of water should be brought to a boil. Cook the fusilli according to the package guidelines. Stir in broccoli 1 min until the pasta is done. Cook for 1 min before draining and rinsing beneath cold water to end the cooking process.
2. In a little food processor, combine basil, Parmesan, oil, mayonnaise, lemon juice, garlic, pine nuts, salt, and pepper. Process until the mixture is practically smooth. Place in a large mixing basin. Toss in the pasta, broccoli, and tomatoes. Toss to coat evenly.

68 Roasted Greek Fish with Vegetables

Ready in 55 min **Servings:** 4 **Difficulty:** Easy

Ingredients

- 5 coarsely chopped garlic cloves
- 1 pound fingerling potatoes
- 2 tbsp of olive oil
- ½ teaspoon of sea salt
- 4 5 to 6-ounce skinless salmon fillets
- 2 medium red, yellow & orange sweet peppers, cut into rings
- ½ teaspoon of ground black pepper
- 2 cups cherry tomatoes
- 1 lemon
- 1 ½ cups of chopped fresh parsley (1 bunch)
- 1 Tbsp crushed dried oregano
- ¼ cup of snipped fresh oregano
- ¼ cup pitted kalamata olives

Instructions

1. Heat the oven to 425 °. In a large mixing basin, place the potatoes. Toss with 1 tbsp oil, garlic, and 1/8 tsp. Salt & black pepper; stir to coat. Cover with foil and move to a 15x10-inch baking sheet. 30 minutes of roasting
2. In the meanwhile, defrost any frozen fish. Sweet peppers, parsley, olives, oregano, tomatoes and 1/8 teaspoon salt and black pepper all go into the same dish. Drizzle the leftover 1 tbsp oil over the top and toss to coat.
3. Rinse the fish and pat it dry. Add the remaining 1/4 teaspoon salt and black pepper to taste. Top potatoes with the sweet pepper mixture and fish. Roast for another 10 minutes, uncovered, or until fish flakes easily.
4. Lemon zest should be removed. Lemon juice should be squeezed over the fish and veggies. Add a dash of zest.

69 Mediterranean Stew in a Slow Cooker

Ready in 6 hrs 45 min **Servings:** 6 **Difficulty:** Easy

Ingredients

- 3 tablespoons of virgin olive oil
- Fresh basil leaves
- 6 lemon of wedges (Elective)
- ½ teaspoon of crushed red pepper
- ¼ teaspoon of ground pepper
- 1 (15 ounces) can rinse chickpeas (no-salt-added)
- 1 bunch lacinato kale, stemmed & chopped (around 8 cups)
- 1 tbsp of lemon juice
- 3 cups of low-sodium vegetable broth
- 1 cup of chopped onion
- ¾ cup of chopped carrot
- 4 minced of cloves garlic
- 1 teaspoon of dried oregano
- ¾ teaspoon of salt
- 2 (14 ounces) cans of fire-roasted diced tomatoes

Instructions

1. In a 4-quart slow cooker, add broth, onion, garlic, tomatoes, oregano, carrot, salt, red pepper, and pepper. Cook on low for six hours, covered.
2. Pour 1/4 cup of the slow cooker's cooking liquid into a small basin. Using a fork, mash 2 tablespoons of chickpeas until smooth.
3. In the slow cooker, combine the mashed chickpeas, lemon juice, greens and the remaining whole chickpeas. To blend, stir everything together. Cover and simmer on low for 30 minutes or until the kale is cooked.
4. Divide the stew into 6 bowls and sprinkle with oil. Serve with basil as a garnish. If desired, garnish with lemon slices.

70 Portobello Mushrooms with Greek Stuffing

Ready in 25 min **Servings:** 4 **Difficulty:** Easy

Ingredients

- 3 tbsp virgin olive oil
- 1 minced clove garlic
- ¼ teaspoon of salt
- 1 cup of chopped spinach
- 1 tbsp of chopped fresh oregano
- ½ cup quartered tomatoes
- ⅓ cup of crumbled feta cheese
- 4 portobello mushrooms (about 14 ounces) stems, clean and gills removed
- 2 tbsp pitted & sliced Kalamata olives
- ½ teaspoon of ground pepper

Instructions

1. Preheat oven to 425 degrees Fahrenheit.
2. In a small bowl, mix 2 tbsp oil, garlic, 1/4 teaspoon pepper, and salt. Apply the oil mixture all over the mushrooms using a silicone brush. Put on a large rimmed baking sheet for 8 to 10 minutes or when the mushrooms are largely tender.
3. In a medium mixing bowl, add feta, tomatoes, spinach, oregano and olives the outstanding 1 tbsp of oil. Remove the mushrooms from oven after they have softened & fill with spinach mixture. After that bake for approximately 10 minutes or when tomatoes have wilted.

71 Ravioli with Artichokes and Olives from the Mediterranean

Ready in 15 min **Servings:** 4 **Difficulty:** Easy

Ingredients

- 2 (8 ounces) packages of frozen or refrigerated spinach & ricotta ravioli
- ¼ cup of sliced Kalamata olives
- ½ cup of drained oil-packed sun-dried tomatoes
- 1 (15 ounces) rinsed of cannellini beans
- 3 tbsp of toasted pine nuts
- 1 (10 ounces) thawed frozen quartered artichoke hearts
- ¼ cup of chopped basil

Instructions

1. A huge pot of water should be brought to a boil. Cook ravioli as directed on the box. Set aside after draining and tossing with 1 tbsp of the leftover oil.
2. Inside a large nonstick skillet, heat the remaining 1 tbsp oil over medium heat. Sauté for 2 to 3 mins, or until artichokes and beans are cooked through.
3. Toss the prepared ravioli, sun-dried tomatoes, pine nuts, olives and basil together in a large mixing bowl.

72 Provençal Baked Fish with Mushrooms and Roasted Potatoes

Ready in 1 hr **Servings:** 4 **Difficulty:** Easy

Ingredients

- 1 pound of cubed red potatoes
- 2 tbsp of extra-virgin olive oil
- 1 pound of trimmed & sliced mushrooms
- ¼ teaspoon of ground pepper
- ¼ teaspoon of salt
- 2 peeled & sliced cloves garlic
- 14 ounces halibut and cut into 4 portions, grouper or cod fillet
- 4 tbsp of lemon juice
- Fresh thyme for garnish
- 1 teaspoon of herbs de Provence

Instructions

1. Turn the oven to 425 ° F.
2. In a large mixing bowl, combine potatoes, mushrooms, 1 tablespoon oil, salt, and pepper. Fill a 9x13-inch baking sheet halfway with the mixture. Roast for 30 to 40 minutes or until the veggies are barely tender.
3. Stir in the veggies, followed by the garlic. Arrange the fish on top. Drizzle with the leftover 1 tbsp. oil and lemon juice. Herbs de Provence should be sprinkled on top. Bake for 10 to 15 minutes, or until the salmon is translucent in the middle and flakes readily. If desired, garnish with thyme.

73 Mediterranean Chicken, Brussels sprouts, and Gnocchi on a Sheet Pan

Ready in 40 min **Servings:** 4 **Difficulty:** Easy

Ingredients

- 2 tbsp of chopped oregano
- 2 large cloves of garlic, minced
- 4 tbsp extra-virgin olive oil, divided
- 1 (16 ounces) package shelf-stable gnocchi
- ½ teaspoon of ground pepper
- 1 pound Brussels sprouts, quartered & trimmed
- 1 cup sliced of red onion
- 4 boneless, trimmed chicken thighs
- 1 tbsp of vinegar
- 1 cup of halved cherry tomatoes
- ¼ teaspoon of salt

Instructions

1. Heat the oven to 450 ° F.
2. In a large mixing bowl, combine 2 tbsp oil, 1 teaspoon oregano, half of the garlic, 1/4 teaspoon pepper, and 1/8 teaspoon salt. Toss in the Brussels sprouts, gnocchi, and onion to coat. Place on a broad-rimmed baking sheet and spread out evenly.
3. In a large mixing bowl, combine 1 tbsp oil, the remaining 1 tbsp oregano, the remaining garlic, the remaining 1/4 teaspoon pepper, and 1/8 teaspoon salt. Toss in the chicken to coat. Place the chicken in the vegetable mixture and tuck it in. 10 minutes of roasting
4. Remove the pan from the heat and mix in the tomatoes. Continue roasting for another 10 minutes or until the Brussels sprouts are soft and the chicken is only cooked through. In a mixing bowl, combine the vegetable combination, vinegar, and the other 1 tbsp oil.

74 Spaghetti Squash with Vegan Pesto, Mushrooms, and Sun-Dried Tomatoes

Ready in 30 min **Servings:** 4 **Difficulty:** Easy

Ingredients

- ⅓ cup of unsalted raw cashews
- 4 tbsp extra-virgin olive oil, divided
- 3-pound squash spaghetti, lengthwise halved & seeded
- 8 ounces of sliced cremini mushrooms
- ½ cup julienned sun-dried tomatoes
- ½ teaspoon of salt
- 2 teaspoons of nutritional yeast
- 1 cup basil leaves fresh
- 2 cloves of coarsely chopped garlic
- 3 tbsp of lemon juice
- ½ teaspoon of ground pepper

Instructions

1. Cut-side down, place squash halves in an oven dish with 2 tbsp water. Microwave on High for 10 to 14 minutes, uncovered, until soft. (Alternatively, cut side down on a baking sheet and bake, put squash halves.) Preheat the oven to 400 degrees F and bake for 40 - 50 minutes, or until the potatoes are soft. You may also use a pressure cooker/multi-cooker to cook the squash.
2. In a large skillet, heat 1 tbsp oil over medium heat. Add the mushrooms, tomatoes, and 1/4 teaspoon salt; simmer, occasionally turning, for 5 to 6 minutes, or until the mushrooms are tender and beginning to brown. Remove the pan from the heat.
3. In a food processor, combine basil, an additional 3 tbsp oil, cashews, lemon juice, Garlic, nutritional yeast, and the remaining 1/4 teaspoon salt and pepper. Process until the mixture is largely smooth.
4. Remove the squash flesh from the shell into a strainer with a fork. To eliminate some of the liquid, softly press on the skin. Squash should be divided among four plates. Place a scoop of basil pesto on top of each dish of the mushroom mixture.

75 Grilled Salmon with Vegetables

Ready in 25 min **Servings:** 4 **Difficulty:** Easy

Ingredients

- 2 red, trimmed, halved and seeded yellow, orange bell peppers
- 1 tablespoon of extra virgin olive oil
- ½ teaspoon of salt
- 1 lemon, cut into 4 wedges
- ½ teaspoon of ground pepper
- 1 medium red onion and cut into 1-inch wedges

- 1 ¼ pounds salmon fillet and cut into 4 portions
- ¼ cup thinly sliced basil fresh
- 1 medium halved lengthwise zucchini

Instructions
1. Preheat the grill to medium-high.
2. Oil the zucchini, peppers, and onion, then season with 1/4 teaspoon salt. Season the salmon with the additional 1/4 teaspoon salt and pepper.
3. Place the veggies and salmon slices on the grill, skin-side down. Cook the veggies for 4 to 6 minutes on each side, stirring just once twice until barely cooked and grill marks form. Cook the salmon for 8 to 10 minutes, without turning it, till it flakes when checked with a fork.
4. Once the veggies have cooled enough to handle, coarsely chop them and combine them in a large mixing basin. If preferred, remove the skin of the salmon fillets and serve with the veggies. Serve with a lemon slice and 1 tablespoon basil on top of each plate.

76 Pizza with goat cheese

Ready in 30 min **Servings:** 2 **Difficulty:** Easy

Ingredients
- 1 (7 inches) crust of the whole wheat pizza
- 1 teaspoon of olive oil
- 1 sliced of Roma tomato
- 2 ounces cooked turkey breast
- 1 cup fresh baby spinach
- ¼ cup sliced red onion
- ¼ cup of crumbled goat cheese
- 2 tbsp of fresh snipped basil

Instructions
1. Using a pastry brush, coat the pizza dough with oil. Tomato, spinach, turkey, goat cheese & red onion go on top. Bake according to the instructions on the crust box.
2. Sprinkle with basil before serving.

77 Soup with Mediterranean Chicken and Chickpeas in a Slow Cooker

Ready in 4 hr 20 min **Servings:** 6 **Difficulty:** Easy

Ingredients
- 1 large finely chopped yellow onion
- 1 ½ cups dried chickpeas, soaked overnight
- 1 (15 ounces) fire roasted diced tomatoes
- 2 tbsp of tomato paste
- 4 cloves of chopped garlic
- 4 teaspoons of ground cumin
- ¼ teaspoon of cayenne pepper
- 1 bay leaf
- ¼ teaspoon of ground pepper
- 2 pounds trimmed chicken thighs & skin removed
- 4 teaspoons of paprika
- 1 (14 ounces) can drain & quarter artichoke hearts
- ¼ cup halved oil-cured olives
- ½ teaspoon of salt
- ¼ cup chopped fresh parsley or cilantro

Instructions

1. Place chickpeas in a 6-quart or bigger slow cooker, drained. Stir together 4 cups water, tomatoes onion, garlic, cumin bay leaf, cayenne, paprika, tomato paste and ground pepper. Toss in the chicken.
2. Cook on medium for eight hours or moderate for 4 hours, covered.
3. Allow the chicken to cool slightly on a clean chopping board. Bay leaf should be discarded. Stir together the artichokes, olives, and salt in the slow cooker. Remove the bones from the chicken and shred them. Add the chicken to the broth and mix well. Serve with parsley on top (or cilantro).

78 Pasta with Whole-Grain Sauce and Parmesan

Ready in 1 hr 55 min **Servings:** 8 **Difficulty:** Easy

Ingredients

- 2 cloves of garlic
- ½ teaspoon of kosher salt
- ½ teaspoon of smoked paprika
- ¼ cup grated Parmesan cheese
- ½ of a (28 ounce) whole peeled plum tomatoes (1 1/3 cups)
- ½ cup of toasted whole almonds
- 3 tbsp of olive oil
- 2 tbsp of chopped fresh Italian parsley, add more for garnish
- 1 tbsp of sherry vinegar
- 12 ounces of whole-grain pasta
- 1 tbsp of honey
- 2 large red bell peppers

Instructions

1. Preheat the oven to 400 Fahrenheit. A baking sheet should be lightly oiled. Remove the stems, seeds, and membranes from bell peppers by cutting them in half lengthwise. Set the pepper slices, cut sides up upon the baking sheet that has been prepared. Roast for 45 minutes until the pepper is tender and the skins easily peel away.
2. Wrap the peppers in plastic wrap and place them in a bowl. Allow for 30 minutes of cooling time or until cold enough to handle. The skins should be peeled off and discarded.
3. To make the sauce, in a blender or food processor, mix the roasted peppers, almonds, tomatoes, oil, 2 tbsp parsley, sherry vinegar, honey, garlic, salt, &smoky paprika. Blend or process until almost smooth, covered. (Because of the almonds, the sauce will have a coarse texture.)
4. Place the sauce in a medium pot and stir to combine. Bring to a boil, and then turn off the heat. Cook for 20 minutes.
5. Meanwhile, cook the pasta as directed on the box; drains. Pour sauce above the spaghetti and top with Parmesan cheese. Garnish with more parsley, if preferred.

79 Farfalle with Tuna, Fennel & Lemon

Ready in 30 min **Servings:** 4 **Difficulty:** Easy

Ingredients

1) 2 tbsp of snipped fresh Italian parsley
2) 1 teaspoon of shredded lemon peel
3) 2 cloves of minced garlic
4) ½ teaspoon of crushed red pepper
5) ¼ teaspoon of salt
6) 2 (14.5 ounces) cans diced tomatoes, un-drained
7) 6 ounces whole grain farfalle pasta
8) 1 (5 ounces) white tuna solid
9) 1 Olive oil
10) 1 cup of sliced fennel

Instructions

1. Drain pasta and cook according to package instructions, avoiding salt. Return the spaghetti to the pan and cover to keep it heated. Meanwhile, drain the tuna and set aside the oil. Add additional olive oil to make 3 tbsp total if required. Set aside the flakes of tuna.
2. Heat the three tablespoons of leftover oil in a medium skillet over medium heat. Cook, stirring periodically, for 3 minutes after adding the fennel. Add the garlic, salt and simmer, crushed red pepper, constantly stirring, for approximately 1 minute, or until the garlic is golden.
3. Toss in the tomatoes. Bring to a boil, then turn off the heat. Cook, uncovered, for 5 to 6 minutes, or until the mixture thickens. Stir in the tuna and continue to cook, uncovered, for another minute or until the tuna is well heated.
4. Pour the tuna mixture over the noodles and toss to incorporate. Parsley & lemon peel should be sprinkled on top of each dish.

80 Chicken on a Sheet Pan with Brussels sprouts

Ready in 35 min **Servings:** 4 **Difficulty:** Easy

Ingredients

- 1 pound of sweet potatoes, cut into 1/2-inch wedges
- ¾ teaspoon of salt
- ¾ teaspoon of ground pepper
- 4 cups quartered Brussels sprouts
- 2 tbsp of virgin olive oil
- 1 ¼ pound trimmed boneless, skinless chicken thighs
- ½ teaspoon of ground cumin
- 3 tbsp of sherry vinegar
- ½ teaspoon of dried thyme

Instructions

1. Preheat the oven to 425 ° F.
2. In a large mixing basin, toss potatoes with 1 tbsp oil and 1/4 tsp salt & pepper. On a lined baking sheet, spread evenly. 15 minutes of roasting
3. In a large mixing basin, toss Brussels sprouts with extra 1 tbsp oil and 1/4 tsp salt and pepper. On the baking sheet, mix into the sweet potatoes.
4. Season, the chicken with the other 1/4 tsp salt & pepper and cumin and thyme. Arrange the veggies on top. Roast for another 10 to 15 minutes, just until the meat is cooked through when the veggies are soft.
5. Arrange the chicken on a plate to serve. Toss the veggies with the vinegar & pour with the chicken.

81 Pasta e Fagioli Soup in a Slow Cooker Freezer Pack

Ready in 8 hr 15 min **Servings:** 6 **Difficulty:** Easy

Ingredients

- 1 (15 ounces) can rinse white beans
- 4 teaspoons of dried Italian seasoning
- 4 cups of baby spinach
- 2 tbsp of extra-virgin olive oil
- ½ cup of grated Parmigiano Reggiano cheese
- 1 pound cooked of Meal-Prep Sheet-Pan Chicken
- 4 cups of cooked wheat rotini pasta
- 6 cups of sodium chicken broth
- ¼ teaspoon of salt
- 2 cups of chopped onions
- 4 tbsp of chopped freshly basil
- 1 cup of chopped celery
- 1 cup of chopped fresh carrots

Instructions

1. In a big sealable plastic bag, combine the onions, carrots, and celery. In a separate bag, combine cooled cooked chicken with cooked pasta. Refrigerate for up to five days after sealing both bags. Before starting, defrost the bags overnight in the refrigerator.

2. Fill a large slow cooker halfway with the vegetable mixture. Combine the broth, Italian seasoning, and salt in a large mixing bowl. Cook on medium for 7 1/4 hours, covered.

3. Combine the beans, spinach, and 2 tablespoons basil, when using, with the refrigerated chicken and pasta in a large mixing bowl. Cook for another 45 minutes. Into bowls, ladle the soup. Drizzle a little oil into each bowl and, if preferred, sprinkle some cheese as well as the remaining 2 tablespoons basil.

82 Baked Turkey Meatballs

Ready in 35 min **Servings: 3 Difficulty:** Easy

Ingredients
- 1 pound of ground turkey
- 1 tbsp of chopped parsley
- ½ tbsp of chopped basil
- ½ cup of fresh Parmesan cheese
- 1 large beaten egg
- Pinch freshly grated nutmeg
- ½ cup of breadcrumbs, white/whole wheat
- 2-3 tablespoons of water or milk
- ½ tbsp of chopped oregano

Instructions
1. Preheat the oven to 350 ° F.
2. Preheat oven to 350°F. Line two baking pans with parchment paper.

3. In a large mixing bowl, crumbs, mix the turkey, cheeses, nutmeg, herbs, egg, salt & pepper, as well as the milk. Depending on how dry the bread is, you might have to vary the quantity of milk you use. The combination should be moist enough to cling together but not soggy, so it falls apart.

4. Roll pieces of the meat into 1-inch balls using only a tsp (for uniformity) or using hands, and place them on a baking sheet. You should have around 25-30 meatballs in the end.

5. Cook the meatballs for about 30 minutes, flipping once until the meat is tender through and lightly browned on both sides.

83 Bean Bolognese in the Crock-Pot

Ready in 4 hr **Servings: 4 Difficulty:** Easy

Ingredients
- 1 chopped normal size of onion
- 2 celery chopped stalks
- 2 cloves of minced garlic
- 1 28-ounce can tomatoes
- Pasta (elective)
- 1 14-ounce can white beans
- 2 carrots chopped & peeled

Instructions
1. In a slow cooker set on low, combine all of the ingredients. Cook for 4-6 hours, or until all of the ingredients are soft. End up serving as a chunky stew (additional 12 cup water if you want a looser texture) or a sauce over cooked spaghetti.

84 Salmon & Cauliflower Rice Bowl for Gut Healing

Ready in 30 min **Servings:** 2 **Difficulty:** Easy

Ingredients
- 3 tbsp olive or coconut oil
- Himalayan salt
- 1 teaspoon of sesame oil
- 1 teaspoon of curry powder
- 2 salmon fillets, sustainably sourced or organic
- ¼ cup of tamari sauce
- 1 teaspoon of Dijon mustard
- 1 teaspoon of honey
- 1 tbsp of sesame seeds
- 10 - 12 Brussels sprouts, chopped in half
- 1 bunch washed & shredded kale
- ½ head cauliflower

Instructions
1. Preheat the oven to 350 degrees Fahrenheit.
2. Spread chopped Brussels sprouts on a baking dish. Season with salt and 1 tbsp of oil. Bake for 20 minutes in the oven.
3. In the meanwhile, create the marinade by whisking together all of the ingredients in a mixing dish.
4. After 20 minutes, remove the Brussels sprouts and put the fillets in the oven pan.
5. Return the salmon fillets to the oven for another 12 - 14 minutes, or until they are cooked to your preference.
6. Heat 1 tablespoon oil in a skillet over medium-high heat while the salmon is frying. Sauté the kale until it has reduced (2 to 3 minutes). Remove the pan from the heat and put it aside.
7. In the same pan, heat the remaining oil and add the cauliflower rice. Sauté until done, seasoning with 1 teaspoon curry powder & salt (2 to 3 minutes).
8. Take the salmon & Brussels sprouts out of the oven and divide them evenly between two dishes. Fill dishes with sautéed kale & cauliflower rice.

85 White Bean & Chicken Chili with Winter Vegetables

Ready in 30 min**Servings: 6 Difficulty:** Easy

Ingredients
- 2 tbsp olive oil
- 1 small chopped onion
- 1 rinsed & chopped leek
- 1 seeded & diced jalapeño pepper
- 2 minced garlic cloves
- 1 tbsp of ground cumin
- Pinch of crushed red pepper flakes
- 1 large, peeled & chopped white potato
- 1 teaspoon of oregano
- 1 cup of chopped Brussels sprouts
- 3 cups of chicken stock
- 1 15-ounce can small white beans
- 1 cup of milk
- 2 cups cooked, shredded chicken breast

Instructions
1. In a big saucepan, heat the olive oil over medium heat. Cook for about 5 min, till the onion & leek is translucent and tender, then mix the onion, leek, & jalapeno.
2. Add the garlic & spices to the pan and simmer for another minute, stirring constantly.

3. In a large saucepan, combine stock, white beans, the potato, Brussels sprouts and chicken.
4. Cook, occasionally stirring, for 20 minutes, or until the potato chunks are cooked.
5. Mix in the milk & heat until it is barely warm. Serve immediately with preferred toppings.

86 Chicken Tenders with Harissa and Yogurt Marination

Ready in 40 min **Servings:** 8 **Difficulty:** Easy

Ingredients
- ¼ cup of dry white wine
- 2 tbsp of Harissa paste
- 2 pounds of boneless chicken tenders
- ¼ cup of plain yogurt

Instructions
1. Combine the Harissa, yogurt, and wine in a mixing bowl. In a shallow baking dish, place the chicken tenders and cover them with the yogurt mixture. Refrigerate after wrapping with plastic wrap. Marinate for at least 2 hours and up to overnight in the refrigerator.
2. Preheat the grill for the chicken. Allow any extra marinade to drain off the chicken before removing it. Cook, the chicken for about 5 minutes on each side on a hot grill.
3. Serve with only a side salad, couscous, rice, or quinoa, or a sandwich with sliced veggies and fresh herbs.

87 Buffalo cauliflower baked

Ready in 35 min **Servings:** 2 **Difficulty:** Easy

Ingredients
- 1 medium size cauliflower, cut into small pieces

- Pinch of salt & pepper
- ¼ cup of water
- ¼ cup of banana flour
- 2 tbsp of melted butter
- ½ cup of hot sauce
- For serving: ranch dressing and blue cheese

Instructions
1. Preheat oven to 425 ° F.
2. In a large mixing basin, flour mixture, water, salt, and pepper.
3. Toss the cauliflower in the flour-water mixture to coat it. Put on some kind of foil-lined baking sheet and bake for about 15 minutes, turning once.
4. In a small mixing dish, combine the butter and spicy sauce. Pour the sauce over cauliflower that has been roasted. Return the pan to the oven and bake for another 20 minutes. If preferred, serve hot with your preferred dressing on the side.

88 Bolognese with Polenta and Wild Mushrooms

Ready in 40 min **Servings:** 4 **Difficulty:** Easy

Ingredients
For Polenta
- ¼ cup of Parmesan cheese
- 2 cups of yellow cornmeal
- 6 cups of vegetable stock
- 2 tbsp of unsalted butter

For Wild Mushroom Bolognese
- 6-ounces assorted wild mushrooms
- 1 teaspoon of salt
- ½ teaspoon of black pepper
- ½ cup of red wine
- 1 28-ounce can tomato

- 1 chopped fresh onion
- 2 peeled & chopped carrots
- 2 peeled & chopped celery stalks
- 2 chopped of garlic cloves
- ¼ cup of olive oil
- ½ teaspoon of dried thyme
- 1 teaspoon of dried oregano

Instructions

1. To prepare the polenta (while the Bolognese is cooking), follow these steps: Bring the water to a boil in the stock.
2. Mix in the cornmeal slowly, scraping up any clots as you need them.
3. Reduce heat to medium-low & simmer the cornmeal for 15-20 minutes or until it has thickened. It should be porridge-like inconsistency.
4. Mix in the butter & Parmesan cheese after removing the polenta from heat. Remove from the equation.
5. To create the Bolognese, onion, celery, pulse the carrots & garlic together in a food processor until finely chopped but not pureed. Remove from the equation.
6. In a big saucepan, heat oil over medium heat. In the same saucepan, add the chopped veggies. Cook for about 5 minutes, or even the vegetables are soft.
7. Add the mushrooms and spices to the pan. Cook for another 5 minutes, or until the mushrooms' water has drained completely.
8. Add inside this red wine, grinding up any brown pieces from the bottom of the pan with a spatula.
9. Bring the mixture to a boil with the tomatoes. Reduce to medium-low heat and continue to cook for another 15 minutes.
10. Spoon the sauce over the polenta and serve.

89 Recipe for Chinese chicken salad

Ready in 25 min **Servings:** 4 **Difficulty:** Easy

Ingredients
For Salad
- ½ cup of cilantro leaves chopped
- 2 tbsp chopped mint leaves
- ¼ cup of cooked edamame
- 4 thinly scallions sliced
- Wonton strips
- 2 cooked shredded chicken breasts (grilled)
- 1 cup of red cabbage
- 1 carrot, cut into thin pieces
- 4 cups of green cabbage

For Dressing of Salad
- 1 tbsp low-sodium soy sauce
- 1 teaspoon of sesame oil
- 2 minced garlic cloves
- ¼-inch chopped & peeled piece of ginger
- Pinch of salt
- ½ cup of vegetable oil
- ¼ cup of unseasoned rice wine vinegar
- 1 tbsp of Dijon mustard

Instructions

1. In a blender, combine all of the dressing ingredients and mix until smooth. Remove from the equation.
2. Inside a large mixing bowl, mix all of the salad ingredients. Toss the salad with the dressing. If desired, garnish with wonton strips.

90 Saag Paneer

Ready in 25 min **Servings:** 4 **Difficulty:**
Easy

Ingredients

- 8 ounces of paneer cheese, cut into 1/2-inch cubes
- 2 tbsp of virgin olive oil
- ¼ teaspoon of ground turmeric
- 2 cups of low-fat yogurt
- 1 finely small onion chopped
- 1 finely jalapeño pepper chopped
- 1 minced of clove garlic
- 1 tbsp of minced ginger
- 2 teaspoons of garam masala
- ¾ teaspoon of salt
- 1 teaspoon of ground cumin
- 20 ounces of chopped spinach

Instructions

1. In a medium mixing basin, mix paneer with turmeric until evenly covered in a nonstick skillet, heat 1 teaspoon oil over medium heat. Cook, tossing once until the paneer is browned on all sides, approximately 5 minutes. Place on a platter to cool.
2. In the same pan, add the rest 1 tbsp of oil. Cook, turning regularly, until golden brown, about 7 to 8 minutes, with the onion & jalapeno. (If the pan becomes dry while cooking, add 2 tbsp of water at a time.) Garlic, garam masala, ginger, & cumin are added to the pan. Cook, constantly stirring, for approximately 30 seconds, or until

aromatic. Season with salt and spinach. Cook, constantly stirring, for 3 minutes, or until heated. Take the pan off the heat and add the yogurt and paneer.

91 Alfredo Spaghetti Squash

Ready in 35 min **Servings:** 2 **Difficulty:**
Easy

Ingredients

- 3-pound of spaghetti squash
- 1 tbsp of olive oil
- 1 cup of milk
- 2 finely garlic cloves
- 2 tbsp of brown rice flour
- 1 tbsp of yogurt
- ½ cup of Parmesan cheese
- Salt & pepper
- 1 teaspoon of dried thyme

Instructions

1. Preheat oven to 350 ° Fahrenheit.
2. Poke a few tiny holes in the squash's exterior with a knife. While roasting the squash, it will allow sufficient steam to escape, preventing it from bursting.
3. Arrange the squash on some kind of baking tray in its whole state. Bake for 45 minutes on average until the squash gets tender to the touch and the liquid has begun to drain.
4. Remove the squash from the oven and let it cool completely before slicing it lengthwise in half. Discard all of the seed as well as any fibrous parts in the center.
5. Prepare the Alfredo sauce in the meanwhile. In a saucepan over medium heat, pour in the oil.
6. Toss in the garlic and cook for about 2-3 minutes, or until fragrant.
7. Stir in the flour in the pan for about a minute to "toast" it.

8. Pour the milk into the pan, constantly whisking to incorporate the flour and scrape up any lumps.
9. Heat the milk to such a low boil, and then remove it from the heat. As it heats up, the sauce will thicken.
10. Once the sauce has reached a boil, remove it from the heat and whisk in the yogurt, Parmesan, and dried thyme. To taste, season with salt and pepper.
11. Gently "shred" the spaghetti squash halves' inside with a fork. It'll have a paste-like texture to it! The sauce should be poured over both halves.
12. Broil until the sauce is gently browned and the halves are bubbling. Remove from the oven and serve immediately.

92 Green Fried Rice

Ready in 20 min **Servings:** 4 **Difficulty:** Easy

Ingredients
- 1 tbsp of olive oil
- 1 diced white onion
- ½ cup chopped broccoli
- 1 minced garlic clove
- 1 teaspoon of honey
- 2 cups of cooked brown rice
- ½ cup of frozen or fresh peas
- 1 tbsp soy sauce
- 1 diced celery stalk
- ¼ teaspoon of fresh lemon zest

Instructions
1. In an oven-safe pan, heat the olive oil over medium-high heat. Cook the vegetables, onion, and broccoli in the pan for about 2 minutes, and when the onions & celery start to soften.
2. Saute for yet another 2 minutes after adding the garlic & rice to the pan.

3. Combine the frozen peas, tamari, and honey in a mixing bowl. Cook, occasionally stirring, for a further 3-5 minutes, and when the rice is somewhat crunchy around the edges.
4. Take the pan off the heat and add the lemon zest.
5. Serve right away.

93 Recipe for Baked Tilapia with Pecan Rosemary Topping

Ready in 33 min **Servings:** 4 **Difficulty:** Easy

Ingredients
- 1/3 cup of chopped pecans
- 1 egg
- 1/3 cup of whole wheat breadcrumbs
- 4 4 ounces of each tilapia fillets
- 1/2 teaspoon of coconut palm sugar
- 1 pinch of cayenne pepper
- 2 teaspoons of fresh rosemary
- 1 teaspoon of olive oil
- 1/8 teaspoon of salt

Instructions
1. Preheat the oven to 350 ° F.
2. Combine nuts, crumbs, thyme, coconut palm sugar, salt, and cayenne pepper in a small baking dish. Toss in the olive oil to cover the pecan mixture.
3. Bake for 7 to 8 minutes, or until the pecan batter is light golden brown.
4. Raise the temperature to 400 degrees Fahrenheit. Using cooking spray, coat a big glass baking dish.
5. Beat the egg white in a small bowl. Starting with one tilapia once a moment, gently cover each side of the fish with the egg yolk but then the pecan mixture. Put the fillets inside the baking dish that has been prepared.

6. Place the leftover pecan slices on top of the tilapia fillets and press down.
7. Bake for 10 minutes, just until the tilapia is only done through. Serve the food.

94 Lentil Shrimp Jambalaya

Ready in 45 min **Servings:** 4 **Difficulty:** Easy

Ingredients

- 1 cup of lentils
- 2 tbsp of butter
- 170 grams of sliced uncooked sausage
- 1 cup chopped celery, bell pepper & onion
- 3 minced garlic cloves
- 1 sliced of jalapeno
- 1 cup of tomatoes
- 1 bay leaf
- 1/2 tsp of seasoning blend Cajun creole
- 1/2 tsp of dried thyme
- 14–16 ounces peeled & deveined medium shrimp
- 1 cup of diced okra
- Sea salt & freshly black pepper
- 1 tbsp of cornstarch mixed with cold water
- Crushed red pepper flakes for gravy
- pinch of paprika

Instructions

1. First, have your lentils ready (if using uncooked lentil). To get the finest results, fully rinse the lentils beforehand. If you're using canned lentils, you may skip the cooking stage.
2. Lentils: Bring 3 cups fluid (water) to either a boil in a big saucepan. 1 1/4 cup drained and washed lentils Cover securely, lower the heat, and cook for 15-20 minutes. Drain the lentils and put them aside in a basin.
3. Heat 1 tbsp oil or butter in the same saucepan over medium to high heat. NOTE: If you're using uncooked sausage, brown it here first and then remove it. If you're using pre-cooked sausage, skip the browning and serve the shrimp and lentils with cooked sliced sausage afterward.
4. Combine the celery, onion, jalapeno, garlic and carrots/bell pepper in a large mixing bowl. To coat the pan, sauté the veggies for a few minutes on moderate to medium-high heat until the onions cook aromatic and slightly caramelized.
5. Combine the cooked lentils, smashed tomatoes, smoked paprika, Cajun spices thyme, and bay leaf in a mixing bowl. Cook until the mixture achieves a gentle simmer. Lower heat to medium-low, cover, and continue to cook for approximately 5 minutes. Simply to let the tastes mingle. Because the lentils are already cooked, you won't have to cook them for long.
6. Finally, add the shrimp and okra. Combine. Mix in a slurry of arrowroot or corn flour for a thicker jambalaya. Recombine the ingredients. Cook for 6-10 minutes on moderate, stirring either once twice or until shrimp are no longer pink. Return the saucepan to low heat and add the chicken sausage. Before serving, remove the bay leaf.
7. Toss in red pepper flakes, a pinch of sea salt, black pepper, and parsley, if preferred, and serve in bowls.

95 Lasagna with Tofu and Winter Squash

Ready in 50 min **Servings:** 6 **Difficulty:** Easy

Ingredients

- 2 cups of mashed winter squash like Acorn
- 1-pound of lasagna noodles
- 1 tbsp of brown sugar
- 16-ounce soft tofu
- Salt & pepper
- ½ cup of non-dairy milk like Almond or coconut
- 2 tbsp of lemon juice
- 1 tbsp of thyme leaves
- Pinch of paprika
- 4 cups of prepared Marinara sauce

Instructions

1. Preheat oven to 350°F.
2. In a large mixing bowl, combine the squash and brown sugar; put aside.
3. In a food processor, combine the tofu, lime juice, milk, thyme, & paprika and process until smooth.
4. Stir in the tofu with the squash mixture. To taste, season with salt & pepper.
5. Apply a thin layer of red sauce on the base of the 9 x 13-inch baking sheet. Add another layer of noodles on top, using about a third of the box. 1/3 of the squash & tofu filling should be on top.
6. Layer in the same sequence as before, finishing with a little quantity of the squash & tofu combination. If desired, top using bread or cracker crumbs.
7. Bake for 40 to 45 minutes, or until hot and bubbly.

96 Buddha Bowls with Chicken and Quinoa

Ready in 30 min **Servings:** 4 **Difficulty:** Easy

Ingredients
Roasted Chicken Thighs

- 5 trimmed boneless, skinless chicken thighs
- ¼ teaspoon of salt
- ½ teaspoon of ground pepper

Quinoa

- 3 cups of chicken broth
- 1 cup of quinoa
- ¼ teaspoon of salt
- 1 tbsp of virgin olive oil

Italian Dressing

- 1 tbsp of sugar
- 1 tbsp of Dijon mustard
- 1 large clove of garlic
- 2 teaspoons basil, dried
- 5 tbsp water
- 2 teaspoons of oregano
- ½ teaspoon of ground pepper
- 1 ¾ cups of virgin olive oil
- ½ teaspoon of salt
- ¾ cup of vinegar

Toppings

- 1 can rinsed chickpeas
- 1 cup of sprouts
- ¼ cup of chopped nuts
- 1 sliced avocado
- 6 thinly sliced radishes

Instructions

1. To cook chicken, follow these steps: Heat the oven to 425 ° F.

2. Place the chicken on some kind of baking pan and bake it. 1/2 teaspoon black pepper & 1/4 teaspoon salt to taste. Roast the chicken for 14 minutes, or until an immediate thermometer inserted within the thickest section registers 165 degrees F. 4 thighs, sliced.

3. Meanwhile, prepare the quinoa as follows: In a large pot, mix broth, 1 tablespoon oil, and 1/4 teaspoon salt. Bring to a boil over high heat, and then reduce to low heat. Return to low heat and stir in the quinoa. Reduce heat to low and continue to cook for 20 minutes, just until the quinoa completely absorbed all of the liquid as well as the grains have burst. Take the pan off the heat, cover it, and set it aside for 5 minutes.

4. To make the dressing, follow these steps: In a blender, combine the lemon juice, sugar, mustard, water, garlic, basil, oregano, salt and pepper. Puree until completely smooth. Slowly drizzle in the oil and purée until the mixture is creamy. Assemble the bowls 3 cups quinoa, divided into 4 big shallow dishes. Sprinkle seeds over the chicken, avocado, radishes, chickpeas and sprouts. Drizzle 3/4 cup dressing on top.

97 Salad of Greek Kale with Quinoa and Chicken

Ready in 15 min **Servings:** 2 **Difficulty:** Easy

Ingredients
- ¼ cup of roasted red peppers
- ¼ cup of Greek salad dressing
- 1 ounce of Crumbled cheese
- 4 cups of chopped kale
- 1 cup of shredded chicken
- 1 cup of quinoa

Instructions
1. In a large mixing bowl, combine the greens, chicken, quinoa, and roasted peppers. Toss in the dressing to coat. If preferred, top with feta cheese.

98 Chicken Fajita Bowls on a Sheet Pan

Ready in 40 min **Servings:** 4 **Difficulty:** Easy

Ingredients
- 4 cups of steamed kale
- 1 can rinse no-salt-added black beans
- ¼ cup low-fat plain yogurt
- 1 tbsp of lime juice
- 2 teaspoons of water
- ½ teaspoon of smoked paprika
- ¼ teaspoon of ground pepper
- 2 tbsp of olive oil
- 1 ¼ pounds of chicken tenders
- 1 medium sliced onion
- 1 medium sliced red bell pepper
- ½ teaspoon powder of garlic
- 1 medium green bell pepper
- 2 teaspoons of chili powder
- 2 teaspoons of cumin
- ¾ teaspoon of salt

Instructions
1. Preheat the oven to 425 ° F. and place a big covered baking tray in it.
2. In a large mixing bowl, combine chili powder, cumin, a pinch of salt, garlic powder, paprika, & ground pepper. Set aside 1 teaspoon of a spice mixture in a medium bowl.
3. In a large mixing bowl, whisk 1 tablespoon of oil into the remaining spice mixture.

4. Toss in the chicken, onion, then red and green bell peppers.

5. Take the pan out of the oven and spray it with cooking spray. On the pan, pour the chicken combination in a uniform layer. 15 minutes of roasting.

6. In a large mixing basin, toss the kale & black beans with the remaining 1/4 teaspoon salt and 1 tbsp olive oil to coat.

7. Turn off the oven and remove the pan. Combine the chicken and veggies in a mixing bowl. Evenly distribute the greens and beans over the top. 5 to 7 minutes of roasting time till the roasted through and the veggies are soft.

8. Meanwhile, whisk together the yogurt, lemon juice, and water in the reserved spice mixture.

9. In four separate dishes, distribute the chicken & vegetable combination. Serve with a dollop of yogurt dressing on top.

Sebastian Young

Chapter 5: Snacks and Quickies Recipes

1. Turmeric bars (paleo, AIP) - Anti-inflammatory

Prep Time: 10 min, Serving: 8, Difficulty: Easy

Ingredients

For the crust

- 1 tbsp coconut oil
- 1 cup shredded coconut
- 10 dates, pitted (soak in water for 10 minutes if hard)
- 1 tsp cinnamon

For the filling

- 1 tsp cinnamon
- 1 1/4 cup coconut butter
- 2 tsp honey
- 1/2 cup coconut oil
- 1 1/2 tsp turmeric powder
- 1/8 tsp black pepper

Instructions

1. Line an 8x8" baking pan with parchment paper.
2. In a food processor, combine the shredded coconut & dates, then pulse multiple times until thoroughly combined. Blend in the coconut oil & cinnamon until smooth.
3. Remove the crust mixture from the bowl and place it in the pan. Press it into the pan until it's flattened evenly. Put the crust inside the refrigerator for 2-3 hours to cool.
4. Prepare a double boiler by filling a saucepot with water and bringing it to a low boil to make the filling. To make a double boiler, lay a stainless steel bowl on top of the pot. Pour the coconut butter into the mixing bowl and swirl to melt it. The coconut butter should

not be melted in the microwave since it will burn.

5. Mix in the coconut oil till the mixture is completely liquid after the coconut butter has partly melted.
6. Allow the mixture to cool for several minutes after removing it from the heat.
7. In a mixing bowl, combine the turmeric, cinnamon, black pepper and honey.
8. Fill the crust with the filling and spread it out evenly with a spoon.
9. Refrigerate for 3-4 hours or overnight to harden.
10. Remove the pan from the refrigerator and set it on the counter for 10 minutes after it has solidified.
11. Carefully cut into 16 squares using a kitchen knife. Some could shatter, but that's ok!
12. Cinnamon should be sprinkled on top of the final bars.
13. Refrigerate and serve cold... with a napkin! Turmeric stains readily.

2. Turmeric Gummies (Anti-Inflammatory, Paleo)

Prep Time: 5 min, Serving: 4, Difficulty: Easy

Ingredients

- 3 ½ cups water
- Pinch of ground pepper
- 1 tsp ground turmeric
- 6 tsp maple syrup
- 8 tsp unflavored gelatin powder

Instructions

1. Combine the ground turmeric, maple syrup, and water in a big saucepan.
2. Heat on high for approximately 5 minutes, often stirring to ensure that the ingredients are evenly distributed.

3. Remove the saucepan from the heat and stir in the gelatin powder to hydrate the gelatin.

4. Return the saucepan to heat and constantly stir with a spoon until all of the gelatin has dissolved.

5. Cover a deep dish with plastic wrap after pouring the liquid mixture in it. Refrigerate the mixture for at least 4 hours or until it is firm.

6. Slice into tiny squares, or your favorite form, after cooled, and serve.

3. Spicy Kale Chips

Prep Time: 8 min, Serving: 4, Difficulty: Easy

Ingredients

- 1/4 tsp ground cayenne pepper
- 1 bunch of curly kale
- 1/8 tsp garlic powder
- spray oil or your favorite healthy oil
- 1/4 tsp sea salt, or to taste
- 1/8 tsp black pepper

Instructions

1. Preheat the oven to 300 degrees Fahrenheit.
2. Thoroughly rinse and dry the kale.
3. Tear kale leaves from their stems/ribs into potato chip-sized pieces.
4. Place on a wire baking rack, spaced apart, on top of a foil-lined cookie sheet.
5. Make two sheets/batches of kale if you're preparing a lot of it so it cooks evenly.
6. Spritz gently with a natural cooking spray or delicately massage a little amount of oil into the kale leaves with your fingertips. To make crispy kale chips, gently cover the leaves in oil without putting too much moisture on them. In addition, the wire baking rack guarantees that the crisp factor is maximized.

7. To taste, sprinkle with garlic powder, cayenne pepper, and salt. It'll be spicier if you add extra cayenne pepper.
Bake for 18-20 minutes on the middle rack or until the edges are crisp.

4. Paleo ginger-spiced mixed nuts

Prep Time: 5 min, Serving: 8, Difficulty: Easy

Ingredients

- Coconut oil spray
- 1/2 tsp fine sea salt
- 1 tsp fresh grated ginger
- 2 large egg whites
- Parchment paper
- 2 cups mixed nuts, raw almonds, pumpkin seeds, goji berries cashew, etc.
- 1/2 tsp ground Vietnamese cinnamon

Instructions

1. Preheat the oven to 250 degrees Fahrenheit.
2. Whip the egg whites until they are foamy. Grate the ginger, season with fine sea salt, and sprinkle with Vietnamese cinnamon.
3. Whip the ingredients until it is well mixed.
4. To the egg white mixture, add uncooked mixed nuts of your choosing. Toss to coat.
5. Lightly sprinkle the parchment paper with coconut oil. On the baking sheet, equally, distribute the nuts. Bake at 250 degrees Fahrenheit for 40 minutes, or until fragrant, rotating the baking sheet pan halfway through.
6. Break the combined nuts into pieces after they have cooled and set. Keep the container sealed. Store them in the fridge if the weather is hot.

5. 10-minute spicy tuna rolls

Prep Time: 10 min, Serving: 6, Difficulty: Easy

Ingredients

- 1/8 tsp salt
- 1 medium cucumber
- 2 slices avocado, diced
- 1 pouch StarKist Selects EVOO Wild-Caught Yellowfin Tuna
- 1/16 tsp ground cayenne
- 1 tsp hot sauce
- 1/8 tsp pepper

Instructions

1. Thinly cut the cucumber lengthwise using a mandolin. Once the cucumber has been thinly sliced down to where the seeds appear, turn it over and finely slice the other side. Remove the cucumber's outermost slices and any slices with seeds. With a paper towel, pat dries the leftover slices (6 total). Set aside.
2. Combine hot sauce, tuna, pepper, salt, and cayenne in a small mixing bowl. Mix until all of the ingredients are evenly distributed.
3. Spoon tuna mixture over cucumber slices one at a time, leaving one inch on every side. Place one slice of avocado on top of the tuna, then wrap the cucumber up gently, closing the end with two toothpicks.

6. Easy Peasy Ginger Date Bars

Prep Time: 10 min, Serving: 4, Difficulty: Easy

Ingredients

- ¼ cup almond milk
- 1 ½ cup almonds or 1 cup almond flour
- ¾ cup dates
- 1 t ground ginger

Instructions

1. Preheat the oven to 350 degrees Fahrenheit.
2. To create the almond flour, pulse the almonds for about 1-2 minutes in a high-powered blender until fine and powdery. If you stir the almonds too much, they'll start to leak their oils, results in nut butter. Remove from the equation.
3. To prepare the date paste, combine the dates and almond milk in the same blender and puree for around 3-5 minutes.
4. Blend the date mixture for 2-3 minutes with almond flour & ground ginger.
5. Bake for 20 minutes after pouring the mixture into a baking dish.
6. Allow it cool before slicing into eight bars of similar size.

7. Vanilla Turmeric Orange Juice

Prep Time: 5 min, Serving: 2, Difficulty: Easy

Ingredients

- ½ tbsp cinnamon
- 3 oranges, peeled + quartered
- Pinch of pepper
- 1 cup unsweetened almond milk
- 1 tbsp vanilla extract
- ¼ tbsp turmeric

Instructions

1. In a blender, combine all of the ingredients.
2. Blend until completely smooth, then serve in a glass.

8. AIP / Paleo Hibiscus Ginger Gelatin Gummies (Sweet n' Sour)

Prep Time: 10 min, Serving: 7, Difficulty: Easy

Ingredients

- 3 tbsp hibiscus flowers cut
- 1 tsp ginger juice
- 1 cup water
- 2 tbsp gelatin powder
- 1½ tbsp honey

Instructions

1. In a small saucepan, take water to a boil.
2. Remove the pan from heat & stir in the hibiscus blossoms.
3. Cover and set aside for 5 minutes to infuse.
4. Using a tiny filter, drain the flowers.
5. Bring the liquid to the saucepan, add the honey and ginger, and whisk to combine.
6. Allow for the gelatin to soften & dissolve after sprinkling it over the liquid's surface. After a few minutes, whisk to ensure that the gelatin is completely dissolved and there are no clumps.
7. Pour into the silicone mold right away.
8. Allow cooling before placing in the refrigerator for at least 2 hrs.
9. To unmold the gummies, just press your fingertips on the bottom of the mold, and the gummies would pop out. Good appetite!

9. Baked Veggie Turmeric Nuggets (Freeze-Friendly)

Prep Time: 10 min, Serving: 6, Difficulty: Easy

Ingredients

- 1/2 tbsp ground turmeric
- 2 cups cauliflower florets
- 1 large pasture-raised egg
- 2 cups broccoli florets
- 1/2 cup almond meal
- 1 cup carrots, coarsely chopped
- 1/4 tbsp black pepper
- 1 t garlic, minced
- 1/4 tbsp sea salt

Instructions

1. Preheat the oven to 400 degrees Fahrenheit and prepare the baking sheet by lining it with parchment paper.
2. In a food processor, combine the cauliflower, broccoli, garlic, carrots, sea salt, turmeric, and black pepper. Pulse until the mixture is fine.
3. Pulse in the egg & almond meal until barely combined.
4. Place in a mixing bowl. Take out a spoonful of the ingredients and shape them into round discs with your palms. Place on a baking sheet that has been lined with parchment paper.
5. Preheat oven to 350°F and cook for 25 minutes, turning after 15 minutes. For dipping, serve with Paleo ranch sauce.

10. Pineapple Ginger Slaw (Creamy)

Prep Time: 40 min, Serving: 12, Difficulty: Medium

Ingredients

- Creamy Ginger Sauce
- 1 cup fresh cilantro, roughly chopped
- 1 cup soaked cashews
- 3 cups pineapple, chopped in small chunks
- 1/2 cup water
- 2 red peppers, thinly sliced (4 cups)
- 1 tbsp + 1 tsp lime juice
- 1/2 head thinly sliced green cabbage
- salt and pepper, to taste
- 2 inches fresh ginger
- 1/2 head thinly sliced red cabbage
- 1/2 tsp red pepper flakes
- Pineapple Slaw

Instructions

1. In a bowl, combine the cashews. Fill the container with water. Allow for at least 30 minutes of soak time, preferably overnight.
2. Prepare the sauce. The cashews should be drained and rinsed. Combine the soaked cashews as well as the remaining sauce in a blender. In a high-powered blender or food processor, combine all ingredients.
3. In a large mixing bowl, combine the red peppers, cabbage, and pineapple. Mix in the sauce well. Stir in the cilantro until it is well incorporated.
4. Have fun!

11. No-Bake Energy Bites with Golden Turmeric

Prep Time: 20 min, Serving: 9, Difficulty: Easy

Ingredients

- 1 t coconut oil
- 1 cup almond or coconut butter
- 2 tbsp turmeric
- 3/4 unsweetened coconut flakes
- 4-6 tbsp plant-based protein powder
- ½ tsp maple syrup

Instructions

1. Add nut butter, almond butter, 1/2 coconut flakes, maple syrup, protein powder, coconut oil, and turmeric to a blender and puree until smooth.
2. Blend on high until the ingredients are evenly distributed.
3. Refrigerate the dough for 30 to 60 minutes to allow it to solidify.
4. Take the dough out from the refrigerator and form it into 12-inch diameter bite-sized balls.
5. Place the balls on a platter lined with parchment paper and refrigerate for 3 to 4 hours.
6. Remove the food from the refrigerator. Roll the balls in the remaining crushed coconut flakes on a dish. Have fun!

12. Ginger Fried Cabbage and Carrots (AIP, Paleo, Vegan)

Prep Time: 5 min, Serving: 4, Difficulty: Easy

Ingredients

- ¼ cup green onion, chopped
- 1 tbsp ginger, minced
- 1 tbsp coconut aminos
- 2 garlic cloves, crushed
- 1 tbsp apple cider vinegar
- 4 cups green cabbage, shredded
- 2 tbsp oil
- 2 carrots, julienned or grated

Instructions

1. Heat the oil in a big skillet over medium-high heat. Garlic and ginger should be added now. Cook for one minute or until aromatic.
2. Toss in the cabbage and carrots. Cook for 6-8 minutes, or until soft.
3. Turn off the heat under the cabbage & carrot mixture. Combine the vinegar, coconut aminos, and green onion in a mixing bowl. Serve the food.

13. Grain-Free Banana Ginger Bars

Prep Time: 15 min, Serving: 2, Difficulty: Easy

Ingredients

- 2 large or 3 small very ripe bananas
- 2 tsp apple cider vinegar
- 1 cup coconut flour
- 1 tsp baking soda
- ⅓ cup coconut oil, ghee or butter, liquified
- 1 tsp ground cardamom
- ⅓ cup raw honey or real maple syrup
- 2 tsp cinnamon
- 6 eggs
- 1½ Tbsp grated fresh ginger

Instructions

1. Preheat oven to 350 degrees
2. Fahrenheit. Grease or line a 9x9" glass baking dish with parchment paper.

3. Blend everything in a food processor until smooth, except the baking soda & vinegar. Combine the baking soda and vinegar in a blender until smooth, then pour into the lined dish.
4. Bake for 30-40 minutes, or until a toothpick inserted in the center comes out clean.

14. Gut-Healing Kombucha Gummies

Prep Time: 15 min, Serving: 5, Difficulty: Easy

Ingredients

- 1 tbsp grapefruit zest
- 1 tbsp grated ginger
- 1/3 cup gelatin powder
- 1 ½ cups plain kombucha
- 1/2 cup grapefruit juice
- 6 tbsp honey

Instructions

1. Wrap plastic wrap over the bottom of a 9x9" glass pan.
2. Bring a medium saucepan of water to a boil with the grated ginger. Allow for a five-minute boil to destroy the protease enzymes in the ginger. Drain the water and put it aside.
3. Mix the grapefruit juice, zest, kombucha, and honey in a large saucepan and stir thoroughly. Spread the gelatin powder on top and set aside for a few minutes to hydrate.
4. Reduce the heat to medium-low and slowly simmer the mixture until the gelatin powder melts. Mix until all of the gelatin has dissolved.
5. In a blender, pulse the gelatin mixture as well as the boiling grated ginger for 20 seconds.

6. Chill the mixture for at least three hours or until solid in the prepared glass pan. After that, cut the cake into little pieces and serve!

15. Spicy nuts (paleo + whole30)

Prep Time: 5 min, Serving: 6, Difficulty: Easy

Ingredients

- 1/2 tsp cumin
- 1 cup almonds
- 1 tbsp olive oil
- 1 cup pecans
- 1/4 tsp cayenne pepper
- 1 cup cashews
- 1/2 tsp sea salt
  - tsp chili powder
- 1/2 tsp garlic powder
- 1/2 tsp black pepper

Instructions

1. Preheat the oven to 350°F and prepare a baking sheet with parchment paper. On the baking pan, arrange the nuts in a single layer. Preheat oven to 350°F and roast for 15 mins, flipping halfway.
2. Prepare the spice combination by mixing garlic powder, chili powder, black pepper, cumin, cayenne pepper, and salt in a small bowl while the nuts are roasting.
3. Remove the nuts from the oven and set aside to cool. With a mixing dish, coat the nuts with olive oil, then in the spice mixture.
4. Keep at room temperature in an airtight container.

16. Apple Cider Vinegar Gummies

Prep Time: 5 min, Serving: 24, Difficulty: Easy

Ingredients

- ½ cup water
- 1 ½ cups organic apple juice
- ½ cup apple cider vinegar
- 5 tbsp gelatin powder

Instructions

1. In a large saucepan over low heat, combine the apple cider vinegar, apple juice, & water and whisk thoroughly. Mix in the gelatin powder with the liquid and set aside for two minutes.
2. Reduce the heat to low and whisk with a spoon for 5 minutes or until the gelatin has dissolved completely.
3. Fill ice cube trays halfway with gelatin mixture and refrigerate for at least 1 hr then serving.

17. Cacao Coffee Protein Bars [copycat RXBAR]

Prep time: 10 min, serving: 12, difficulty: easy

Ingredients

- 3 tbsp instant coffee or espresso powder (can adjust to taste)
- 2 cups nuts
- 1/4 cup cacao nibs, optional
- 1 cup egg white protein powder
- 3–5 tbsp water, as needed to blend
- 1/4 cup cacao powder (or unsweetened cocoa)
- 18 large Medjool dates, pitted (10 ounces)

Instructions

1. Set aside an 8x8 pan lined with parchment paper or a square silicone pan.
2. Process nuts, egg white protein, cacao powder, and coffee powder in a food processor bowl until nuts are broken down into tiny bits. It's important not to over process the nuts since they'll keep breaking down in the following stage.
3. Add the pitted dates and pulse until smooth– the mixture will be touch dry at this point. 1 tbsp of water at a time, with the engine running, until the mixture is sticky & everything comes together. You may also need less or more water depending on whether your dates were juicy or dry.
4. Remove S-blade and whisk in cacao nibs if using after the mixture has come together and is sticky.
5. Place the mixture in an 8-inch square pan that has been lined with parchment paper. Press evenly into the pan with somewhat damp palms.
6. Before cutting into bars, chill the pan for 1 hour or freeze it for 30 minutes. Cut the bars into 12 or 16 squares using a big sharp knife & cutting board.

18. Garlic Plantain Chips

Prep time: 12 min, serving: 2, difficulty: easy

Ingredients

- 2 tsp garlic powder
- 3 cups plantain chips
- 3 tbsp coconut oil or avocado oil
- 1 tbsp lemon juice

Instructions

1. Preheat the oven to 250 degrees Fahrenheit.
2. Using parchment paper, line a baking pan.
3. Combine the coconut oil, garlic, and plantain chips in a large mixing basin. Toss the chips carefully with your hands so that they are equally covered. When the oven is heated, pour in the lemon juice & mix it in as well.
4. Using the prepared baking pan, spread the plantain chips evenly. Bake for 12 minutes or until just starting to brown, then drain on a paper towel for a min or two to absorb any leftover oil before eating.

19. Roasted Chickpeas with Tumeric

Prep time: 20 min, serving: 2, difficulty: easy

Ingredients

- 1 tsp salt
- 1 tsp turmeric
- 1 can chickpeas (garbanzo beans)
- 1/2 tsp paprika
- 1/4 tsp black pepper
- 2 tsp olive or grapeseed oil

Instructions:

1. Chickpeas should be soaked overnight or for at least 8 hours. Open & rinse the chickpea can.
2. Mix chickpeas with high-temperature oil, salt and spices on a parchment or Silpat-lined baking sheet.
3. Preheat oven to 250°F and bake for 20 minutes. To achieve consistent cooking, shake the pan to stir the chickpeas around. Remove from the oven and set aside to cool for another 20 minutes.
4. Keep them at room temperature in a BPA-free or glass container, and try not to eat them all.

20. Mediterranean roasted chicken with fennel and turmeric

Prep Time: 15 min, Serving: 4, Difficulty: Easy

Ingredients

- ½ cup extra virgin olive oil
- 3 tbsp brown sugar, more for later
- 2 tbsp yellow mustard
- 1 lime juice
- ½ cup orange juice
- ½ cup dry white wine
- 1 tsp ground coriander
- 1 tbsp garlic powder
- 6 pieces skin on, bone-in chicken
- 1 tsp sweet paprika
- ¾ tbsp ground turmeric spice
- 1 large fennel bulb, cored, sliced
- 1 lime, thinly sliced (optional)
- 1 large sweet onion, sliced into half-moons
- Salt and Pepper
- 2 Oranges, unpeeled, sliced

Instructions

1. Preparing the marinade is the first step. Combine the first six ingredients in a large mixing bowl: white wine, mustard, olive oil, lime juice, orange juice, and brown sugar.
2. Combine the coriander, garlic powder, salt, paprika, turmeric, and pepper in a small bowl. Half spice mix should now be added to the marinade. To mix, stir everything together.
3. Dry the chicken slices and season thoroughly with the remaining spice mix. Hold the chicken skins and rub part of the spice mixture beneath the skin.
4. To the big bowl of marinade, add the seasoned chicken as well as the additional ingredients. Incorporate the chicken well into the marinade. Cover and marinate for 1-2 hours.
5. Preheat the oven to 470 degrees F when ready. Transfer the chicken, along with the marinade and the rest of the ingredients, to a large baking sheet and arrange everything in one layer. Make sure the skin of the bird is facing up. If desired, season with a pinch of salt and additional brown sugar.
6. Roast the chicken for 45 minutes, or until it's cooked through and the skin is well browned. The internal temperature of the chicken must be 170 degrees F.

21. Baked Turkey Meatballs (Makes 25-30 mini meatballs)

Prep Time: 10 min, Serving: 2, Difficulty: Easy

Ingredients

- Pinch freshly grated nutmeg
- 1 large egg, beaten
- ½ tbsp chopped fresh oregano
- ½ cup fresh breadcrumbs, white or whole wheat
- ½ cup fresh grated Parmesan cheese
- 1 tbsp chopped fresh parsley
- ½ tbsp chopped fresh basil
- 1 pound ground turkey
- 2-3 tbsps milk (or water)

Instructions

1. Preheat the oven to 350 degrees Fahrenheit.
2. Line two baking pans with parchment paper.
3. In a big mixing bowl, combine the breadcrumbs, turkey, herbs, cheese, nutmeg, egg, salt, & pepper, as well as the milk. Depending on how dry the bread is, you may need to vary the quantity of milk you use. The mixture should be moist enough to cling together but not soggy, so it falls apart.

4. Roll pieces of the meat into 1-inch balls using a tsp, and place them on a baking sheet. You should have around 25-30 meatballs in the end.
5. Bake the meatballs for about 30 minutes, flipping once, until the meat is cooked through and lightly browned on both sides.

22. Crock-Pot Bean Bolognese

Prep Time: 10 min, Serving: 4, Difficulty: Easy

Ingredients

- 2 cloves garlic, minced
- 1 medium-size onion, chopped
- Pasta (optional)
- 2 carrots, peeled and chopped
- 1 28-ounce can crushed tomatoes
- 2 celery stalks, chopped
- 1 14-ounce can white beans (such as Great Northern, Cannellini, or Navy)

Instructions

1. Take a crockpot, set it on low, and combine all ingredients in it.
2. Cook for 4-6 hours, or until all of the ingredients are soft.
3. Serve as a chunky stew (add 1/2 cup water if you want a looser consistency!) or a sauce over cooked spaghetti.

23. Gut-Healing Salmon & Cauliflower Rice Bowl

Prep Time: 10 min, Serving: 2, Difficulty: Easy

Ingredients

- 2 salmon fillets, sustainably sourced or organic

- Himalayan salt
- 10 to 12 Brussels sprouts, chopped in half
- 1 tsp curry powder
- 1 bunch kale, washed and shredded
- ½ head cauliflower, pulsed into cauliflower rice (you can use a whole cauliflower head if you wish)
- 3 tbsp olive or coconut oil

For marinade

- 1 tsp sesame oil
- ¼ cup tamari sauce
- 1 tbsp sesame seeds
- 1 tsp Dijon mustard
- 1 tsp honey or maple syrup (optional)

Instructions

1. Preheat the oven to 350 degrees Fahrenheit.
2. Line a baking pan with parchment paper and add the Brussels sprouts, chopped. Season with salt and 1 tbsp of oil. Roast for 20 mins in the oven.
3. In the meanwhile, create the marinade by mixing all of the ingredients in a basin.
4. After 20 minutes, remove the Brussels sprouts and put the salmon fillets in the oven pan. Return the salmon fillets to the oven for another 13 to 15 minutes, or until they are cooked to your preference.
5. Heat 1 tbsp oil in a skillet over medium-high heat while the salmon is frying. Sauté the kale until it has wilted (2-3 minutes). Remove the pan from the heat and put it aside.
6. In the same pan, heat the remaining oil and add the cauliflower rice. Sauté until done, seasoning with 1 tsp curry powder & salt (2 to 3 minutes).
7. Take the salmon & Brussels sprouts out of the oven and divide them between two dishes. Fill dishes with sautéed kale & cauliflower rice.

24. White Bean and Chicken Chili with Winter Vegetables

Prep Time: 25 min, Serving: 4, Difficulty: Easy

Ingredients

- 2 garlic cloves, minced
- Pinch of crushed red pepper flakes (optional)
- 2 tbsps olive oil
- 1 cup milk (any type of milk will work here, including nut milk)
- 1 small onion, chopped
- 2 cups cooked, shredded chicken breast
- 1 leek, rinsed and chopped
- 1 15-ounce can small white beans
- 1 large white potato, peeled and chopped
- 1 cup chopped Brussels sprouts
- 3 cups chicken OR vegetable stock
- 1 jalapeño pepper, seeded and diced
- 1 tbsp ground cumin
- 1 tsp dried oregano
- To serve: Additional shredded cheese, jalapeño slices, hot sauce, tortilla chips

Instructions

1. In a large saucepan (or Dutch oven) placed over medium heat, heat the olive oil. Cook for about 5 minutes until the onion & leek are translucent and tender, then add the leek, onion, and jalapeno.
2. Cook, stirring, for another minute after adding the garlic & spices to the pan.
3. In a large saucepan, combine the Brussels sprouts, potato, white beans, stock, and chicken. Cook, occasionally stirring, for 20 minutes, or until the potato chunks are cooked.
4. Stir in the milk and heat until it is barely warm. Serve immediately with preferred toppings.

25. Blender Olive Oil Hollandaise Sauce

Prep Time: 10 min, Serving: 12, Difficulty: Easy

Ingredients

- ½ cup mild extra-virgin olive oil
- Dash of cayenne pepper
- ½ cup pure olive oil
- ⅛ tsp granulated sugar
- 3 large egg yolks
- ½ tsp white pepper
- 5 tbsp warm water, divided
- 2 ½ tbsp fresh lemon juice
- ½ tsp kosher salt

Instructions

1. In a small saucepan over low heat, bring both olive oils to 120 degrees F.
2. In a blender, combine the yolks, 3 tablespoons of warm water, lemon juice, salt, white pepper, sugar, and cayenne. Pulse until everything is thoroughly combined. Fill a spouted measuring cup with hot oil.
3. Slowly drizzle in the oil in a steady, thin stream while the mixer is running. If the sauce is too thick, add up to 1 tbsp at a time, 2 tbsp warm water, until it reaches the appropriate consistency.

26. Spinach-Salmon Salad

Prep Time: 10 min, Serving: 1, Difficulty: Easy

Ingredients

- ½ tsp toasted sesame seeds
- ⅓ cup flaked canned wild salmon
- ⅛ tsp kosher salt
- ⅓ cup Sautéed Asparagus

- 2 tbsp Rice Vinaigrette
- ¼ cup Sautéed Mushrooms
- 1 ½ cups baby spinach
- ¼ cup diagonally sliced carrot

Instructions

1. Combine salmon, spinach, mushrooms, carrot, and asparagus in a bowl; sprinkle with vinaigrette. Drizzle with sesame seeds and salt, if desired.
2. Serve and Enjoy.

27. Easy Roasted Chicken Breasts with Tomatoes and White Beans

Prep Time: 15 min, Serving: 4, Difficulty: Easy

Ingredients

- 2 bone-in, skin-on chicken breasts
- 1 tsp chopped fresh rosemary leaves
- 1 tsp black pepper
- 1 tsp lemon zest
- 2 tsp kosher salt, divided
- 1 cup pitted Castelvetrano olives
- 2 tbsp extra-virgin olive oil
- 2 pints cherry tomatoes
- 2 (15-oz.) cans cannellini beans, rinsed and drained

Instructions

1. Preheat the oven to 425 degrees Fahrenheit. Chicken breasts should be patted dry and sliced in half crosswise. Season the breast pieces with pepper & 1 teaspoon salt. Remove from the equation.
2. In a 13 x 9-inch baking dish, combine the tomatoes, olive oil, olives, beans, rosemary, lemon zest, and the remaining 1 tsp salt.
3. Put seasoned chicken breast sliced on top of the tomato mixture, skin side up. Bake in a preheated oven for 50 minutes, or until

chicken is cooked through and skin is golden brown and crispy, turning veggies halfway through.

28. Citrus-Salmon Salad

Prep Time: 10 min, Serving: 4, Difficulty: Easy

Ingredients

- 4 lemongrass stalks, bruised and cut into 4-inch pieces
- 1 fennel bulb (about 14 oz.), sliced
- 4 scallions, halved crosswise
- ⅓ cup water
- ⅓ cup dry white wine
- 1 (2-lb.) center-cut, skin-on salmon fillet
- 1 ½ tsp kosher salt, divided
- ¾ tsp black pepper, divided
- ¼ cup white wine vinegar
- ¼ cup thinly sliced shallots
- ⅓ cup extra-virgin olive oil
- 2 tbsp fresh orange juice
- 1 tsp honey
- 1 tsp Dijon mustard
- ½ tsp orange zest
- 6 ounces torn butter lettuce, torn
- 2 cups Belgian endive, sliced
- 1 ½ cups orange segments
- 1 ripe avocado, chopped
- ¼ cup sliced almonds, toasted

Instructions

1. Fold a 30x18-inch sheet of parchment paper in half lengthwise, then crosswise to make a four-layer thick sheet. Fold the parchment and place it in the bottom of a slow cooker, allowing the ends to stretch slightly up the sides.

2. In a slow cooker, arrange fennel, half of the lemongrass, & scallions in an equal layer on parchment paper. Pour in the wine & the water. Place fish on lemongrass mixture and season with 1/2 tsp pepper & 1/2 tsp salt. Finish with the remaining lemongrass, fennel, and scallions on top of the salmon. Cover and simmer on HIGH for 1 to 2 hours, or until salmon flakes easily with a fork. Lift the salmon from the slow cooker using the parchment paper liner as handles, letting the liquid drain. In the slow cooker, toss out the mixture. Remove the salmon from the pan & put it aside.

3. In a small dish, mix white wine vinegar & shallots; set aside for 5 minutes. Combine the orange juice, olive oil, honey, orange zest, Dijon mustard, 1/2 teaspoon salt, & 1/4 teaspoon pepper in a mixing bowl. 4 plates each with butter lettuce, orange segments, and chopped avocado, Belgian endive, and 8 oz flakes of salmon drizzle the dressing over the salad & top with sliced almonds.

29. Crispy Sheet Pan Salmon with Lemony Asparagus and Carrots

Prep Time: 20 min, Serving: 4, Difficulty: Medium

Ingredients

- 4 (6-oz.) skin-on salmon fillets
- Lemon wedges
- ¼ cup mayonnaise
- 2 tbsp melted unsalted butter
- 2 tbsp Dijon mustard
- ¾ tsp divided black pepper
- ¼ cup panko
- 1 (8-oz.) pkg. small carrots with tops
- 1 tbsp fresh chopped dill
- ½ pound fresh asparagus, halved and trimmed crosswise
- 1 ½ tsps lemon zest, divided
- Cooking spray
- ¾ tsp kosher salt, divided

Instructions

1. Preheat the oven to 425 degrees Fahrenheit. Using parchment paper, line a baking sheet. Place the salmon on half of the baking sheet that has been prepared. In a medium mixing bowl, combine mustard, mayonnaise, 1 teaspoon lemon zest, 1/4 teaspoon salt, dill, and 1/4 teaspoon pepper. Spread a uniform layer of mayonnaise over the salmon fillets; top with panko and softly press to adhere. Cooking spray should be used.

2. In a medium mixing bowl, combine the butter, carrots, asparagus, and the remaining 1/2 teaspoon each of lemon zest, pepper, and salt. Place the veggies on the baking sheet's empty side. Bake for 18 minutes in a preheated oven until fish is cooked through & veggies are soft. Serve with lemon slices on the side.

30. Easy Kimchi

Prep Time: 10 min, Serving: 2, Difficulty: Easy

Ingredients

- 1 Napa cabbage, sliced into 2-inch strips
- 2 tbsp minced ginger
- 1 tsp sugar
- 1/2 cup kosher salt
- 3 tbsp water
- 2 tbsp minced garlic

- 4 tbsp Korean red pepper flakes
- 1 large daikon radish, peeled and cut into 1-inch matchsticks
- 2 bunches of green onions, cut into 1-inch pieces

Instructions

1. Salt the cabbage and place it in a large mixing dish. Allow cabbage to remain for 2 hours until wilted & water has been released, then cover with a heavy pot or pan and weights.
2. After 1-2 hours, discard the water. Allow the cabbage to drain in a strainer for a further 15-20 minutes after rinsing it 2 to 3 times in the sink to remove the salt.
3. Mix the cabbage with the rest of the ingredients (through water). Next, put on the gloves and start mixing and rubbing the Korean red pepper flakes into the mixture. Next, stir in the daikon radish & green onions until well combined.
4. Place the mixture in a jar, pushing it down and compressing it tightly so that it is completely buried in its liquid. Place the lid on the jar and set it aside for 2–5 days at room temperature. Because the mixture can bubble over during fermenting, set the jar on a plate.
5. Remove the lid every day of fermentation to let gases escape and to keep the mixture submerged.
6. Refrigerate kimchi once it has fermented for 2-5 days.

31. Matcha Green Tea

Prep Time: 10 min, Serving: 1, Difficulty: Easy

Ingredients

- 6 ounces hot water, divided
- 1 tsp Matcha powder

Instructions

1. 6 ounces water, brought to a boil Mix matcha powder & 1 ounce boiling water in a mixing bowl. Whisk the ingredients rapidly with a bamboo whisk until it makes a thin paste.
2. Add additional hot water to the mixture until it reaches the required consistency.
3. Serve and enjoy.

32. Roasted Haloumi-Stuffed Broccoli Recipe

Prep Time: 10 min, Serving: 4, Difficulty: Easy

Ingredients

- 1/3 cup dill fresh
- 1/2 thinly sliced red onion medium
- 1 broccoli big head, sliced into 4 large florets
- 200 g sliced haloumi

Anti-Inflammatory Dressing Drizzle

- 1/2 tsp ground cumin
- 2 tbsp extra-virgin olive oil for drizzling
- 1/2 cup full-fat Greek yogurt
- 2 tsp ground turmeric
- salt & pepper to taste

Instructions

1. Preheat the oven to 425 degrees Fahrenheit and prepare a baking sheet with parchment paper.
2. Place broccoli in a dish of boiling water & cook for 2 minutes, or until slightly softened. Drain and put on a baking tray lined with parchment paper.
3. Make three slices across the length of the broccoli heads. It will provide room for the fillings to be stuffed into the broccoli.

4. Fill every cut with haloumi, red onion, and dill slices.
5. Season with some crunches of sea salt & freshly ground pepper, and drizzle with olive oil.
6. Roast for almost 10 minutes until the haloumi has melted.
7. In a separate bowl, combine the rest of the ingredients (cumin, turmeric, yogurt, and olive oil) to make the anti-inflammatory dressing drizzle.

33. Anti-Inflammatory Coconut Fish Curry

Prep Time: 10 min, Serving: 2,: Easy

Ingredients

- 1 lime, sliced into wedges.
- 1 5cm knob ginger, fresh, chopped.
- Extra chili, fresh.
- 1 tbsp turmeric, ground.
- Coriander leaves.
- 2 tsp fennel seeds.
- 1 cup basmati rice.
- 1 tsp coriander, ground.
- 600 g white fish fillets.
- 1/4 tsp cumin, ground.
- 2 bunches of broccolini, sliced in half lengthways.
- 1 tbsp curry powder.
- 500 ml homemade chicken, fish or vegetable stock.
- 1 long red chili, seeds removed, chopped.
- 400 ml full-fat coconut milk.
- 1 tbsp fish sauce.
- 1 small bunch coriander, leaves removed and stems finely chopped.
- 1/2 tsp sea salt.
- 1 tbsp coconut oil.
- 4 cloves garlic, peeled and chopped.
- 1 red onion, finely chopped.

Instructions

1. To begin, place the rice in a saucepan with 2 cups boiling water, bring to a boil, then decrease the heat to low and simmer, covered, until the water has been absorbed. To serve, fluff with a fork. Alternatively, a rice cooker may be used.
2. Prepare a paste with the ginger, garlic, fennel seeds, turmeric, cumin, coriander, chili, curry powder, salt, fish sauce, and 30ml boiling water in a small food processor.
3. In a large saucepan, heat the coconut oil over medium heat, then add the onion & coriander stems and cook for almost 5 minutes, or until aromatic. Cook for 5 minutes, until the paste is aromatic, then add the coconut milk & stock. Bring to a boil, covered.
4. Reduce heat to a low setting and gently add the fish and broccolini to the liquid. Allow to cook for 7–10 minutes on low, uncovered, or until salmon is cooked through.
5. Serve with a scoop of rice, coriander leaves, a pinch of chili, & a squeeze of lime on top.

34. Winter Sausage Stew (Gluten-Free)

Prep Time: 10 min, Serving: 1, Difficulty: Easy

Ingredients

- 1 tsp olive oil extra virgin
- 1/6 cup buckwheat (raw)
- 1/2 onion (brown) diced
- 1/2 lemon juiced
- 1/2 pork sausage (roughly chopped)
- 1/2 cup parsley (fresh) chopped
- 1 cup kale chopped & destemmed
- 25 grams sliced mushroom
- 200 grams diced tomato (canned)
- 1/2 grated carrot

Instructions

1. Cook the buckwheat according to the package instructions while you prepare the veggies.
2. In a medium saucepan over low-medium heat, combine the olive oil and onion.
3. Cook for 5 minutes or until the onion is tender.
4. Bring to a slow boil with the mushrooms, sausages, carrot, tinned tomatoes, kale, and cooked buckwheat.
5. Cook for 10 minutes on low heat.
6. Remove the pan from the heat and add the parsley & lemon juice.

35. Dan Buettner's coconut cherry parfait recipe

Prep Time: 10 min, Serving: 4, Difficulty: Easy

Ingredients

- Zest from one lemon
- 1 package silken tofu
- 2 tbsp brandy (optional)
- 1 can coconut milk
- 1/3 cup honey
- 1/3 cup maple syrup
- 1 cup pitted cherries

Instructions

1. To prepare the silken tofu, cut it into cubes. In a blender, combine the coconut milk, tofu, lemon zest, and honey. If using, add the brandy as well. Combine everything in a blender. It should have a rich, thick texture.
2. To serve, spoon the mixed ingredients into tiny cups or bowls.
3. In a small saucepan, combine the cherries & maple syrup. Heat the syrup over low heat until it begins to develop a glaze-like texture.

In each bowl, sprinkle the cherries on the parfait. Enjoy!

36. Tofu and Winter Squash Lasagna

Prep Time: 40 min, Serving: 6, Difficulty: Medium

Ingredients

- 1-pound "no-boil" lasagna noodles
- Seasoned bread or cracker crumbs
- 2 cups cooked, mashed winter squash, such as Acorn or Butternut variety
- 4 cups prepared marinara sauce
- 1 tbsp packed brown sugar
- Salt & pepper
- 1 16-ounce package soft tofu
- Pinch smoked paprika
- ½ cup non-dairy milk such as Almond or Coconut, or Hemp
- 2 tbsp fresh lemon juice
- 1 tbsp fresh thyme leaves

Instructions

1. Preheat the oven to 350 degrees Fahrenheit.
2. In a large mixing bowl, combine the squash and brown sugar; put aside.
3. In a food processor, combine the milk, tofu, thyme, lemon juice, and paprika, then process until smooth.
4. Combine the tofu with the squash mixture. To taste, season with salt and pepper.
5. Spread a thin layer of tomato sauce on the bottom of a baking dish. Add a layer of noodles on top, using about a third of the box. 1/3 of the squash & tofu filling should be on top.
6. Layer in the same way as before, finishing with a little portion of the squash & tofu combination. If desired, top with bread or cracker crumbs.
7. Preheat oven to 400°F and bake for 40-45 minutes, or until hot & bubbling.

37. Harissa & Yogurt Marinated Chicken Tenders

Prep Time: 10 min, Serving: 6, Difficulty: Easy

Ingredients

- ¼ cup dry white wine
- 2 tbsp harissa paste
- ¼ cup plain Greek yogurt
- 2 pounds skinless, boneless, chicken tenders

Instructions

1. Combine the yogurt, harissa, and wine in a mixing bowl. In a deep baking dish, put the chicken tenders and cover them with the yogurt mixture. Refrigerate after wrapping with plastic wrap. Marinate for two hours and up to overnight in the refrigerator.
2. To prepare the chicken, preheat your grill. Allow any extra marinade to drain off the chicken before removing it. Cook chicken for about 5 minutes on every side on a hot grill.
3. Serve with a side salad, rice, couscous, or quinoa, or a sandwich with sliced veggies and fresh herbs.

38. Ground Turkey Sweet Potato Stuffed Peppers

Prep Time: 10 min, Serving: 4, Difficulty: Easy

Ingredients

- crushed red pepper to taste - optional
- fresh parsley - for garnishing
- 2 cups grass-fed ground turkey
- feta cheese - for garnishing
- 2 cloves garlic - minced
- 2 large bell peppers - cut in half
- ½ cup onions - diced
- salt and pepper
- 1⅔ cups sweet potatoes - diced
- ½ cup homemade tomato sauce
- 1 tbsp extra virgin olive oil

Instructions

1. Preheat the oven to 350 degrees Fahrenheit.
2. Heat the olive oil in a pan over medium-high heat.
3. Combine the ground turkey & garlic in a mixing bowl. Cook for approximately 10 minutes, stirring occasionally. As the meat cooks, be careful to break it up with a wooden spoon.
4. Cook, occasionally stirring, until the onions are golden brown.
5. Cook until the sweet potatoes are cooked, covered in the skillet. It takes roughly 8 minutes to complete.
6. Don't forget to stir from time to time. Toss in the crushed red pepper, tomato sauce, salt, and freshly ground black pepper to taste. To cook the potatoes, add extra olive oil or a splash of water if required.
7. Place the peppers in a prepared baking dish, cavity side up, in a baking dish.
8. Fill each half of bell pepper with the ground turkey and sweet potato mixture.
9. Bake for 30 minutes, uncovered, or until the peppers are tender and cooked.
10. Remove the dish from the oven and top with feta cheese and parsley.

39. Polenta with Wild Mushroom Bolognese

Prep Time: 10 min, Serving: 4, Difficulty: Easy

Ingredients

For the polenta:

- ¼ cup grated Parmesan cheese
- 2 tbsps unsalted butter
- 6 cups vegetable stock
- 2 cups yellow cornmeal

For the wild mushroom Bolognese:

- ½ cup red wine
- 1 tsp salt
- 1 tsp dried oregano
- 2 garlic cloves, chopped
- ½ tsp dried thyme
- 2 celery stalks, peeled and chopped
- ¼ cup olive oil
- 1 onion, chopped
- 1 28-ounce can chopped tomatoes
- 2 carrots, peeled and chopped
- 6-ounces assorted wild mushrooms
- ½ tsp black pepper

INSTRUCTIONS

1. Bring the water to a boil in the stock.
2. Mix in the cornmeal slowly, scraping off any lumps.
3. Reduce heat to medium-low and cook the cornmeal for 15-20 minutes, or until it has thickened. It should be porridge-like inconsistency.
4. Stir in the butter & Parmesan cheese after removing the polenta from the heat. Set aside.

5. In a food processor, pulse the celery, carrots, onion, and garlic until the veggies are finely chopped but not pureed. Set aside.
6. In a large saucepan, heat the oil overheat. In the same saucepan, add the chopped veggies. Cook for almost 5 mins, or until the vegetables are soft.
   In the same pan, put the spices and mushrooms. Cook for another 5 minutes, or until the mushrooms' water has drained completely.

40. Baked Buffalo cauliflower recipe

Prep Time: 15 min, Serving: 3, Difficulty: Easy

Ingredients

- 1 medium cauliflower, cut into bite-size pieces
- For serving (optional): blue cheese or ranch dressing
- ¼ cup banana flour
- ½ cup hot sauce
- ¼ cup water
- Pinch of salt & pepper
- 2 tbsps butter, melted

Instructions

1. Preheat oven to 425 degrees Fahrenheit.
2. In a large mixing bowl, combine the water, flour, salt, & pepper.

3. Toss the cauliflower in the flour-water mixture to coat it. Put on a foil-lined rimmed baking sheet for about 15 minutes, flipping once.

4. Meanwhile, in a small bowl, combine the butter and spicy sauce. Sprinkle the sauce over the cauliflower that has been roasted. Return the pan to the oven and cook for another 20 minutes. If preferred, serve warm with the preferred dressing on the side.

7. Scrape up any brown pieces that have gathered at the bottom before putting in the red wine.

8. Bring the mixture to a boil with the tomatoes. Reduce to medium-low heat and continue to cook for another 15 minutes.

9. Serve the polenta with the sauce on top.

41. Glowing spiced lentil soup

Prep Time: 15 min, Serving: 7, Difficulty: Easy

Ingredients

- 2 cups (280 grams) diced onion (1 medium/large)
- 1 (5-ounce/140-gram) package baby spinach
- 2 large garlic cloves, minced
- Red pepper flakes or cayenne pepper to taste (for a kick of heat!)
- 2 tsp ground turmeric
- Freshly ground black pepper, to taste
- 1 1/2 tsp ground cumin
- 1/2 tsp fine sea salt, or to taste
- 1/2 tsp cinnamon
- 3 1/2 cups (875 mL) low-sodium vegetable broth
- 1/4 tsp ground cardamom
- 3/4 cup (140 grams) uncooked red lentils, rinsed and drained
- 1 (14-ounce/398 mL) can diced tomatoes, with juices

- 1 1/2 tbsp (22.5 mL) extra-virgin olive oil
- 2 tsp (10 mL) fresh lime juice, or more to taste
- 1 (14-ounce/398 mL) can full-fat coconut milk

Instructions

1. Combine the onion, oil, and garlic in a big saucepan. Add a bit of salt, stir, and cook for 4 to 5 minutes over medium heat until the onion softens.

2. Combine the cumin, turmeric, cardamom, and cinnamon in a large mixing bowl. Cook for another minute or so until aromatic.

3. Add the chopped tomatoes (with juices), coconut milk (entire can), red lentils, broth, salt, and pepper to taste. Taste and season with red pepper flakes or cayenne, if desired. To blend, stir everything together. Raise the heat to high & bring the mixture to a low boil.

4. Reduce heat to medium-high and continue to cook, uncovered, for 18 to 22 minutes, or until the lentils are bubbly and soft.

5. Remove the pan from the heat and whisk in the spinach until it has wilted. To taste, add the lime juice. If desired, season with extra salt and pepper. Serve with toasted bread & lime wedges, ladled into bowls.

42. Chinese chicken salad recipe

Prep Time: 10 min, Serving: 2, Difficulty: Easy

Ingredients

For the dressing:

- Pinch of salt
- ¼ cup unseasoned rice wine vinegar
- ¼-inch piece of ginger, peeled, chopped
- 1 tbsp Dijon mustard
- 2 garlic cloves, minced
- 1 tbsp low-sodium soy sauce

- ½ cup vegetable oil
- 1 tsp sesame oil

For the salad:

- 2 cooked (grilled or roasted) chicken breasts, shredded
- Wonton strips (optional)
- 4 cups shredded green cabbage
- 4 scallions, thinly sliced
- 1 cup shredded red cabbage
- 2 tbsp chopped mint leaves
- 1 small carrot, cut into thin strips
- ¼ cup cooked edamame
- ½ cup chopped cilantro leaves

Instructions

1. In a blender, combine all the dressing ingredients and mix until smooth. Remove from the equation.
2. In a large mixing bowl, combine all the salad ingredients. Toss the salad with the dressing. If desired, garnish with wonton strips.

43. Sweet potato and crispy kale tostadas recipe

Prep Time: 10 min, Serving: 3, Difficulty: Easy

Ingredients

- 2 medium-size sweet potatoes, chopped and cleaned
- Fresh chopped mint (optional)
- 2 tbsps olive oil
- Dried coconut (optional)
- Pinch of cayenne pepper
- Yogurt
- 6-8 stems kale, roughly chopped
- Corn tortillas
- 1 tbsp olive oil
- 1 tsp honey

- Pinch of salt
- 10-12 Brussels sprouts, finely chopped
- 1 tbsp lime juice

Instructions

1. Preheat oven to 400 degrees Fahrenheit.
2. Put the sweet potatoes on a baking sheet lined with foil. Toss with cayenne pepper and olive oil. Place the kale on a second foil-lined baking sheet in the meanwhile. Combine the salt and olive oil in a mixing bowl. Preheat the oven to 350°F. Put both pans in the oven. Roast the kale for 5-10 minutes, or until crisp but not browned on the edges. While sweet potatoes continue to cook, remove them from the pan and put them aside. Roast the sweet potatoes for 35-40 minutes, or until they are soft.
3. Mix the Brussels sprouts with lime juice & honey while the potatoes and greens are cooking.
4. Put the corn tortillas on a piece of tin foil and cook in the oven for 2-3 minutes, or until gently toasted.
5. Put sweet potatoes & crispy kale on a tortilla to form the tostadas. If preferred, garnish with Brussels sprout slaw, a sprinkle of yogurt, toasted coconut, and mint.

44. Easy Saag Paneer

Prep Time: 25 min, Serving: 4, Difficulty: Easy

Ingredients

- 1 tbsp minced fresh ginger
- 8 ounces paneer cheese, cut into 1/2-inch cubes
- 2 cups low-fat plain yogurt
- ¼ tsp ground turmeric
- ¾ tsp salt
- 2 tbsp extra-virgin olive oil, divided

- 20 ounces frozen spinach, thawed and finely chopped
- 1 small onion, finely chopped
- 1 tsp ground cumin
- 1 jalapeño pepper, finely chopped (Optional)
- 2 tsp garam masala
- 1 clove garlic, minced

Instructions

1. In a medium mixing bowl, toss paneer and turmeric until evenly coated. In a big nonstick skillet, heat 1 tablespoon of oil over medium heat. Cook, tossing once until the paneer is browned on all sides, approximately 5 minutes. Place on a platter to cool.
2. In the same pan, add the rest of 1 tbsp oil. Cook, occasionally flipping, until golden brown, about 7 to 8 minutes, with the onion and jalapeno (if using). (If the pan becomes dry during cooking, add 2 tbsps of water at a time.) Garlic, ginger, garam masala, and cumin are added to the pan. Cook, constantly stirring, for approximately 30 seconds, or until fragrant. Season with salt and spinach. Cook, constantly stirring, for 3 minutes, or until heated. Take the pan off the heat and add the yogurt and paneer.

45. Spaghetti Squash Alfredo

Prep Time: 50 min, Serving: 2, Difficulty: Medium

Ingredients

- 2-3 pound spaghetti squash
- Salt & pepper to taste
- 1 tbsp olive oil
- 1 tsp dried thyme
- 2 garlic cloves, finely minced
- ½ cup grated Parmesan cheese
- 2 tbsp brown rice flour

- 1 cup low-fat milk
- 1 tbsp Greek yogurt

Instructions

1. Preheat the oven to 350 degrees Fahrenheit.
2. Poke several tiny holes on the squash's exterior using a knife. While roasting the squash in the oven, this will let some steam escape, preventing it from exploding!
3. On a baking sheet, place the whole squash. Bake for 45 mins to 1 hour, or until the squash is tender to the touch and the liquid has started to drain.
4. Remove the squash from the oven and set it aside to cool before slicing it in half lengthwise. Extract all of the seeds from the center, as well as any fibrous parts.
5. Prepare the Alfredo sauce in the meanwhile. In a saucepan over medium heat, heat the oil.
6. Cook for about 2-3 minutes, or until fragrant, after adding the garlic to the pan.
7. Add the flour to the pan and whisk for about a minute to "toast" it.
8. In a separate bowl, whisk together the flour and milk, scraping off any lumps.
9. Bring the milk to a low simmer. As the sauce heats, it will thicken.
10. Once the sauce has reached a boil, remove it from the heat and whisk in the yogurt, Parmesan cheese, and dried thyme. Season to taste with pepper and salt.
11. Gently "shred" the inside of the spaghetti squash pieces with a fork. It'll look like spaghetti! Over each side, pour the sauce.
12. Broil the halves until the sauce is gently browned and the halves are bubbling. Serve immediately after taking it out of the oven.

46. Homemade Green Fried Rice

Prep Time: 10 min, Serving: 2, Difficulty: Easy

Ingredients

- ¼ tsp fresh lemon zest
- 1 celery stalk, diced
- 1 tsp honey
- 1 small white onion, diced
- 1 tbsp tamari sauce
- ½ cup chopped broccoli
- ½ cup frozen peas
- 1 garlic clove, minced
- 1 tbsp olive oil
- 2 cups cooked brown rice

Instructions

1. In an oven-safe pan, heat the olive oil over medium-high heat. Cook the onion, celery, and broccoli in the pan for about 2 minutes, or until the onions and celery soften.
2. Cook for the next 2 minutes after adding the garlic & rice to the pan.
3. Combine the frozen peas, tamari, and honey in a mixing bowl. Cook, occasionally stirring, for a further 3-5 minutes, or until the rice is lightly crisp around the edges.Remove the pan from the heat and add the lemon zest.
4. Serve right away.

47. Baked Tilapia Recipe with Pecan Rosemary Topping

Prep Time: 15 min, Serving: 4, Difficulty: Easy

Ingredients

- 1 1/2 tsp olive oil
- 1 pinch cayenne pepper
- 1/8 tsp salt
- 1/2 tsp coconut palm sugar or brown sugar
- 1/3 cup chopped raw pecans
- 4 4 ounces each tilapia fillets
- 1/3 cup whole wheat panko breadcrumbs
- 1 egg white
- 2 tsp chopped fresh rosemary

Instructions

1. Preheat the oven to 350 degrees Fahrenheit.
2. Combine pecans, breadcrumbs, rosemary, coconut palm sugar, salt, and cayenne pepper in a small baking dish. Toss in the olive oil to coat the pecan mixture.
3. Bake for 7 to 8 minutes, or until the pecan mixture is light lightly browned.
4. Raise the temperature to 400 degrees F. using cooking spray, coat a big glass baking dish.
5. Mix the egg white in a small dish. Working with one tilapia at a time, gently cover each side of the fish with the egg white and afterward the pecan mixture. Put the fillets in the baking dish that has been prepared.
6. The leftover pecan mixture should be pressed into the tops of tilapia fillets.
7. Bake for approximately 10 minutes or until the tilapia is cooked through. Serve the food.

48. Sweet potato and chickpea stew recipe

Prep Time: 10 min, Serving: 4, Difficulty: Easy

Ingredients

- Pinch of salt and pepper
- 1 tsp paprika
- 1 tsp cumin
- 2 tbsp olive oil
- 1 14-ounce can coconut milk
- 1 small white onion, chopped

- 2 14-ounce cans of chickpeas
- 2 carrots, chopped
- 2 medium-size sweet potatoes, peeled and diced
- 2 garlic cloves, minced
- 1 cup vegetable stock
- 1-inch piece of ginger, minced
- ¼ tsp ground turmeric

Instructions

1. In a big Dutch oven or saucepan, heat the olive oil over medium heat. Cook, frequently turning, until the onion & carrots are soft, about 8-10 minutes.
2. Cook for another minute after adding the ginger, garlic, and spices to the saucepan.
3. Bring the rest of the ingredients to a boil in the same saucepan. Cover and decrease the heat to low after the water has reached a boil. Simmer for about an hour, or until the potatoes have begun to break apart and "blend" into the stew.
4. If preferred, serve over rice alongside lime wedges & fresh mint.

49. Lentil Shrimp Jambalaya {Grain Free}

Prep Time: 10 min, Serving: 5, Difficulty: Easy

Ingredients

- 1 cup to 1 1/4 cup lentils (uncooked)
- 1 cup diced okra (frozen or fresh)
- 1 1/4 cup sliced precooked
- 14–16 ounces medium shrimp – peeled and deveined
- 1 –2 tbsp oil
- 1 bay leaf
- 2/3 to 1 cup each onion, chopped celery, and bell pepper
- pinch of smoked paprika

- 3 garlic cloves, minced
- 2 sprig fresh thyme
- 1 jalapeno – sliced
- 1 cup crushed tomatoes
- 1/2 tsp Cajun creole seasoning blend

Instructions

1. First, have your lentils ready. To get the finest results, fully rinse the lentils beforehand. If you're using canned lentils, you may skip the cooking stage.
2. Lentils are a legume. Put 3 cups of liquid to a boil in a big saucepan. 1 1/4 cup drained and washed lentils Cover securely, lower the heat, and cook for 15-20 minutes. Drain the lentils and put them aside in a bowl.
3. Over medium-high heat, put 1 tbsp oil or butter in the same saucepan. If you're using pre-cooked sausage, skip the browning and serve the shrimp and lentils with cooked sliced sausage afterward.
4. Combine the celery, onion, jalapeno, carrots/bell pepper, and garlic in a large mixing bowl. To coat the pan, sauté the veggies for a few minutes on medium to medium-high heat. Or until the onions are fragrant and slightly caramelized.
5. Next, add the cooked lentils, crushed tomatoes, smoked paprika, thyme, Cajun spices, and bay leaf in a large mixing bowl. Cook until the mixture achieves a gentle simmer. Decrease the heat to medium-low, cover, and continue to cook for approximately 5 minutes. Simply to let the tastes mingle. Because the lentils are already cooked, you won't have to cook them for long.

50. Turmeric Ginger Smoothie with Coconut Oil

Prep Time: 5 min, Serving: 1, Difficulty: Easy

Ingredients

- 2 tbsp pure or Manuka honey
- 1½ cups unsweetened coconut milk
- 1 cup ice, optional
- 1 tbsp turmeric
- 1 tbsp chia seeds
- 1 tbsp coconut oil, softened
- 1 tbsp ginger, peeled and chopped

Instructions

1. In a blender, combine coconut milk, honey, ice, coconut oil, turmeric, and ginger. Blend on high until the mixture is smooth and frosty.
2. Pour into a glass and add chia seeds to taste. Allow a few minutes for the chia seeds to bloom before drinking.

51 Turmeric Bars

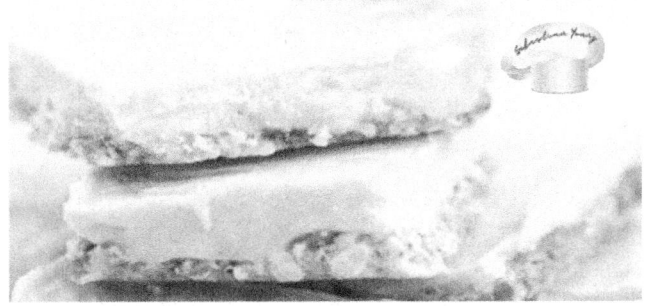

Ready in 30 min Servings: 16 bars Difficulty: Easy

Ingredients
For Filling
- 1/2 cup of coconut oil
- 2 teaspoon honey
- 1 1/2 teaspoon turmeric powder
- 1 teaspoon cinnamon
- 1/8 teaspoon black pepper
- 1 cup coconut butter

For Crust

- 1 cup of shredded coconut
- 1 tbsp coconut oil
- 1 teaspoon cinnamon
- 10 dates

Instructions
1. Preheat oven to 350°F and line an 8-inch four-sided baking sheet with parchment paper.
2. In a food processor, pulse the shredded coconut & dates several times until thoroughly combined. Blend in the cinnamon & coconut oil until smooth.
3. Remove the crust mixture from the bowl and place it in the pan. Press it into the pan until it's flattened evenly. Put the crust inside the refrigerator for 2-3 hours to cool.
4. Prepare the double boiler by half-filling a wide saucepot with water and bringing it to a low boil to make the filling. To make a double boiler, lay a stainless bowl on top of the pot. Pour the coconut butter into a mixing bowl and swirl to melt it. The coconut butter should not be melted in the microwave since it will burn.
5. When the coconut butter is almost completely melted, add the coconut oil and whisk until the mixture is completely liquid.
6. Remove the pan from the heat and set it aside to rest for a few minutes.
7. Toss the filling mixture with turmeric, cinnamon, black pepper & honey.
8. Using a spoon, evenly distribute the mixture over the crust.
9. Refrigerate for 3-4 hours or overnight to harden.
10. Remove the plate from the fridge and set this on the counter for 5-10 mins after it has solidified.

11. Carefully cut into 16 squares with a sharp kitchen knife. Some could shatter, but that's ok!
12. Cinnamon should be sprinkled on top of the final bars.
13. Refrigerate & serve cold! Turmeric stains readily.

52 Turmeric Gummies

Ready in 4 hrs 10 min **Servings:** 4 **Difficulty:** Easy

Ingredients

- 3 ½ cups of water
- 8 tbsp gelatin powder
- Pinch of pepper
- 1 tbsp turmeric
- 6 tbsp maple syrup

Instructions

1. Mix ground turmeric, water, & maple syrup in a big saucepan.
2. Cook for approximately 5 minutes on medium-high, often stirring to ensure that all spices are well dispersed.
3. Turn off the heat & distribute some gelatin powder over the liquid, thoroughly mixing to hydrate the gelatin.
4. Return the saucepan to heat and constantly stir with just a wooden spoon till all the gelatin has dissolved.
5. Put the liquid into a large mixing bowl and cover with plastic wrap.
6. Refrigerate the mixture for at least 4 hours or until firm.
7. When completely cooled, cut into tiny squares or any desired form and serve.

53 Spicy Tuna Rolls

Ready in 10 min **Servings:** 6 Rolls **Difficulty:** Easy

Ingredients

- 1 medium cucumber
- 1 pouch StarKist
- 1/8 teaspoon pepper
- 1/16 teaspoon cayenne
- 2 slices avocado
- 1 teaspoon hot sauce
- 1/8 teaspoon salt

Instructions

1. Finely sliced the cucumber lengthwise using a mandolin. Once the cucumber has been thinly sliced down to where the seeds emerge, turn it over and finely slice the other side. Remove the cucumber's outermost slices and any slices with seeds.
2. With a paper towel, pat dries the leftover slices (6 total). Remove from the equation.
3. Combine tuna, spicy sauce, salt, pepper, & cayenne in a small mixing bowl. Mix until all of the ingredients are well combined.
4. Spoon tuna mixture over cucumber slices one at a time, leaving one inch per side. Place one slice of avocado over the tuna, then wrap the cucumber up gently, closing the end with two toothpicks.

54 Mixed Nuts with Ginger Spice

Ready in 45 min **Servings:** 8 **Difficulty:** Easy

Ingredients

- 2 egg whites
- 1 teaspoon ginger
- 1/2 teaspoon fine sea salt
- 2 cups mixed nuts, cashew, raw almonds, goji berries, pumpkin seeds, etc.

- 1/2 teaspoon cinnamon
- Coconut oil spray
- Parchment paper

Instructions

1. Preheat the oven to 250 degrees Fahrenheit.
2. Whisk the egg whites until they are foamy. Grate the ginger, season with fine sea salt, and sprinkle with Vietnamese cinnamon. Whip the ingredients until it is well mixed.
3. Toss in your favorite raw mixed nuts into the egg white combination. Toss to coat.
4. Lightly mist the parchment paper using coconut oil spray. On the baking sheet, equally, distribute the nuts. Bake at 250 degrees Fahrenheit for 40 minutes, or until fragrant, rotating the baking sheet pan halfway through.
5. Break the combined nuts into pieces after they have cooled and stiffened. Keep the container sealed. Keep them in the fridge if the temperature is high.

55 Spicy Kale Chips

Ready in 26 min **Servings: 4 Difficulty:** Easy

Ingredients
- 1 cluster of curly kale
- spray oil
- 1/8 teaspoon garlic powder
- 1/4 teaspoon sea salt
- 1/4 teaspoon of cayenne pepper
- 1/8 teaspoon black pepper

Instructions

1. Preheat oven to 300 ° F.
2. Thoroughly rinse your kale. Air dry, blow dry inside a salad spinner, and pat dry with paper towels are all options.
3. Cut kale leaves from their stems/ribs into potato chip-sized pieces.

4. Arrange on a wire cooling rack, spaced apart, on top of a foil-lined cookie sheet.
5. If you're cooking a lot of kale, divide it into two sheets or batches, so it cooks evenly.
6. Delicately spritz with such a simple cooking spray or lightly massage a little amount of oil into kale leaves with your fingertips. To make crispy kale chips, gently cover the leaves in oil without putting too much moisture on them. In addition, its wire baking rack guarantees that the crisp factor is maximized.
7. Pinch of salt, garlic powder, & cayenne pepper. They'll be spicier if you add extra cayenne pepper.
8. Do you want them to be mild? Instead of cayenne pepper, use sweet paprika!
9. Bake for 18-20 minutes on the middle rack or until the edges are crisp.

56 Ginger Date Bars

Ready in 20 min **Servings:** 8 Bars **Difficulty:** Easy

Ingredients
- ¼ cup of almond milk
- 1 teaspoon of ground ginger
- 1 ½ cup almonds
- ¾ cup of dates

Instructions

1. Preheat oven to 350 ° degrees Fahrenheit.
2. To produce the almond flour, pulse the almonds for about 1-2 minutes in a high-powered blender until fine and powdery. If you stir the almonds too much, they'll start to leak their oils, ending in nut butter. Remove from the equation.
3. To prepare the date paste, combine the dates and almond milk in the same blender and puree for around 3-5 minutes, or till you have a puree.

4. Blend the date mixture for 2-3 minutes with the almond flour & powdered ginger.
5. Pour the sauce into an oven-safe baking dish & bake for 20 minutes.
6. Allow it cool before slicing into eight bars of similar size.

57 Orange Juice with Vanilla and Turmeric

Ready in 5 min **Servings:** 2 **Difficulty:** Easy

Ingredients
- 3 peeled oranges
- Pinch of pepper
- 1 t vanilla extract
- 1 cup of almond milk
- ½ teaspoon of cinnamon
- ¼ tbsp turmeric

Instructions

1. In a blender, combine all of the ingredients.
2. Puree until smooth, and then strain into a glass to serve.

58 Gelatin Gummies with Hibiscus and Ginger

Ready in 12 min **Servings:** 28 Gummies **Difficulty:** Easy

Ingredients
- 1 cup of water
- 1 teaspoon ginger juice
- 2 tbsp gelatin powder
- 3 tbsp hibiscus flowers cut
- 1½ tbsp honey

Instructions

1. In a small saucepan, bring water to a boil.

2. Turn off the heat and stir in the hibiscus blossoms.
3. Cover and set aside for 5 minutes to infuse.
4. Using a tiny sieve, drain the flowers.
5. Restore the liquid to a saucepan, add the honey and ginger, and whisk to combine.
6. Scatter the gelatin over the surface of the liquid and wait for it to soften & dissolve. After several minutes, whisk to ensure that gelatin is completely dissolved and there are no clumps.
7. Pour into the silicone mold right away (or a rectangular baking dish creased with parchment paper).
8. Allow cooling before placing in the refrigerator for at least two h.
9. To remove your gummies from the mold, just press down on the bottom of the mold with your fingertips.
10. Welcome to the table.

59 Baked Turmeric Veggie Nuggets

Ready in 35 min **Servings:** 24 Nuggets **Difficulty:** Easy

Ingredients
- 1 cup of chopped carrots
- 1 tbsp garlic
- 2 cups of cauliflower florets
- 2 cups of broccoli florets
- 1/2 teaspoon ground turmeric
- 1/2 cup of almond meal
- 1 pasture-raised egg
- 1/4 teaspoon sea salt
- 1/4 tbsp black pepper

Instructions

1. Preheat oven to 400 degrees Fahrenheit and line a pan with parchment paper.
2. In a food processor, mix the carrots, garlic, cauliflower, turmeric, sea salt, broccoli, and black pepper. Pulse until the mixture is fine.

3. Pulse in the almond meal & egg until barely combined.
4. Pour into a mixing basin. Scoop out a spoonful of the ingredients and shape them into round discs with your palms. Place on a baking sheet that has been lined with parchment paper.
5. Cook for 25 minutes, rotating halfway through. For dipping, serve additional Paleo ranch sauce.

60 Slaw with Pineapple & Ginger Cream

Ready in 40 min **Servings: 12 Difficulty:** Easy

Ingredients
Pineapple Slaw
- 1/2 slice of red cabbage
- 2 red peppers
- 3 cups pineapple chunks
- 1 cup chopped cilantro
- 1/2 head green cabbage

Creamy Ginger Sauce

- 1 cup of soaked cashews
- 1/2 teaspoon of red pepper flakes
- salt and pepper
- 1/2 cup of water
- 2 teaspoon lime juice
- 2 inches ginger

Instructions

1. Put cashews in a mixing bowl. Fill the container halfway with water. Allow for at least 30 minutes of soak time, preferably up overnight.
2. Begin preparing the sauce. The cashews should be drained and rinsed. In a high-powered blender or food processor, combine the soaked cashews and the additional sauce ingredients.
3. In a large mixing bowl, combine the red peppers, cabbage, & pineapple. Mix in the sauce well. Stir in the cilantro until it is well incorporated.
4. Have fun.

61 Muffins with Turmeric & Coconut Flour

Ready in 30 min **ervings:** 8 Muffins **Difficulty:** Easy

Ingredients
- 1 teaspoon of vanilla extract
- 2 tbsp of coconut flour
- ½ teaspoon of baking soda
- 2 teaspoon of turmeric
- 6 eggs
- ½ cup of coconut milk
- ⅓ cup of maple syrup
- ½ teaspoon of ginger powder
- salt and pepper

Instructions
1. Preheat oven to 350 degrees Fahrenheit. Make 8 muffin liners in a muffin tray.
2. Combine eggs, maple syrup, milk & vanilla extract in a large mixing basin. Blend until everything is fully blended and the eggs start to bubble.
3. Sift up coconut flour, turmeric, ginger powder, baking soda, pepper, & salt in a small basin.
4. Gradually whisk in the dry ingredients till the mixture is smooth and thick.
5. Divide the batter equally among the muffin cups in the prepared muffin tray.
6. Cook for 25 minutes, or until the edges are gently browned.
7. Remove the muffins out from the oven and cool on a wire rack.

62 No-Bake Golden Turmeric Energy Bites

Ready in 5 hrs 20 min **Servings:** 18 Bites **Difficulty:** Easy

Ingredients
- 1 cup almond
- ½ teaspoon maple syrup
- 2 teaspoon turmeric
- 3/4 coconut flakes
- 4-6 tbsp plant-based protein powder
- 1 teaspoon coconut oil

Instructions

1. Blend nut butter, 12 coconut oil, maple syrup, almond butter, coconut flakes, protein powder, and turmeric in a blender.
2. In a high-powered blender, combine all of the ingredients until they're uniformly dispersed.
3. Allow 30-60 minutes for the dough to solidify in the refrigerator.
4. Take the dough out of the fridge and shape it into 12-inch diameter bite-sized balls.
5. Place the balls on a parchment-lined dish and chill for 3-4 hours.
6. Take it out of the fridge. Toss the ball in the remaining crushed coconut on a dish. Enjoy.

63 Coconut Oil with Turmeric Ginger Smoothie

Ready in 5 min **Servings:** 1 **Difficulty:** Easy

Ingredients
- 1 teaspoon of turmeric
- 1 teaspoon of chia seeds
- 1 cup ice
- 1 tbsp of coconut oil
- 2 tbsp pure
- 1½ cups of coconut milk
- 1 teaspoon of ginger

Instructions
1. In a blender, combine the ice, turmeric, coconut oil, coconut milk, honey, and ginger. Blend on high until the mixture is smooth and frosty.
2. Dilute into a glass & add chia seeds to taste. Allow a few minutes for the chia seeds to grow before drinking.

64 Banana Ginger Coconut Flour Bars

Ready in 10 min **Servings:** 1 **Difficulty:** Easy

Ingredients
- ⅓ cup of raw honey
- 6 eggs
- 1½ tbsp of ginger
- 2 tbsp of cinnamon
- 3 small of bananas
- 1 cup of coconut flour
- ⅓ cup of coconut oil
- 1 teaspoon of ground cardamom
- 1 teaspoon of baking soda
- 2 teaspoon of apple vinegar

Instructions
1. Preheat oven to 350 ° degrees Fahrenheit. Grease or line a 9x9 glass baking sheet with parchment paper.
2. In a food processor, add all ingredients and process until smooth. Combine the baking soda and vinegar in a blender until smooth, then drop into the prepared dish.
3. Bake for 30-40 minutes, or until a toothpick inserted in the center comes out clean.

65 Kombucha Gummies for Gut Healing

Ready in 3 hrs 25 min **Servings:** 25 Gummies **Difficulty:** Easy

Ingredients
- 1 teaspoon grated ginger
- 6 tbsp honey
- 1/3 cup of gelatin powder
- 1 ½ cups kombucha
- 1/2 cup of grapefruit juice
- 1 tbsp grapefruit zest

Instructions
1. Use plastic wrap to line the bottom of just a 9x9-inch glass pan.
2. Bring a medium saucepan of water to a boil with the grated ginger. Allow for a five-minute boil to destroy the protease enzymes in the ginger. Drain the water and put it aside.
3. Mix the kombucha, zest, grapefruit juice, & honey in a large pot and stir thoroughly.
4. Spread the gelatin powder on top and set aside for a few minutes to hydrate.
5. Reduce the heat to medium-low & slowly simmer the mixture until the gelatin powder melts. Mix until the entire gelatin has dissolved.
6. In a blender, pulse the gelatin mixture as well as the boiling grated ginger for 20 seconds.
7. Chill the mixture for at least 3 hours until it's solid in the prepared glass pan. After that, cut the cake into little pieces and serve!

66 Protein Bars with Cacao Coffee

Ready in 10 min **Servings:** 12 **Difficulty:** Easy

Ingredients
- 2 cups nut 1 cup egg white protein powder
- 1/4 cup cacao powder
- 1/4 cup cacao nibs
- 3 tbsp instant coffee
- 18 large Medjool dates
- 3–5 tbsp water

Instructions
1. Preheat oven to 350°F. Line an 8-inch square baking sheet with just a square silicone baking pan; put aside.
2. Mix egg white protein, nuts, cacao powder, and coffee powder in a food processor bowl until nuts are broken down into tiny bits. It's important not to over-process the nuts since they'll try to set down in the following stage.
3. Add the pitted dates and blend until smooth–the mixture may seem dry at this point. 1 tsp of water at a time, with the engine running, until the mixture is thick and all comes together. You would need less or more water depending on whether your dates are juicy or dry. I used a total of 6 tablespoons.
4. Remove S-blade and whisk in cacao nibs if using after the mixture has come together, which is sticky.
5. Pour the mixture into an 8-inch square pan that has been lined with parchment paper. Push evenly into the pan with somewhat damp palms. To get it extra flat, I use his adorable tiny pastry roller.
6. Chill for 1 hour or freeze for 30 min before chopping into bars in the pan.

67 Spicy Nuts

Ready in 20 min **Servings:** 6 Snacks
Difficulty: Easy

Ingredients

- 1 cup almonds
- 1.5 teaspoon chili powder
- 1/2 teaspoon garlic powder
- 1 cup of pecans
- 1 cup of cashews
- 1/2 teaspoon cumin
- 1/4 teaspoon cayenne pepper
- 1 tbsp olive oil
- 1/2 teaspoon black pepper
- 1/2 teaspoon sea salt

Instructions

1. Preheat the oven to 350°F and prepare a baking sheet with parchment paper. On the baking pan, arrange the nuts in a single layer. Preheat oven to 350°F and roast for 15 min, flipping halfway.
2. In a small bowl, combine chili powder, cumin, black pepper, salt, and cayenne pepper while the nuts are roasting.
3. Remove the nuts from the oven and set them aside to cool. With a mixing dish, coat the nuts with olive oil and in the spice mixture.
4. Keep at room temperature in an airtight container.

68 Gummies with Apple Cider Vinegar

Ready in 1 hr 10 min **Servings:** 24
Difficulty: Easy

Ingredients

- 1 ½ cup apple juice
- ½ cup of apple cider vinegar
- ½ cup of water
- 5 tbsp gelatin powder

Instructions

1. In a large saucepan over low heat, mix the apple cider vinegar, apple juice, and water and whisk thoroughly. Mix in the gelatin powder with the liquid and set aside for two minutes.
2. Reduce the heat to low and constantly whisk for five minutes until the gelatin gets completely dissolved.
3. Fill ice cube trays halfway with gelatin mixture and place in the fridge 1 hr earlier serving.

69 Recipe for Lemon-Blueberry Bread

Ready in 1 hr 5 min **Servings:** 16 **Difficulty:** Easy

Ingredients

- 1 cup Knudsen Sour Cream
- 1/2 cup of oil
- 1 teaspoon lemon zest
- 1/2 teaspoon vanilla
- 1 cup blueberries
- 1-1/2 cups plus 1 tbsp flour
- 2 teaspoon baking powder
- 1/2 teaspoon salt
- 3 eggs
- 1 cup of sugar

Instructions

1. Preheat the oven to 350 degrees Fahrenheit.
2. In a large mixing basin, mix baking soda, 1-1/2 cups flour, and salt. Whisk together the sour cream, oil, sugar, lemon zest, eggs, and vanilla extract until well combined. Pour to flour mixture and whisk until just combined.
3. Toss the blueberries with the remaining flour and gently fold them into the batter. Fill an oiled & greased 9x5-inch loaf pan halfway with batter.

4. 1 hour to 1 hour 5 minutes in the oven, or until a toothpick inserted in the middle comes out clean. Allow 10 minutes for cooling. Then, remove the bread from the pan and place it on a wire rack to cool it entirely.

70 Shortbread Cookies with Lavender

Ready in 40 min **Servings:** 4-8 **Difficulty:** Easy

Ingredients
- 1/2 cup ghee
- 1/4 cup coconut oil
- 1/4 cup of maple syrup
- 1/4 teaspoon sea salt
- 1 teaspoon lemon zest
- 1/4 cup honey
- 1 cup of cassava flour
- 1/4 cup of nut flour
- 1/2 cup of arrowroot flour
- 1/4 cup of coconut flour
- 1 teaspoon dried lavender food grade

Instructions
1. In a large mixing bowl, combine the dry ingredients. Cream together ghee, maple syrup, coconut oil, & honey in a separate bowl. Combine the wet and dry ingredients in a mixing bowl. Mix until everything is properly combined.
2. Roll dough into a 2-inch-diameter log & freeze for 15-30 min, or until solid. A baking sheet should be greased.
3. Heat the oven to 325 ° F. Slice the cookies 1/4-inch thick & space them approximately an inch apart on the prepared baking sheet.
4. Bake or until the sides are browning and the bottoms of the cookies are crisp and golden.

71 Energy Balls

Ready in 15 min **Servings:** 23 Balls **Difficulty:** Easy

Ingredients
- 1/4 cup of sunflower seeds
- 2 tbsp chia seeds
- 2 tbsp ground flaxseeds
- 3/4 cup Medjool dates
- 3/4 cup of almonds
- 3/4 cup chopped dried fruit
- 1/2 teaspoon vanilla extract
- 1/4 teaspoon cinnamon

Instructions
1. Set aside a sheet pan lined with parchment paper.
2. Mix the pitted dates & almonds in the food processor. Pulse until the mixture resembles coarse crumbs.
3. Combine the remaining ingredients in a food processor and mix until smooth. The paste should be thick and readily stick together when two fingers are pressed together. Adding 1 tbsp of freshwater if the batter seems dry.
4. A spoonful of the ingredients should be rolled into a 1-inch ball. Rep till all the mixture is already rolled out on the prepared sheet pan.
5. Refrigerate the balls for approximately an hour until once they are firm. Refrigerate in an airtight container. This recipe makes 20-23 balls.

72 Peanut Butter Chocolate Chex Bars

Ready in 45 min **Servings:** 32 **Difficulty:** Easy

Ingredients

- 1 cup of corn syrup
- 6 cups of Honey Nut cereal
- 1 bag of milky chocolate chips
- 2 tbsp butter
- 1 cup of sugar
- 1 1/4 cups of butter peanut
- 1/4 teaspoon of salt

Instructions

1. Coat a 13x9-inch baking pan using cooking spray.
2. Microwave corn syrup & sugar, uncovered, on High 2 min 30 seconds, mixing every 30 seconds, until the liquid just starts to boil in a large microwaveable basin.
3. Mix in 1 cup of peanut butter as well as the salt until well combined.
4. Toss in the grains until it is uniformly covered. Make sure the surface is even by pressing the mixture firmly into the pan.
5. Heat chocolate chips, leftover 1/4 cup peanut butter, and butter uncovered in a medium microwaveable dish for 1 minute on high; stir until smooth. Distribute across the bars. Refrigerate for at least 30 minutes or until the chocolate has hardened. Cut 8 lines by 4 rows for the bars.

73 Yogurt with Almonds and Blueberries

Ready in 5 min **Servings:** 1 **Difficulty:** Easy

Ingredients

- 2 teaspoon Slivered almonds
- 1/4 cup 0 Greek yogurt
- 1/3 cup of Blueberries

Instructions

1. Mix all materials in a bowl & enjoy.

74 Cottage Cheese with Applesauce

Ready in 5 min **Servings:** 1 **Difficulty:** Easy

Ingredients

- Cinnamon and ginger
- 2 teaspoon Almonds
- 1/4 cup Applesauce
- 1/4 cup cottage cheese

Instructions

1. Combine applesauce as well as cottage cheese in a mixing bowl.
2. Cinnamon and ginger should be sprinkled on top.
3. Serve with sliced almonds on top.

75 Salad with Asparagus and Artichokes

Ready in 20 min **Servings:** 4 **Difficulty:** Easy

Ingredients

- 2 tbsp Dr. Sears' Zone Virgin Olive Oil
- 1 teaspoon of Garlic powder
- 1-pint of cherry tomatoes

- 1 can Artichoke hearts canned in water
- 3 slices of red onion
- 3 tbsp of lemon juice
- 1 1/4 pounds of asparagus
- Salt and pepper

Instructions

1. Soak the onions in lime juice in a large mixing dish. Remove from the equation.
2. Preheat the microwave to 400 degrees Fahrenheit.
3. Cut off the rough ends of the asparagus bottoms (approximately 1/2 to 1 inch). Season the asparagus stalks with salt and olive oil frying spray.
4. Place on a foil-lined baking dish in a single layer and roast for 8-10 minutes, or until lightly browned & fork tender.
5. Take the asparagus out of the oven and chop it into little pieces.
6. Combine the asparagus, the other ingredients, including the onions including lemon juice, in a mixing dish. To blend, stir everything together.
7. Serve at room temperature or cooled.

76 Sauce for Barbecue

Ready in 45 min **Servings:** 4 **Difficulty:** Easy

Ingredients

- 1 teaspoon of Worcestershire sauce
- 3/4 cup of Chicken stock
- 3 tbsp of cider vinegar
- 1 cup of tomato puree
- 1/3 cup of applesauce
- 1 tbsp of liquid smoke
- 4 teaspoon of garlic
- 1/4 teaspoon of chili powder
- 4 teaspoon of cornstarch

Instructions

1. To make the sauce, combine all of the components in a small pot. (Before adding cornstarch to the pot, mix it with some cold water to dissolve it.)
2. Warm sauce to a low simmer, stirring regularly with either a whisk until everything thickens.
3. Transfer the sauce to a container, set aside to cool, and the fridge.

77 Freezer Pops of Berries

Ready in 5 min/Overnight **Servings:** 6
Difficulty: Easy
Ingredients

- 1 cup of Strawberries
- 3 cups of yogurt
- 1 1/2 tbsp of almonds

Instructions

1. In a food processor, combine the strawberries and almonds until they are very minute bits.
2. Pulse some few times to incorporate the yogurt.
3. Divide the yogurt mixture evenly into 6 tiny paper cups.
4. In the center of the yogurt, place a Popsicle stick.
5. Place in the freezer for at least one night.
6. Remove the paper cup before eating.

78 Berry good snack

Ready in 5 min **Servings:** 1 **Difficulty:** Easy
Ingredients

- 1 teaspoon of Walnuts
- Stevia for taste
- 5 Blueberries
- 1 teaspoon of Vanilla
- 5 Strawberries
- 1/4 cup of ricotta cheese
- 1 teaspoon of lemon juice

Instructions

1. Set aside strawberries that have been cleaned and hulled.
2. Ricotta, lemon juice, vanilla, crumbled walnuts, and stevia are combined in a mixing bowl.
3. Top each strawberry with a spoonful of the ricotta mixture.
4. Sprinkle each strawberry with just blueberry and put them in a dish on their sides to form a star, with the blueberry in the center and strawberries on the edges.

79 Salad with Blackberries and Shrimp

Ready in 10 min **Servings:** 1 **Difficulty:** Easy

Ingredients

- 2 drops of Agave Nectar
- 1/2 cup of Baby Spinach
- 1/2 teaspoon of Dr. Sears' Virgin Olive Oil
- 2 teaspoon of Lemon Juice
- 1/2 cup of chopped Yellow Bell Pepper
- Salt and Pepper
- 1/2 cup of Blackberries
- 2 chopped medium Shrimp

Instructions

1. To prepare the dressing, mix olive oil, lemon juice, and agave nectar using a fork.
2. Transfer the spinach & bell peppers to a salad dish and toss with the dressing.
3. Serve with blackberries & shrimp on the side.

80 Breakfast with Blueberries and Yogurt

Ready in 5 min **Servings:** 1 **Difficulty:** Easy

Ingredients

- 1 cup of Strawberries
- 1 cup of yogurt
- 2 tbsp of Walnuts
- 3/4 cup of Blueberries

Instructions

1. Stir fruits & nuts into the yogurt.

81 Brussels Sprouts in a Garlic-Black Bean Sauce

Ready in 15 min **Servings:** 3 **Difficulty:** Easy

Ingredients

- 2 1/2 cups of Brussels sprouts
- black pepper
- 1 1/2 teaspoon of Dr. Sears' Zone Extra Virgin Olive Oil
- 1/2 teaspoon of red pepper flakes
- 1 1/2 tbsp of Black bean garlic sauce

Instructions

1. The Brussels sprouts should be quartered lengthwise.
2. In a large pan, heat the oil and chili flakes over medium-high heat.
3. Cook the Brussels sprouts in the pan for approximately 3-5 minutes or until they start to color a little. They may absorb all of the oil. If this is the case, add a spoonful of water or broth.
4. Stir throughout black bean garlic sauce until all of the Brussels sprouts are thoroughly covered.
5. Add a dash of black pepper to taste. Cook for a further 30 seconds.
6. Remove from the heat and serve right away.

82 Strawberries and Cacao Greek Yogurt

Ready in 5 min **Servings:** 1 **Difficulty:** Easy

Ingredients

- 1/4 cup of Greek yogurt
- 2 teaspoon of Almonds
- 1 1/2 tbsp of Cacao Powder
- 1/4 cup of Strawberries

Instructions

1. In a mixing bowl, combine the Greek yogurt and cacao powder.
2. Blend in the strawberries & almonds gently.

83 Dirty Rice in Cajun Style

Ready in 20 min **Servings:** 4 **Difficulty:** Easy

Ingredients

- 2 teaspoon of Dr. Sears' Zone Virgin Olive Oil
- 1 cup of green bell pepper
- 1 cup of red bell pepper
- 3 cups of Cauliflower
- 1 teaspoon of fresh thyme
- 1 Bay leaf
- Salt and pepper
- 4 cloves of Garlic
- 1 cup of white onion
- 2 chopped celery stalks
- 3 tbsp of unsalted vegetable stock
- 1/2 teaspoon of Chili powder
- 1/2 teaspoon of Cumin

Instructions

1. In a large skillet, heat the olive oil on medium heat.
2. Sauté the garlic, onion, celery, & peppers until they are tender.
3. Add the rice cauliflower, thyme, bay leaf, chili, salt, pepper, and cumin, and stir to combine.
4. To combine the flavors, add a tiny quantity of stock (1 tbsp at a time).

84 Dressing with Carrots and Ginger

Ready in 10 min **Servings:** 8 tbsp of servings **Difficulty:** Easy

Ingredients

- 3 tbsp of soy sauce low sodium
- 2 tbsp of Ginger root
- 1 tbsp of Sesame oil
- 2 Carrots
- 1/4 cup of vinegar
- 2 teaspoon of Virgin Olive Oil
- 1/4 cup of Water
- 1 tbsp of Tahini
- For taste Stevia

Instructions

1. In a blender, puree everything except the carrots.
2. Add the carrots just a few pieces to the blender while it's running and mix till smooth before pouring more.
3. If the dressing is too thick, add 2 teaspoons of water at a time until you get the appropriate consistency.

85 Popcorn made with cauliflower

Ready in 35 min **Servings:** 1 **Difficulty:** Easy

Ingredients

- 2 teaspoon of Olive oil
- 4 cups of cauliflower
- Salt for taste

Instructions

1. Cut into buds after removing the core.
2. Toss to coat with olive oil.
3. Season to taste with a good quantity of salt.
4. Roast at 450°F for 25-30 minutes.
5. Drizzle with virgin olive oil before serving.

86 Cauliflower-Mash

Ready in 15 min **Servings:** 2 **Difficulty:** Easy

Ingredients

- 1 16-oz of bag cauliflower
- 1 teaspoon of Dr. Sears' Zone Virgin Olive Oil
- Salt and Pepper
- 2 tbsp of chicken stock
- 3 1/2 tbsp of Greek yogurt

Instructions

1. Microwave the cauliflower in the stock for 10 - 15 minutes, or until it's cooked but still crisp, not mushy.
2. In a blender, stick blender, or food processor, purée all of the ingredients, except the olive oil, until they have the texture of mashed potatoes.
3. Pour with the olive oil before serving.

87 Hummus with celery

Ready in 5 min **Servings:** 1 **Difficulty:** Easy

Ingredients

- 2 tbsp of Hummus spread
- 6 stalks Celery
- 3 tbsp of Salsa
- 1 oz of chicken breast cooked

Instructions

1. Fill the celery stalks' wells with hummus and chicken bits.
2. Cut chicken into hummus, then use the celery as a spoon if you wish.

88 Chard Salad with Parmesan

Ready in 20 min **Servings:** 4 **Difficulty:** Easy

Ingredients

- 3 tbsp of Lemon Juice
- 1 1/2 tbsp of Virgin Olive Oil
- 1/2 cup of Parmesan (grated)
- Pepper
- 2 tbsp of Water
- 2 teaspoons of Lemon Zest
- 1/4 teaspoon of salt
- 1/2 teaspoon of Garlic Powder

Instructions

1. Remove the stems from the chard and coarsely chop them, leaving the leaves alone.
2. In a small bowl, mix the lemon zest, water, lemon juice, 1/4 teaspoon salt, and garlic powder to form a dressing. Whisk in the olive oil slowly. Remove from the equation.
3. Toss the chard stems & leaves firmly with the Parmesan & roughly 2/3 of the lime dressing in a large mixing basin; serve the remainder on the side.
4. Season with black pepper to taste.

89 Plum & Cheese Snack

Ready in 25 min **Servings:** 4 **Difficulty:** Easy

Ingredients

- 1 Low-fat of cheese stick
- 1 Plum

Instructions

1. Mix these two ingredients.

90 Lemon Zucchini with Cheesy Sauce

Ready in 20 min **Servings:** 4 **Difficulty:** Easy

Ingredients

- 2 teaspoons of dried oregano
- 3 lbs. of Zucchini
- 1/2 teaspoon of Lemon zest
- 1/2 teaspoon of pepper flakes red
- Cooking spray, olive oil
- 2 teaspoons of Virgin Olive Oil
- 1/4 teaspoon of Cayenne pepper
- 2 oz Fat-free creamy cheese
- 2 tbsp of vegetable stock
- Salt and pepper

Instructions

1. Cooking oil should be sprayed onto a pan. In a large pan, heat the olive oil over high heat and add the zucchini, lemon zest, & red pepper flakes.
2. Cook for another 2 minutes, adding more stock if necessary.
3. Continue cooking until zucchini is soft, approximately 5 minutes, after adding salt, black pepper, & cayenne pepper.
4. Add cheese into zucchini combination and simmer for 1 minute, or until cream cheese starts to melt.
5. Remove the pan from the heat and add the oregano.

91 Fruit & Cottage Cheese

Ready in 5 min **ervings:** 1
Difficulty: Easy

Ingredients

- 1/3 cup of Mandarin oranges
- 1 1/2 teaspoon of Slivered almonds
- 1/4 cup of cheese Low-fat cottage

Instructions

1. Mix the mandarin orange sections in a bowl with the low-fat cottage cheese.
2. Top with slivered or sliced almonds.

92 Chicken Gravy with a Country Flair

Ready in 25 min **Servings:** 3 Cups
Difficulty: Easy

Ingredients

- 2 1/2 cups of chicken stock
- 1/2 teaspoon of Garlic
- 1/2 teaspoon of Celery salt
- 2 1/2 cups of Onions

- 6 teaspoons of Cornstarch
- 1 tbsp of White wine
- 1 teaspoon of Parsley flakes
- 1 teaspoon salt and pepper for taste

Instructions

1. Mix all of the ingredients.

93 Yogurt with cucumber and cashews

Ready in 5 min **Servings:** 1 **Difficulty:** Easy

Ingredients

- 1 cup of Cucumber
- 1/4 cup of Greek yogurt
- 2 teaspoons of Cashews
- 2 teaspoon of squeezed lemon juice
- 1 teaspoon of chopped fresh dill

Instructions

1. Cucumbers should be sliced.
2. Combine yogurt, cashews, lemon juice, and dill in a mixing bowl.

94 Cucumber Cups

Ready in 10 min **Servings:** 3 **Difficulty:** Easy

Ingredients

- 1 cucumber
- 1/4 cup of sour cream
- 1 tbsp of Horseradish mustard
- 1 sprig fresh dill
- 1/3 cup of Hummus
- 6 halved of Cherry tomatoes

Instructions

1. Split the cucumber into 12 pieces using a knife.
2. Cut the cherry tomatoes in half.

3. Scoop out the interior meat, being cautious not to go all the way to the bottom with your scoop.
4. Drain the pieces on paper towels or cotton towels.
5. In the meanwhile, mix the mustard & sour cream until smooth and put aside.
6. 1 teaspoon of hummus in each cup, followed by the sour cream mix.
7. Serve with a dill sprig as a garnish.

95 Hummus-Dipped Devilled Eggs

Ready in 15 min **Servings:** 1 **Difficulty:** Easy

Ingredients

- 2 Egg
- 4 tbsp of Hummus
- Paprika to taste

Instructions

1. Slice the eggs in half, discard yolks, and fill each egg white half with one-fourth of the hummus.
2. Top with paprika to taste.

96 Dill Sauce

Ready in 15 min **Servings:** 1 **Difficulty:** Easy

Ingredients

- 3/4 teaspoon of Virgin Olive Oil
- 1 teaspoon of Garlic
- 1 teaspoon dill
- 1/3 cup of Greek yogurt
- 2 teaspoons of dry white wine
- Salt and pepper
- 1 1/2 teaspoon of Cornstarch

Instructions

1. Combine yogurt, white wine, garlic, olive oil, & dill in a small saucepan. Reduce the heat to a low setting. Boiling is not recommended.
2. Combine the cornstarch and a little water to make a slur (thin paste).
3. Frequently whisk the cornstarch mix into the yogurt. Return to very low heat after bringing to a simmer (when the sauces will thicken). Boiling is not recommended.

97 Easy Creamy Spinach Dip

Ready in 25 min **Servings:** 5 **Difficulty:** Easy

Ingredients

- 1 tbsp Shallot
- 1/2 cup of cottage cheese
- 1/4 cup of Greek yogurt
- 1 tbsp of lemon juice
- 1 (5 oz) can Water chestnuts
- 1/3 cup of cream
- 1/2 teaspoon of salt
- Black pepper - to taste
- Zone-favorable vegetables for dipping
- 8 oz Baby spinach
- 2 tbsp fresh chives

Instructions

1. In a food processor, roughly chop the shallot and water chestnuts.
2. Pulse together the cream cheese, yogurt, lemon juice, cottage cheese, salt, and pepper until well blended.
3. Pulse in the spinach & chives until well combined.
4. Cut up some Zone-friendly vegetables, and you're good to go.

98 Eggplant Caviar

Ready in 30 min **Servings:** 4 **Difficulty:** Easy

Ingredients

- 2 1/2 lbs. Eggplants (same size)
- 1/2 cup of Scallions
- 1 tbsp of lemon juice
- 1/2 teaspoon of dried basil leaves
- 2 cloves of Garlic
- 2 tbsp of vegetable stock
- Black pepper
- 2 1/2 teaspoon of Virgin Olive Oil

Instructions

1. Preheat the oven to 400 degrees Fahrenheit (or grill).
2. Cut the eggplants in half lengthwise and set them cut-side down on a baking pan. Preheat oven to 350°F and bake for 20 minutes, or until fork-tender.
3. In a blender or food processor, purée the pulp from the skin.
4. Blend in the other ingredients, except the olive oil, until smooth.
5. Add the olive oil and mix well.
6. Chill for 1 hour or serve at room temperature.

My Recipes And Notes

Recipe Name _____

Preparation Time: Serving: Difficulty Level:

Ingredients

....
....
....
....
....
....

Steps for preparation

_____
_____
_____
_____
_____
_____
_____
_____

Recipe Name _____

Preparation Time: Serving: Difficulty Level:

Ingredients

....
....
....
....
....
....

Steps for preparation

_____
_____
_____
_____
_____
_____
_____
_____

Recipe Name _____

Preparation Time: Serving: Difficulty Level:

Ingredients

....
....
....
....
....
....

Steps for preparation

_____
_____
_____
_____
_____
_____
_____
_____

Recipe Name _____

Preparation Time: Serving: Difficulty Level:

Ingredients

....
....
....
....
....
....

Steps for preparation

_____
_____
_____
_____
_____
_____
_____
_____

Recipe Name _____

Preparation Time: Serving: Difficulty Level:

Ingredients

....
....
....
....
....
....

Steps for preparation

_____
_____
_____
_____
_____
_____
_____
_____
_____

Recipe Name _____

Preparation Time: Serving: Difficulty Level:

Ingredients

....
....
....
....
....
....

Steps for preparation

_____
_____
_____
_____
_____
_____
_____
_____
_____

Recipe Name _____

Preparation Time: Serving: Difficulty Level:

Ingredients

....
....
....
....
....
....

Steps for preparation

_____
_____
_____
_____
_____
_____
_____
_____

Recipe Name _____

Preparation Time: Serving: Difficulty Level:

Ingredients

....
....
....
....
....
....

Steps for preparation

_____
_____
_____
_____
_____
_____
_____
_____

Recipe Name _____

Preparation Time: Serving: Difficulty Level:

Ingredients

....
....
....
....
....
....

Steps for preparation

_____
_____
_____
_____
_____
_____
_____
_____
_____

Recipe Name _____

Preparation Time: Serving: Difficulty Level:

Ingredients

....
....
....
....
....
....

Steps for preparation

_____
_____
_____
_____
_____
_____
_____
_____
_____

Printed in Great Britain
by Amazon